# BEDSPREADS TO BROADLOOM

## The Story of the Tufted Carpet Industry

THOMAS M. DEATON
Color Wheel
Post Office Box 21726
Chattanooga, TN 37424

*Tapestry Press*
*Acton, MA 01720*

Printed in the United States of America.

1-56888-038-3

About the back of the dust jacket:

"A Visit from the Hauler" was painted by John Clymer in 1968 for the American Cyanamid Co. It represents the start of the bedspread and carpet industry in our area by showing the way spreads were made in the homes until the 1930s.

The original painting was given to the Whitfield-Murray Historical Society and hangs in their headquarters, Crown Gardens and Archives, 715 Chattanooga Ave., Dalton Ga.

# CONTENTS

# FOREWORD

The Carpet and Rug Institute is continually asked, "Why is tufted carpet production centered around Dalton, Georgia?" The quick answer is always that it began here with Catherine Evans Whitener's hand tufting a bedspread. However, that short answer is insufficient considering that the carpet industry has continued to be centered here. Why has a multi-billion dollar business evolved in an area miles away from major financial, transportation, and marketing centers? These challenges were met and overcome, but how?

Historian Tom Deaton has uniquely woven a history of the tufted carpet industry and its development by telling the stories, almost lost, of the lives of the people who made it happen. These are stories of creative decisions, practical inventions, hard work, and the evolution of an American contribution to the world. In a world noted for mega-corporations it is a modern-day Horatio Alger rags-to-riches industry. Persistence, good work habits, team work, and creativity produced new products, styling innovations, and wealth. Dr. Deaton has drawn lessons of success from the leaders of the industry which could benefit anyone trying to succeed in their chosen field. He has brushed the historical canvas with colors of humor, fascinating participants, contrasting philosophies, and competing companies. While it is impossible to tell it all, it is a representative story of the men and women; pioneers and the newcomers; leaders and line workers; tufters and haulers; friends and rivals. It is a story that will leave the reader with a thirst to know more.

Ronald E. VanGelderen
President, The Carpet & Rug Institute

# PREFACE

This book is the story of the people of the industry and it is dedicated to them. When Truett Lomax of the Carpet & Rug Institute first asked me to write the history of the industry in 1979, I did not realize the magnitude of the task nor the multi-faceted faces of the story. When I first started Vernon Foster walked me through Masterpiece Finishing and taught me the difference between a hyster and a dye beck. He gave me his love for the industry. Although I have interviewed hundreds of participants, I have only scratched the surface. There are many more with whom I hope to talk in the future. It is my greatest hope that I have done justice to the story and that the reader will relive the memories of the hard work, creative contributions, incredible successes, and humorous incidents which abound in its history. This is a people history. The story is told not through volumes of historical numbers, dates, and facts, but through the lives of its people. If those who have been part of this experience can proudly say of the book, "This is my story," then I have succeeded.

I would also like to express my appreciation to my wife, Debra, who supported me, prodded me, and believed in me. The readability of the work is the result of two excellent proof readers: Bobbie Carmical, whose writing ability and knowledge of the industry was needed, and Pam Deaton, whose grammatical ability coupled with her outsider's view of the industry made it more understandable to the layman. I also must acknowledge the individuals in the book who proofed their own story to insure its correctness. I cannot thank everyone, but I do want to express particular appreciation to Warren Sims, Bill Wiegand, Jack Bandy, Reg Burnett and Amy Cruse, Al Wahnon, Shaheen Shaheen and the people of Cobble. There are many whose names do not appear in the book, but helped with details or shared stories at the bank, in the grocery stores or at a carpet market. Their help was just as important.

The Carpet & Rug Institute helped initiate the study and their constant support, particularly Betty Hickman, insured its completion. The pictures which Brenda Murry provided from the CRI archives insured a more enjoyable book. All the carpet journals and their staffs have created a wealth of history through their articles and they have treated me with kindness and support. They do the gritty work daily so that historians have it easier.

Without the help of Polly Boggess and others at the Crown Garden and Archives most of the first chapters would not have been possible. They and others of the Whitfield-Murray County Historical Society have preserved the documents and oral histories of the pioneers as well as the artifacts of this great industry. I hope that the trustees are successful in their goal of creating a tufting and carpet museum and research center. Jean Manly's rich memories to tour groups that I brought to the museum inspired me to continue to write the chapters. My first chapters cannot capture the romance and excitement which a visit to Crown Garden will impart to the visitor. The reader must visit it.

Finally, I must thank the faculty and staff of Dalton College for the assistance which they provided. The Dalton College Enrichment Award helped start the long odyssey and the office computer/word processor which I received two years ago insured its completion. I also thank George Jones, Tom Veve, Jack Waskey, and Neal McKenzie for their support and various contributions. Without the secretarial help of Martha Poteet and numerous student aides its completion would have taken much longer. I trust that the reader will notify me of any corrections or share their personal stories with me in the future.

Throughout the fourteen years a number of persons have spurred me toward completion with their belief in me and the project. At times, it appeared that I would research forever, but their requests for a copy of the book shoved me forward. To all of these and the people whose work created this unique American success story I am eternally grateful.

# INTRODUCTION

Historians called the 1950s the Age of Affluence, the 1960s the Age of Turmoil, and the 1980s the Age of Conservatism. In the last few years world events have shaken our world. The Berlin Wall was torn down, the Soviet Union has disintegrated, the Communist hold on Eastern Europe has been broken, and the Middle East has exploded in violence. Even the carpet industry has been rocked by mergers, changes in consumer buying habits, and new manufacturing developments. Undoubtedly, the 1990s will be the Age of Change: rapid, unpredictable, nerve-shattering change.

In the past historians, economists, and philosophers had the luxury of change proceeding at a measured pace which allowed them to predict the future. Today, the rate of change is accelerating exponentially, shifting so fast it is tough to make even short-term predictions accurately.

The carpet industry is in the midst of turmoil due to technological expansions, mergers and consolidations, and changing demands. Most modern tufting machines are producing 100,000 square yards of carpet quickly and the former Communist nations offer vast new carpet markets. Woven, tufted, and sculptured rugs are encountering growing demands. Shaw Industries has expanded to Great Britain and Australia, strategic locations for quicker delivery to the former Soviet countries, and the Pacific Rim territories. Queen Carpet has added Cumberland Carpets to its Patcraft purchase. To date, Mohawk acquires a new company nearly every six months in its quest to challenge Shaw. Dixie Yarns has acquired Masland Carpets to compliment its earlier purchases of Carriage Industries and Suncraft Mills. Carpet consultant Reg Burnett predicts that in the next five years "approximately 50% of all the existing carpet companies will either be acquired by other mills or will just fade away."

One might ask if the history of the tufted carpet industry is the story of what once was, but will never be again. Before such a study is dismissed, the value of historical analysis should be considered. Playwright Eugene O'Neill in *Long Day's Journey into Night* has Tyrone telling Mary to forget the past. Mary responds:

"Why? How can I? The past is the present, isn't it?
It's the future, too. We all try to lie out of that
but life won't let us."

Hispanic philosopher George Santayana reminds us that "Those who cannot remember the past are condemned to repeat it." Could it be that within the seeds of the marvelous rags-to-riches story of the tufted carpet industry may lie the secrets of survival and renewal?

The only way that anyone can understand the present movements in the carpet industry is through a careful consideration of the past. When the tufted carpet industry began to dominate the floor covering business in the 1950s, many firms such as RCA and Armstrong hurriedly bought the fledgling companies, only to discover that it was not an ordinary manufacturing business. Standard business practices did not work in the carpet industry and its profit margins were vastly smaller. The U.S. Patent Office told many inventors that certain carpet machinery would not work and could not be patented, but machines were already producing carpet.

Many of the machine and management developments are somewhat unique to the tufted carpet industry such as the business partnership which created the Beaulieu Group. Bob Shaw is working to create a world-class corporation without moving to a financial, transportation, and marketing center like Atlanta. Some new ideas today such as flocking are actually old ideas from the pioneers of the tufted carpet industry such as Gene Barwick. The journey to the present has been along numerous roads, some of which were dead-ends. To appreciate the present and prepare for the future anyone who is going to participate and make an impact, must understand the historical ground upon which they stand.

Regardless, the story of the inception and growth of this American contribution to the world is a magical account of people and companies who participated. The industry is not a monolithic structure which has clearly defined forms of growth and a few selected leaders. It is much more vast. To tell the story is like trying to control the arms of an octopus or pick up a huge square of jello. Where do you start? How do you get a handle on it?

Therefore, we are faced with trying to tell a story which began with a fifteen-year-old teenager's handtufting a bedspread in 1895 which developed into an industry which has produced over one billion square yards of carpet yearly since the beginning of the decade. The story of the carpet industry is not merely one of square yards produced, but it is also the story of the people who worked, dreamed, and created the companies, the machines, and the carpet. Every story can not be told, so some were selected to represent both the present and the past of those who created the tufted carpet industry. Its pioneers came from all walks of life: housewives, farmers, mechanics, store owners, and teachers. They brought their own unique abilities to invent machinery, sell products, organize business and work with people. So many contributed to the growth and expansion of the carpet industry, and whether the impact was minor, major, or magnificent this is their story.

# *Chapter One*

# BEDSPREAD BEGINNINGS

America has always been regarded as the land of opportunity where the reward for hard work, diligence and persistence is often the experience of prosperity. It's where the Horatio Alger story of rags to riches can come true. But, unfortunately for some, the dream has become jaded and for many, a lie. The average American has learned to settle for less, rather than achieving the realization of his dreams. The people of North Georgia, however, have seen the relatively recent development of the tufted carpet industry which has made the American dream come true for many and within the reach of others. The tufting industry has literally transformed both the region and the lives of its inhabitants.

According to historian James Young, the skill of tufting material was introduced to America during the Colonial Period by immigrants from France and England, while the art of rug-making was an ancient Egyptian skill. Another expert, historian Gene Stafford, gives credit to the women of New England for developing tufting. As these women darned areas in counterpanes (bedspreads) and tablecloths, they found that decorative effects could be achieved by fluffing the ends of the thread and adding a design around the tuft. This decorative practice expanded into household linens.

Peter Ellis in the *Ciba Review* said that the early settlers saved the trimmed-off wicks from home-made candles and worked them into the spreads. On Southern plantations tufting reached a high degree of perfection. Hand-tufted spreads were not unusual in homes of the eighteenth and nineteenth centuries, but declined in use and almost disappeared after the Civil War. It was the revival of this art in 1895 that initiated the intriguing story of tufted carpet.

In 1895, Dalton, Georgia, had no reason to believe that it would develop into a modern Eldorado, the city of gold. Although it had two textiles mills which produced threads, the town was not considered a bustling industrial area. C. C. Bemis, owner of the Dalton Grocery Company, was selling Solid Gold Flour for $1.85 per 100 lbs. and Best Rio Coffee at 5 lbs. for $1.00. St. Joseph's Sarsaparilla was the "greatest Cleanser and Purifier of the Age." It could cure rheumatism, scrofula, tetter, eczema and neuralgia by purifying the blood. Banking was done at the older F.T. Hardwick & Co. or the newer First National. Most stylish women wore the season's new sailor dresses over featherbone corsets and were members of the Lesche Club for the study of the classics. Will Harbin was again writing—this time *From Clue to Climax* for J.B. Lippincott Publishers. A proper young lady might go to the Dalton Female College which would mold her into "a high grade teacher." October Beans,

Sweet Taters, Cracklin' Bread, Tame Gooseberry Pie or Blackberry Cobbler and two or three meats graced Sunday dinner tables. After evening church services the children scurried to Horan's Ice Cream Parlor.

Fifteen miles to the west of Dalton, Catherine Evans started a story of unbelievable dimensions. She was born August 10, 1880, one mile west of the hamlet of Rio. At the age of twelve, Catherine visited "cousin Milton Tate" in McCuppy, and saw an old tufted bedspread which the family had saved from pre-Civil War days. The design was in squares, laid off by quilting frames. Catherine was so impressed that she stitched one in 1895, at the age of fifteen.

> I got the material, seamed it together, placed it on the floor, took quilting frames and marked it off in squares of about 3 inches. Then I got white thread which was in skeins and ran it off on the spinning wheel to make 12 strands of number 8 yarn. I put it in a bodkin needle and started working. My mother told me I had started something that I would never finish. But, I did finish! It was like the Irish chain quilt pattern in squares.

Muslin or squares of sheeting was used for the first bedspreads. The yarn was Ace Cotton Yarn, possibly from one of Dalton's two textile mills. Catherine used 12 plys or strings to make the large tufts from the soft yarn. The bodkin needle, three or four inches long with a very large eye, was usually used to pull ribbon through lace netting. She made a stitch along a pencil line she had drawn, and then skipped a half-inch or so to make another stitch. After stitching the entire spread she cut between each stitch, leaving the spread covered with small tufts. Catherine boiled the spread three times in a cast iron wash pot in the backyard causing the base fabric to shrink and bind the yarn. The spread was hung on the line, and the sun dried it and helped bleach both the sheeting and the yarn. The breeze fluffed the yarn and further locked the tufts in place.

Ignoring how much trouble it had been to make, Catherine completed her second spread a year later, which she called a "Spear and Circle." When her oldest brother married Lizzie Creamer of Trion, Catherine presented them with a spread as a wedding present. Later, when Catherine's new sister-in-law, Mrs. John Lange, saw the spread, she wanted one of her own.

> I told her I could make it but I did not know what it would be worth because I had never heard of one being sold. She told me to make it and whatever I said it was worth would be alright with her. So, I made it. The cloth and thread cost $1.25 and I charged $1.25 for my work which made a total cost of $2.50. She wanted to pay more, but I did not want to charge too much. Then, a man worked for a dollar a day.

Catherine Evans Whitener

Others in Trion ordered bedspreads, and when Mrs. Lange moved to Summerville orders began to come from there. Marking the patterns on the base material proved to be a major problem, so Catherine developed a rather unusual solution. Placing a new sheeting over her finished spread, she rubbed the sheeting with a Calumet Baking Powder tin lid which had been greased from fat on a meat skin. The pattern appeared in stamped black dots. The marks would wash off later.

Her marketing area increased in 1909 when her father bought a farm four miles southeast of Dalton on Riverbend Road. As her orders increased, she had to have some help. "Then I started showing the neighbors how to make them so they could help me. I would stamp the spreads and the ladies would take them home and bring them back finished and get more to make." Catherine would then boil, bleach and fluff the spreads before delivering them to her customers.

The first bedspreads were made of pieced muslin, shrunk to hold in the tufts. Thomaston and Dalton's Crown Cotton Mills began making sheeting especially for hand-made bedspreads which would shrink in both directions. The stamping process evolved into the following method: a finished spread was placed on the floor with the wrong side up. New sheeting was placed on top of this and tacked down to hold the fabric tight. Markers at first were can lids or pie pans. Later, markers were made of sheet lead shaped around blocks of wood by Ollie Cavender and others. They still had to be greased with lard or the fat from ham or bacon. The meat skin was held in one hand to regrease the marker while stamping. The grease mark faded quickly, so the invention of the wax marker made this part of the process faster and longer lasting. The marker was made from paraffin, sterick acid and wool violet dye melted and molded to be cut into blocks or bars. Many were attached to wooden handles.

The stitching was still done with a large bodkin needle which would hold the heavy twelve-strand yarn. The mountain women called this "turfin." A stitch was taken through each dot on the pattern with a continuous running stitch. Spreads were beginning to be fluffed by brushing with a broom or beating with a cane, forming the separate tufts.

For her first spreads, Catherine had to spin the yarn on an old-time spinning wheel into the 12 ply tufting yarn. As demand grew, she contracted with Dalton's Elk Cotton Mill to produce 25-pound lots for her needs. In response to a demand for colored tufting, she wrote numerous mills asking for information about color-fast yarns. Eventually, she picked out her colors and sent white thread for dyeing to the Franklin Process Dye Company in Providence, Rhode Island. In later years the demand became so great that Franklin built a plant in Chattanooga, Tennessee for the dyeing of yarn.

Patterns and new designs presented another challenge. Since there were no patterns for the emerging industry, Catherine made her own. Plates, saucers or anything round provided the desired curves for her conventional patterns. Many of her floral designs were tediously copied from curtains. "The

Washbowl," a favorite pattern, was drawn literally from a large washbowl and another popular number, "The Saveall," was taken from an old quilt. The early patterns carried such names as "Square Circles," "Star Circles," "Wild Rose," "Bowknot Rose," "Flower Basket," "Acorn," "Daisy," "Interlacing Rings," "Donut Hexagon," and "Wedding Ring." Many patterns were obtained from previous quilts. In early 1922, Catherine added another dimension to her life; she married W.L. Whitener.

It is generally believed that the second person to enter the tufting business and hire others to work for them was Mrs. Eugene Evans, Catherine's sister-in-law, who lived on an adjacent farm. It has been said that she was one of the first to "make a business of the business." She recalled the early days:

> I would put my young children in the buggy and go throughout the countryside and teach people how to tuft. I'd teach the man, the woman and the child if they showed that they wanted to learn. I took them the sheeting and the yarn and on a regular schedule I'd return to pick up the finished product.

Mrs. Evans remembered July 3, 1918, as the day her business really began to boom.

> I was getting ready to go on a picnic when a fashionably dressed lady drove up in my driveway.... She said, 'You don't know me, but I know you and know about your bedspreads. I want to sell them for you.' She, a Mrs. Parmalee, was on the next train for Atlanta. She went to Rich's Department Store and came away with an order for 24 spreads....

At about the same time, local ladies like Mrs. H.L. Jarvis saw the opportunity for widely marketing the spreads. Mrs. Jarvis had married a local dentist, Harry Lee, who was a widower with two young daughters to raise. Since dentists were often paid in produce and what money Dr. Jarvis did make he spent on fancy cars, she realized that she would have to raise the tuition money to send her new daughters to Georgia State College for Women. Having been a major agent for Pruden Insurance Company until she married at 38, she had a knack for business. At a friend's home, Eugenia Jarvis happened to see a bedspread, and the possibilities sparked her interest.

Ultimately, she became Catherine Evans Whitener's agent. Eugenia stamped out the spreads at her home and then would take them to other women to be made. Also she typed out countless letters to individuals and business firms to acquaint them with the spreads, their prices, and to ask for orders. When the first "large" order came (one dozen from John Wanamaker's

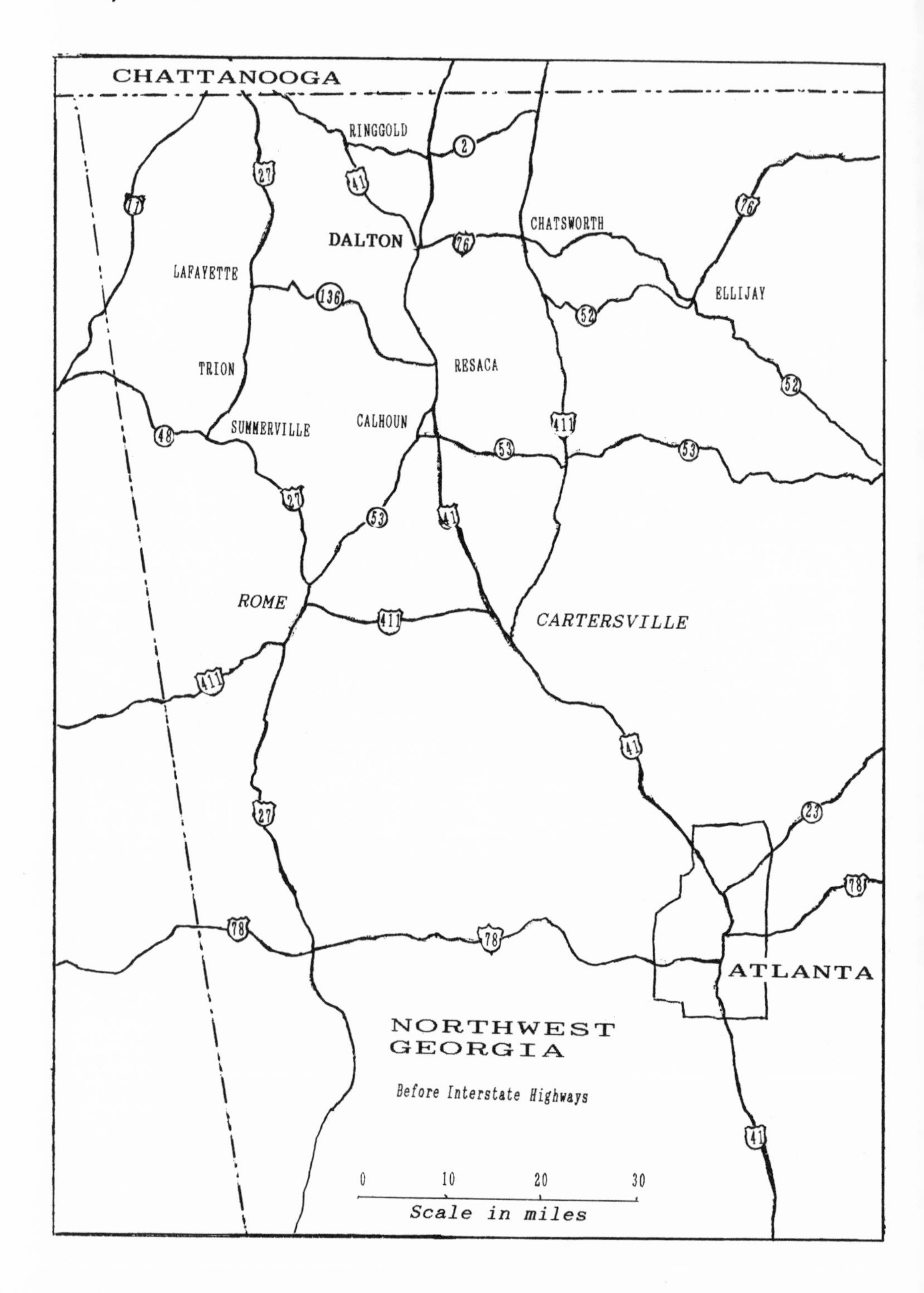
CHATTANOOGA
RINGGOLD
2
27
41
11
DALTON
76
CHATSWORTH
76
LAFAYETTE
136
ELLIJAY
52
TRION
RESACA
52
48
SUMMERVILLE
CALHOUN
411
53
53
27
53
41
ROME
411
CARTERSVILLE
411
41
27
23
78
78
78
ATLANTA
NORTHWEST
GEORGIA
Before Interstate Highways
41
0
10
20
30
Scale in miles

Department Store in Philadelphia) Eugenia knew that she was on her way. "And when the check came in payment for that order, it looked like a fortune."

Many stories exist about those early days which seem to credit different people with similar deeds. The Wanamaker story is a good example. Another account which involved Jessie Bates is equally colorful and demonstrates the vision of these early entrepreneurs. Displaying keen business courage, Jessie packaged fifteen spreads, made out an order on a piece of tablet paper, and shipped them unsolicited to John Wanamaker's Department Store. Within weeks a check for the correct amount was received with an order for more. Jessie then wrote to Chambers of Commerce around the country for names of department stores. His wife Nettie would make the spreads and he would ship fifteen to a store along with an invoice. According to the story, no store ever failed to pay for them.

Other accounts have attributed the first organized selling to Mrs. Gilford Cannon, Jr., whose husband owned a local dry goods store. When a traveling salesman from Cincinnati called on them at their home, she talked him into selling bedspreads for her. After visiting Cincinnati and Columbus the salesman sent back an order for 100 spreads. To meet the demand Mrs. Cannon had to look for help from ladies outside of Dalton.

One example of the early workers is the story of a young boy, Frank Strain, who was put on the noon train from Hill City to Dalton (about 12 miles) with a cardboard suitcase full of finished spreads. He would deliver them to Mrs. Cannon and return on the evening train with more sheeting and yarn for his mother Edna Redwine Strain and Aunt Mamie Redwine. However, these ladies soon saw the potential and began to make and sell spreads for themselves.

Exactly when widespread marketing developed is difficult to determine. The Evans Manufacturing Company dates its existence from 1917 and records indicate that Mrs. Jarvis was also selling at that date. Others feel that the first commercialization of the home crafting industry was done by Mrs. G.M. Cannon, although one state history cites her beginning date as late as 1919.

Regardless, the demand was there and as times were hard, there were plenty of workers available. World War I temporarily inflated the price of cotton, but by 1920 the price plummeted and drove farmers into desperate straits. As evidence of the difficult times, one person recalled awakening to early morning sounds of people walking around in the front rooms looking for a spread to work before other tufters could get there. Even a little money was better than none. Some can remember finishing an entire spread for a nickel. Payment usually depended upon the difficulty of the pattern sewed. Some bedspreads brought the worker as much as $2.50 and in a day when Garrett Sweet Snuff cost 10 cents a can, that was good money.

An early pioneer whose family made the transition from bedspread to rugs was B.J. Bandy. Growing up as a farm boy, he quickly decided that plowing was too hard; so he "learned to telegraph." Bandy married a school teacher,

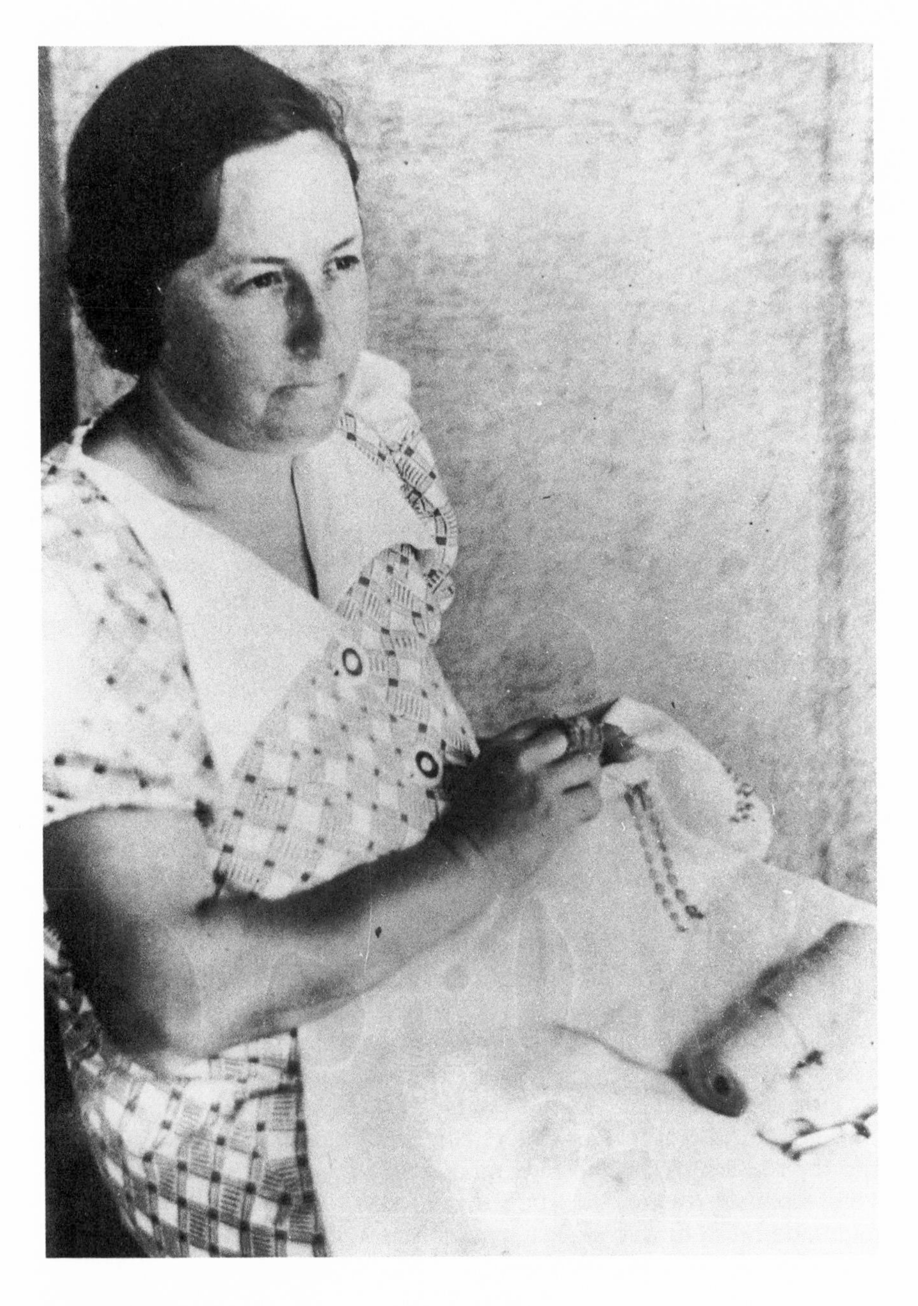

**Hand tufting**

and also taught her to telegraph for the railroad. B.J. and Dicksie saved their money and started several small dry goods stores in Sugar Valley, Calhoun and Hill City. He also did a lot of trading, and he loaned every dollar that he could.

The post-World War recession hit the community hard and many started declaring personal bankruptcy. Since no one was paying him, B.J. had a hard time paying his bills; at one point he owed his suppliers $20,000. Yet he was too stubborn or too proud to go into legal bankruptcy. He had heard about Catherine Evans Whitener and the money she was making with spreads. If Mrs. Whitener could go out and sell them then he was sure that his wife could too. Mrs. Whitener not only agreed to help them but also gave them three or four spread patterns with which to get started.

Armed with one bedspread and aided by a railway pass, Dicksie climbed aboard a northbound train. She remembered sitting up all night on the day coach. She got off in Washington, D.C. and walked with her suitcases to the first department store she could find, Woodward & Lothrop. To the buyer she announced, "I'm Mrs. Bandy from Dalton, Georgia, and this is my spread. Would you like to buy any?" Even though this was all new to her, they ordered 400 spreads at $4.00 each, which meant she would double her money. She immediately left for Baltimore before the buyer could call and change his mind. There she sold 200 more to Hothscheld & Kohn. She was so excited, but rather than go on to New York, she figured she'd "better come on back home and hire the people to tuft those 600 bedspreads." They set up a shop in a tin building on Thornton Avenue in Dalton and began to figure out how to stamp the spreads and get them all tufted.

Other early pioneers included the Walter Kenners and G.H. Rauschenbergs of Dalton, Dr. and Mrs. John Boston of Calhoun, Mrs. R.M. Herron, Sr. of Dalton, the George Muses of Sugar Valley, the Decks, and Misses Grace and Francis Fleminster.

By the early 1920s the demand was increasing so rapidly that expansion was occurring. Back rooms, garages and sheds were no longer large enough. Homes or large rooms were turned into "spread houses" where the spreads were stamped, sorted, packaged and shipped. Often the spreads were not in the best condition when they were retrieved. As one of these early marketeers related:

> When I'd go back to get the spreads sometimes I would find babies sleeping on my spreads, snuff spit on them, and even find them used as bed covers; but when we boiled them in the huge pots they came clean as a whistle and sold like hot cakes. Goodness, we made money.

The demands for a greater labor force led to more developments. "Haulers" began to fill their Model T Fords with sheeting and yarn and would drive

A hauler delivers materials

throughout North Georgia, East Tennessee, Eastern Alabama and even parts of the Carolinas to find people to sew the spreads. Mrs. Fred Caldwell of Resaca would mark off the patterns on 100 pieces of sheeting, gather enough yarn and then leave at each hired house the number of spreads that they thought they could finish before she came back the next week with a new load. Carl Babb, who worked as a hauler for 7 years for Jessie Bates, would carry about 150 spreads a week to workers out in the Mill Creek area west of Dalton. He earned a salary of $11 a week while most of those working in the spread houses made a $1 a day.

Mrs. Caldwell and the Strain-Redwines paid in cash, but the Bandys and others developed a different method of payment. They paid the workers in due bills or coupons which were redeemable in goods from one of the Bandy stores. They could either come to the stores or the Bandy haulers would deliver sugar, snuff, coffee out of a barrel or whatever, along with the next load of materials.

Although some men like Fred Caldwell thought it was women's work and farming was still the man's activity, other men were attracted by the money. One spread house in the 1920s in Hill City had $75,000 in sales in its first year and even after living off its cash bag, it ended the year with $15,000 profit. If this kind of money could be earned by a home craft, how much could be made if machines could be adapted to sew and cut the tufts? With this in mind the door lay open to the next development in the story—the invention of simple tufting machines.

# *Chapter Two*

# INVENTIONS, BANDY AND CABIN CRAFT

In 1929 the country plunged into the worst depression in its history. Farmers of North Georgia were barely surviving. Because of marginal farming in the northern part of the state and the generally depressed conditions of the nation's farmers as a whole since the World War, agriculture had not fashioned a very high standard of living. The basic crop, cotton, had suffered first from the post-war drop in prices which was followed by the ravages of the destructive boll weevil, often described as "a cross between a termite and a tank." The Great Depression caused the farmer's condition to further deteriorate. Between 1929 and 1932 farm prices fell 60% and the gross yearly cash income of each farm person in Georgia went from $206 to $83. For the first time since the 1890's cotton dropped to 5 cents a pound. Many had to stop farming because they no longer had the credit to purchase seed and fertilizer.

The emerging bedspread industry was a lifesaver to the "dirt poor" farmer. Small spread houses dotted the dusty roads of North Georgia. Haulers enlisted whole farming families to tuft. By the end of the decade, Model T's were delivering thousands of spreads each week to homes all over Appalachia. As an indication of the volume, B.J. Bandy has been credited for making the first million dollars in handmade bedspreads. However, he was one of the very few to be that prosperous.

As the depression deepened, America turned to Franklin D. Roosevelt and the New Deal which caused the industry to again change dramatically. On June 16, 1933, the President signed the National Industrial Recovery Act, with Section 7a stipulating that labor codes in every major industry should set minimum wages and maximum hours. Immediately, the tufted industry reacted.

Previously, an informal bedspread association, the forerunner of the Tufted Textile Manufacturers Association (TTMA), had concerned itself with protecting bedspread patterns. Since there were only so many ways you could use circles, squares and stars on a spread, there had been a strong competitiveness over designs. According to R.E. Hamilton, an early leader in the industry and in the TTMA, they were able to work out grievances by changing designs slightly so that no one would be economically injured.

Regardless of their past competitiveness, the specter of the impact of a wage and hour law brought them together. Two issues seized their attention. As long as tufting was done in the homes it was difficult to determine the proper pay. Yet, more importantly, the average pay had been 5 to 10 cents an hour at the very most - far from the 32 cents an hour and $13.00 for a 40 hour week suggested by Washington. B.J. Bandy, G.H. Rauschenberg, Sam Hurowitz,

**Bedspread Code Hearing, Washington, D.C. 1934, Judge Tarver Standing**

Fred Westcott, Pete Lumpkin (the first president of the association), and Judge Tarver, their local Congressman, hurried to the Capitol for the code hearing. Unable to stop the minimum wage law they were able to slow down governmental policing of the codes until 1936 and to get some reduced pay rates for training people. Regardless, the new wages codes meant that hand tufting would inflate the selling price of spreads and reduce their attractiveness to the customer. This threat accelerated the development of a tufting machine.

In 1943 the Georgia State Legislature passed a resolution placing "the first single needle chenille machine" in a glass case in the state museum. The official document states that it had been invented by Glenn Looper in 1936 in the Looper Foundries in Dalton. Actually, it is hard to pinpoint the "first," but the Glenn Looper story is an extraordinary account that needs to be told.

A 1922 honor graduate from the Georgia Institute of Technology, Glenn learned to be an inventor from a master. As a student, he was required to attend a reception honoring Thomas Edison. While there, he engaged in a lengthy conversation with a very uncomfortable looking man. Later he discovered that he had been talking with Edison. That dialogue initiated the steps which led to his employment by Edison's New Jersey Laboratories after graduation.

Since he had married Frances Kenner, daughter of the co-owner of the Kenner-Rauschenberg Bedspread Company, he returned to Dalton to apply his talent to the industry. After a brief experiment with his own bedspread company, Glenn started Looper Foundries. It was at this point that he invented his machine. Just before his death in August, 1970, he talked with journalist Ron Gunter:

> Looper recalled that his father-in-law stated 'Damned if we're not going broke on a million a year volume! Glenn, can't you build us a machine to do this tufting work?' Looper said he went back to Georgia Tech and paid $35 entrance fee in order to have access to precision equipment for his work and experiments.

He created a single needle tufting machine which sewed in the large yarn and cut the tufts with a scissors mechanism. A number of other unique inventions must be credited to Glenn. He developed a very small hand-held gun with which an operator could trace patterns with a type of blue chalk on a towel or on sheeting. He designed a machine for mending rugs and developed the apparatus by which a bedspread could be made in a single pass, though he never patented the latter. The story is that one of his mechanics took the concept, patented it, and made a fortune.

An interesting family story revolves around the development of one of his other ideas. His first machine patents were on electric motor operated units and in later years he experimented with air-operated units. One day the family heard him in the bathroom, and one member said, "he kept flushing the john and we thought something was wrong with him." Actually he had been trying to figure out how to get the air to spin in a tube and thus twist the yarn. He noticed that when he flushed the toilet the water would circle as it went out and he felt that "the same principle would work on a machine with air." This idea is the basis of the principle used to drive the yarn coming from the creel, through plastic tubing to repair broken threads on a tufting machine.

Glenn also invented in other areas. He developed a suspension for a car that would keep it level in curves and one that would keep a bed level regardless of how heavy or light the second person in the bed was. He developed a type of thermostat for the radiator cap of a Model A Ford which would change colors as the engine got hot. At the time of his death he was working on a self-propelling mechanism for a child's scooter. He would literally send the children out to test it and have them come back to his bedside and tell if his adaptation was successful. It is difficult to place each invention in its proper historical context or to determine how many other developments stood upon his pioneering foundation, but the industry definitely profited from his contributions.

Actually, the progressive propagation of tufting machines had been occurring for some time. The oldest patented tufting machine was created by Casper Wood of Bismarck, Illinois, in 1882. In 1889, an invention using a gooseneck sewing machine was developed by H. Hubert Humphery of Detroit, Michigan, but these early inventions had no effect on the tufting industry. As early as 1926 Carter Brothers in Chattanooga developed a single needle tufting machine which was invented by August Carter. A.J. Cook was in charge of manufacturing the bedspreads and Payton L. Carter was the brains behind merchandising them. Incidentally, Chattanooga was considered at the turn of the century as being the most industrialized city of its size in the nation. In 1900 there were nine furnaces, seventeen foundries, and numerous machine shops within the city limits.

Meanwhile, Hank Ingram, owner of the Thomas Henry Company, entered the scene. Formerly, a Philadelphia producer of merino yarns used in thermal clothing, the company had moved to Nashville in 1926 because of the cheaper labor market. Ingram converted it into the Ingram Company, a producer of bath mats and face cloths on terry cloth looms. Hearing that there was a Chattanooga firm making bath mats on a sewing machine he drove to that city to try to buy or lease one. When Carter flatly turned him down, Hank turned to his electrical engineer Ernest Moench and told him to create a similar machine even though he had not seen one nor any blueprints. For a year Ernie worked on a prototype. Each night he would bring home a "little swatch of what they had developed that day" to have Mrs. Moench give her opinion. She remained so critical that he finally cut a piece from one of Carter's rugs and brought it home. She got down on her hands and knees and looked at the front and back and said, "I think you've got it!" So he went back to work.

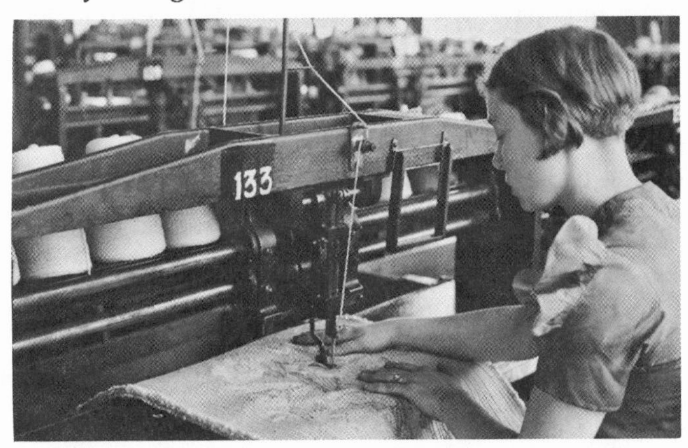


**Ernest Moench's Single Needle Machine, 1928**

By 1928 he had invented a two foot wide machine with the sewing part in the middle supported by beams on either end. It could accommodate 16 needles but used only one at the start. It had a circular cutting head as opposed to the scissor-type of Carter's. Ingram would not venture into production without a patent search.

Although there were similar inventions, the patent attorney thought it was patentable. Not desiring to do things halfway Hank and Ernest carried the 200 lb. model machine to Washington using a separate berth in the Pullman car and leather straps on their shoulders which allowed them to carry it between them. Ultimately they built and put into production 20 machines and successfully fought off a challenge by Carter.

Shortly after that, Ingram eased Moench into leaving the Ingram company and taking the tufting division. The Ingrams held 50% of the new Tennessee Tufting stock and a Miss Snell, his spread designer, invested $2,000 while Ernest contributed $4,000. Things were "nip and tuck" at times but they made money from the start, producing bedspreads and then later rugs and bath mats.

**Tufted on single needle machines and hand trimmed—1938**

Although the machines were very simple, they could do some amazing things with them. The full rug in the picture was tufted on two single needle machines—one was a low pile and the other was a higher pile. Then the rug was hand trimmed to have a carved effect.

Probably the first machine-made bedspread in Dalton was completed on a rented machine in the shops of Kenner-Rauchenberg, an early pioneer in the handmade tufting business. As a railroad employee in Dalton, G. H. Rauchenberg saw how many box loads of spreads were being shipped north, and he responded. He leased his first machine from Carl Stiegers of Delton Rug Company of Oskosh, Wisconsin who was using it to make area rugs.

While all the inventing and adapting was taking place, B.J. Bandy heard of a process which gave the same look as hand tufted. The Boycell Manufacturing Company of Gastonia, North Carolina, was using a machine which produced a product very similar to what he was looking for. Erskine Boyce had developed an early machine known as "the Boyce Knotter," used on looms in the weaving of rugs. In 1932, while everybody was concerned with bedspreads, he was producing 24" and 36" wide rug mats on multi-needle machines. Bandy bought the company and all the patents which would or could be applied to tufted chenille products. He enlarged the plant there and also built similar machines in Rome, Georgia, at Southern Craft, which he owned. In 1940, he moved the Boycell operation to a new plant in Cartersville. Basically he had two different types of machines. One was a skip stitch type which nearly duplicated the hand tufted design. The other was a scissors type machine since tufted bedspreads were cut pile.

As the demand for spreads grew, other inventors experimented with some crude machines. Many were not practical nor successful, but "they could be used". Every tinkerer and mechanic in the tufting rooms tried to develop a machine; many of these first tufting machines were built from a converted Singer or Union Special sewing machine. Most started with the old goose-neck 3115 Singer head, which was used for sewing heavy textiles such as overalls and tents. Using a hacksaw they would cut off the raceway, bobbin and hook and replace them with a series of make-shift attachments. "They made an attachment where the needle would come down, a hook would take that thread off the needle after it went through the sheeting, hold the thread and the needle would go back up and pull more thread in." Then the process would be repeated. The hook or "looper" would be holding four or five loops at a time. A cutter blade, with a scissors action, came along cutting four or five loops behind it. The cutter blade could not cut yarn off simultaneously or the thread would jerk out causing the machine to quit sewing.

Both loop and cut pile were fairly simple tufting procedures. Possibly a simple explanation of loop and cut pile at this time would aid in understanding. (Tufted carpets are made by machines which stitch the pile yarns by vertically- reciprocating needles into a pre-woven fabric backing.) In operation, the tufting machines behave like giant sewing machines with hundreds of needles. Whereas looms and knitting machines fabricate the entire carpet, including backing and pile, tufted construction is concerned only with the pile. The essential principle of pile formation by a tufting machine may be understood by considering the action of a single needle. The formation of a pile loop may be divided into three stages.

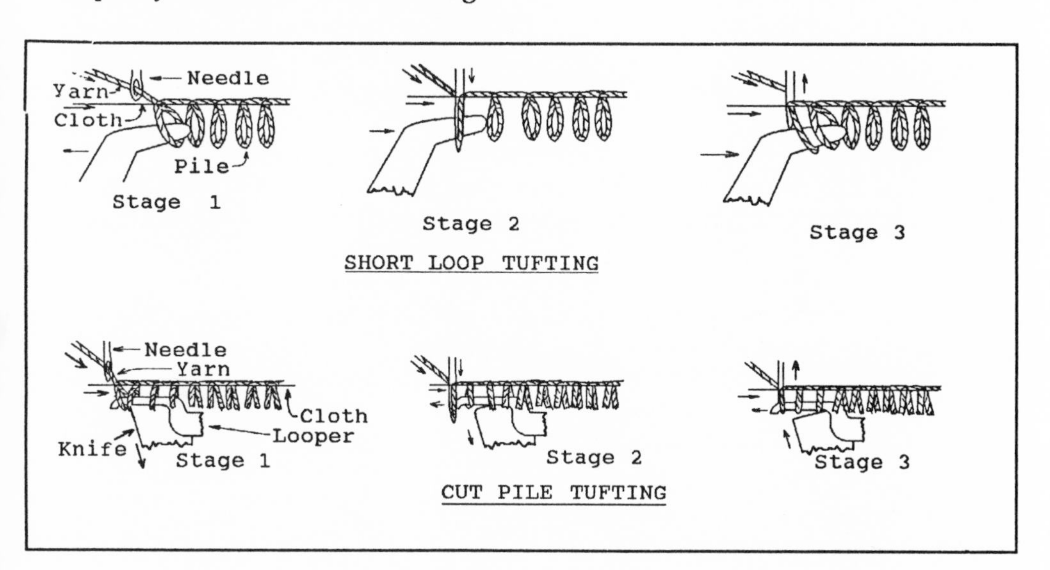


To form a looped pile, the needle in stage 1 begins to descend as the looper is starting its backward movement out of the previously inserted yarn loop and away from the path of the needle. In stage 2, the needle has passed the yarn through the backing fabric and is at the lower point of its motion.

The looper has started forward to enter between the needle and the yarn. During stage 3 the looper has entered the yarn loop and the needle has moved to the upper end of its motion. As the needle descends again, the looper moves from the loop thus avoiding interference with the needle. The fabric is then moved forward and the cycle repeated.

When cut pile is produced, the fabric is moved toward the looper. In stage 1, the looper holds two loops while the knife is cutting the third previously-inserted loop against the sharpened edge of the looper. At this stage the knife, after cutting the loop, is moving downward to begin its next cycle. The looper is moving to enter the loop made as the needle descends through the fabric. In stage 2, the needle has passed through the fabric and delivered the correct amount of yarn to the looper as it moves forward to pass between the needle and the yarn. The knife is moving away from the cutting edge of the looper to allow the next uncut loop to enter the cutting area. In stage

3, the needle is moving upward leaving a loop on the front cutting edge of the looper which begins to withdraw from the loop. The knife is moving upward to cut the third (previously inserted) loop.

**Singer 3115 adapted single needle machine**

The demand for sewing heads caused a Cincinnati merchant, R.G. Miller, in 1937 to begin filling his car with old 3115 sewing machines and heading toward Georgia. On one of these early trips a nearly fatal car accident in Trion, Georgia, left him with his chest and foot crushed and his head badly cut. Mrs. Miller called for help from their future son-in-law, Jim Feighery, who was working in an electrical/plumbing wholesale business in Cincinnati. Jim shuttled machines southward while R. G. recuperated. The business continued to grow so that R.G. moved his family to Dalton, replacing his car with a panel truck for hauling. This, in turn, was replaced by a two-and-one-half ton stake truck, and finally, by a tractor and trailer vehicle. Jim Feighery's heart ruled over his plumbing job and he followed his future wife and father-in-law to Dalton. At one point he covered 32 states delivering sewing machines for the company. He recalled, "Things were so good then, you did not have time to unload them in a store. People would come up with their trucks and we would just count them off."

The feeder head in the early days cost Mr. Miller only fifty cents. NRA, which brought the wage and hour law, also closed down textile production in prisons as they were in competition with outside industry. This allowed Miller to buy their now-idled machines cheaply. Before the war, the price for a machine went as high as $7.50 and after 1945 it peaked at $50.00. As the price rose, interest in machine development increased. Once the machines got to the area, mechanics made the tufting changes. Much of this was accomplished by I.E. Bills in his shop, (everybody called him I.0. Bills, since he owed everyone), or Roy Windon, who worked for B.J. Bandy, or Lawson Jaquith, who worked for Kenner-Rauschenberg. Their basic tools were a screwdriver, pliers, soldering irons heated by blow torches, and cutting wheels. They would cut everything with a 1/32 cutting wheel. Some mechanics were fortunate enough to have some milling machines and bench grinders. Men would sit for hours forming hooks and their fingers would become like leather from the constant heat.

With a small number of mechanics developing slightly different adaptations in Dalton, it was unavoidable that similarities would exist. B.J. Bandy felt that many of the developments in the Dalton area were infringing on his patent rights. Most of the demand was for cut pile tufting on bedspreads as there was little interest in rugs. The scissors type machine created cut pile tufting easily and most of the developments seemed to be an adaptation of his scissor type patent. His attorneys proved to be quite successful in winning litigations to protect his patents.

B.J. heard of a company called Polly Prentiss in South Carolina that might be infringing. However, the lawyers were able to ascertain that the hacksaw invention of O.C. Moore was not covered. They suggested that B.J. and Polly Prentiss join forces to cover the field. Litigation built a strong position and a great deal of ill will. The other companies then sued claiming monopolization. Jack Bandy tells of hearing his father and O.C. Moore talking one day while playing golf. O.C. said, "you know, B.J., if we died tomorrow no one would come to our funeral." Based on this combination of reasons they decided not to enforce the patents, thus giving the industry "a free tufting ride," except for the patterning and combination devices.

In the early 1930s there was a new development in tufting for spreads—the needle punch style. In this style the sheeting was clamped on an oversized embroidery hoop or wagon wheel which was on an axis so that the operator could move the four-foot hoop around to craft the design with the needle. The machine was shaped sort of like "a water pistol made of lightweight aluminum." It used a hypodermic needle through which the yarn came from a bin overhead and was held in the material by the tension of the fabric. A variable speed motor similar to what a dentist used for his drill powered the stitching. The trigger started the needle and the operator could make almost any design. Glenn Looper developed a model, but his looked more like a screw driver, and later a pistol. There were two basic companies that had created the needle punch machine in the early 1930s. Mrs. Louise Vandyke for many years sold needle punch spreads made from a machine probably developed by her brother Billy. The bigger development came from Cabin Crafts.

Cabin Crafts was the work of Bob McCamy, Fred Westcott and G.L.(Lamar) Westcott. They were partners in the Westcott Hosiery Mill. Lamar came to Dalton in 1917 when he was 22 years old and started the mill (originally Dalton Hosiery Mill). He had studied hosiery production in Philadelphia. When Lamar began in Dalton, he discovered that no one in town or even in Westcott Hosiery knew anything about manufacturing hosiery. There were only about 3,000 residents in town so he went into the countryside, hired employees and trained them. His younger brother Fred took charge of sales and Bob McCamy was chief mechanic and superintendent of the plant. When the brothers sold it in 1928-29 to Real Silk of Indianapolis, Bob was left out of work. Bob had done a good deal of electrical and mechanical engineering work at Georgia Tech, and now turned to the spread industry. He started a small spreadhouse with two sample spreads in an old rented building on Emery Street. His wife Mary Stuart came up with the business name "Cabin Craft" since it was a home craft and the alliteration of cabin had a "nice sound". She also supplied most of the early designs of floral, Indian and modern patterns, using her one year in art school at Parsons in New York as her knowledge base. In these early days Bob's wife, Mary Stuart McCamy (now Dixon), said they were also helped by B.J. Bandy who advanced yarn and sheeting to the young company.

In 1932, Fred returned from Indianapolis where he had been trying to help Real Silk salvage the mess it had made of the Westcott Hosiery operations. With his money and marketing ability Cabin Craft began to expand. Later Lamar, who had been in New York licensing his patents on hosiery machines, came in to help manage the financial side. Lamar asked to work and be paid only half-time, so that he could work in the community for the other part. Fred's salesmanship helped him win major accounts like Lord & Taylor's, probably their first big customer. Fred went to the California coast where he sold to Bullock's specialty shop and became a close personal friend of its buyer, Fred Peters. Fred Peters was Clark Gable's brother-in-law and this is one reason why the bedspreads used in *Gone With The Wind* were made by Cabin Crafts. When the picture premiered in Atlanta, Fred Westcott and Mary Stuart McCamy were in the Fox Theater box with Clark Gable and Carole Lombard.

After 1932 the partnership of Bob, Lamar, and Peek Smith (brother of Mrs. G.L. Westcott) developed a needle punch machine which became the hallmark of their early years. The machine was versatile and produced beautiful spreads. Campbell Petty, who joined Cabin Craft in 1941 to help with advertising, said "They guarded that thing like Fort Knox." Only certain personnel were allowed into the locked front room to see and use the machine.

Since the firm did not have their own laundry or dye house, they would send a guard along with their loads to the Dalton Spread Laundry so no one could steal their designs.

Since the early spreads were spoken of as chenille or candlewicking or punch work, the terms need clarification. Chenille is a thread woven into blanket strips which are then cut into yarn, wound and used. Actually, chenille was never used but the terms came to mean any tufting which looked like a row of caterpillars. Punch work or candlewicking was entirely different and implied the use of the needle punch machine which created a more intricate design.

There was one further adaptation of the needle punch machine by B.J. Bandy's son-in-law, Joe McCutchen. After graduating from Georgia Tech, he worked on a variation of a candlewick bedspread machine, but Mr. Bandy suggested he do something in needle punch. He went to Chattanooga and worked with machinists John Turley and Joe and Albert Cobble who were rapidly becoming major contributors in machine development. He developed a machine which was not an infringement on the two other patents. He established 40 machines in the Bandy plant in Gastonia, and then he and his wife Christine went into business in Ellijay in 1937. He landed a major Sears order and in less than 2 years was running over 400 machines in 2 shifts with about 950 employees. Mechanization had appeared in the industry but growth was slow in the late 1930s.

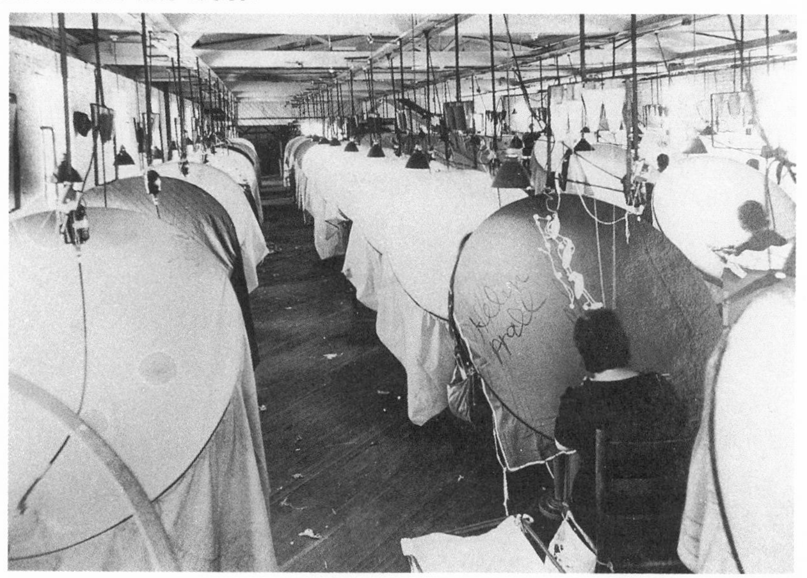

Needle Punch Machines and Hoops

# *Chapter Three*

# TINKERS, TUFTERS AND BOMB COVERS

With the introduction of machines to the bedspread industry, the rhythm and tone of the people involved began to change. Mechanics, machine operators, and just tinkers began to create new developments under the pressure of necessity. Home tufting was replaced by single-needle sewing machines run by a common power source and operated by farmers' wives who drove to work together in carloads. Equally important, new faces were drawn into the region by the possibility of a bedspread bonanza.

An interesting example of the new people drawn into the area was the Lewis Rosen family. In 1934, while attending the Frankfurt Textile Fair, Lewis perceived that the "madman" Adolf Hilter's move toward militarism would ruin his import business. Since handmade bedspreads were beginning to become popular, some of his friends suggested, "Go to Dalton and see what they might have." He met Dr. Woods' wife, Mrs. Joe Wrench of Colonial Spreads, and J.T. Bates' nephew, Chester Underwood, all very active in the "spread" business.

The prospects seemed good enough so that in June 1935 his son Ira opened the LaRose Spread Company on Hamilton Street in Dalton. He contacted a hauler to take the sheeting and yarn to the hand tufters in the area. He mentioned to friends that the hauler looked just like Snuffy Smith in the comic strips, never doing a lick of work while his large wife picked up the bundles and delivered them. Then, just like all the other spread houses on Hamilton Street, spreads were taken to Dewey Wright of Crown Laundry to wash them. One of the first problems that they encountered was how to deal with demand. The greatest demand from the stores came in the fall, which unfortunately coincided with cotton picking time. Instead of three or four weeks for delivery, it would take two to three months. Rosen tried to build an inventory the following year but the problem continued. The answer had to be in the use of machines to create a larger product base. In 1937 LaRose introduced their first single needle tufting machine. Sarge Houston was a mechanic and a tinkerer, so using "good ole American ingenuity" he built their first machine.

By 1939 they had built the first brick tufting plant in Dalton, employing 200-300 workers. Their one to four needle machines were producing spreads, housecoats and small rugs. Still, each spring and summer the business slowed down. Many in the business wondered how long the demand would last, while others tried to expand their product line.

Mrs. Fred Caldwell, 20 miles south in Resaca, entered the housecoat business by seizing an opportunity. A lady from North Carolina had bought a spread at her shop and wrote asking for a housecoat of chenille. She sent a "skeleton picture" of what she wanted and the color. Mrs. Caldwell worked up

**Inspection Table**

a pattern until "it measured out to what she wanted," and she soon was selling all the housecoats that she could make.

Her story is an excellent example of the transition from handcrafted to machines. Mrs. Caldwell began as a hauler for the Bandys, marketing, delivering and picking up as many as a hundred spreads at a time. Then she went to work for "Super" Jones who had one of the largest spread houses in the Calhoun area. She said the "word" was that they made a fortune in it, but "they were bad to drink, and they'd drank themselves to death and threw the fortune away." When machines began to appear, Mrs. Caldwell went to "Super" and told him she was quitting and going into the "Candlewick stuff" on a machine she was having made. She felt that she could get the materials and sheeting, but she was worried about getting the yarn. Then she said, "He looked at me right hard and said, "Now I'Il let you have all the thread you can hook up if you'll make yourself some money. But if you just go out and trade dollars, I've not got any for no damn man.'" That year the river had "washed my husband's cotton and corn away and he lost everything. And he owed for his fertilizer, mules and on the car. We were just desperate as to what we could do." In addition. her father had gotten sick and since he was out of work, he was worried about losing his 200-acre farm. Faced with these overwhelming problems she resolved to get "my own business and pay the note on the farm."

Jim Starr, a Calhoun furniture store owner, trusted Mrs. Caldwell and loaned her the money, while mechanic John Hunt "who could do anything with his hands" made her first machine for $150. Since there was no electricity on their farm, they rented a vacant service station at the crossroads of Resaca. She developed her own patterns and made spreads, capes, housecoats, shawls and whatever people wanted. Ultimately, she put in 14 more machines and ran them all on one line shaft employing as many as 38 people at one time. When the war came and materials were hard to get, she stopped the business and retired. She was an example of the drive of many of the early women who helped get the industry rolling.

Not all the manufacturing activity by women was treated with appreciation. Some men liked the money, but resented that housework did not get done. This attitude is seen in a poem by Earnest Parker of Ellijay written in 1937 and found in George Gordon Ward's *The Annals of Upper Georgia.*

**Working Spreads**

*When the morning meal is over,*
*And the chickens have been fed*
*Then the women grab a needle,*
*Go to working on a spread.*
*back and forth they wield the needle,*
*Filled with blue and white and red;*
*Till they've covered all the surface*
*Of a 'leven quarter spread.*
*'Tis a rush from morn till evening.*
*With no time for baking bread:*
*For it takes the daylight hours*
*For the working of a spread.*
*But it's great to be a tufter-*
*You can surely earn your bread;*
*You can make a quarter daily*
*If you are fast at working spreads.*

As more small spread houses tried to increase their production through the use of machines, the suppliers and mechanics grew in importance. Many had learned their trade in textiles or as tinkers. Teenager George Hanson started sweeping floors in a textile mill in Thomaston, Georgia, but very quickly decided that he wanted "to learn a job that could make some money and you didn't have to work all your life." He went to school at night and took International Correspondence Courses while working his way through the grading, stapling, carding and drawing of cotton. He worked with the overhaulers so that he could tear down a piece of machinery, find out what was wrong with it and then put it back together. Meanwhile, he finished a correspondence course in mechanical engineering. His success also must be credited to his father, a mechanic and a contractor, who always told him, "Son, don't ever say you can't. There is no such word as can't. You first make up your mind that you can do it, then do it and do it right. Anything worth doing is worth doing it right." In 1930 he came to Cartersville to work with Candlewick Yarns. It was there he created a winder which would twist the yarns for women who were hand tufting. Instead of giving the ladies single strands of yarn it twisted 12 and 24 strands together. George was representative of many of the early tinkers who used natural instinct and experience to help the industry in the transition.

**Bedspread factory**

Unfortunately, the industry grew faster than the supply of pre-trained mechanics. Roy Windham, a mechanic working for Bandy's Southern Craft Company in Rome wrote a "how-to" book to help new mechanics. He had sent letters to manufacturers offering twice the highest local salary and practically begging for help from machine repairers for their new plant. His plight was clear in these lines, "Please, Mr. Dealer, answer right back and tell us how to get our machines to sew. Out of the 10 machines you sent us, we can only keep 3 sewing." They were months behind on orders. Ultimately, he was forced to develop a manual. In 1938 he composed 8 sheets of instructions, but his later book was an extremely thorough attempt to solve their dilemma. He concentrated solely on the Singer 3115 as to the workings of the head; how to dismantle, repair and re-assemble. He discussed the theory of the machine and after showing the adjustments of the parts, he explained problems and remedies for the single and multi-needle machines. As further support for the demands and problems, numerous supply houses and machine shops were listed.

The Jim Feighery Company was considered to be the largest second-hand sewing machine dealer in the United States. Along with Battey Machinery Company in Rome, Feighery supplied the basic motors, belts, shafts and parts for the machines. Machine shops scattered over North Georgia and Chattanooga provided custom work, machined parts and made attachments. John Peacock in Chickamauga worked extensively on small machine works and coil springs of different sizes. Chesley Parker at the Hill City Machine Shop in Rome focused on pattern making, fabricating and casting structural steel work. Wilbur Jackson of Chatsworth Manufacturing crafted small to medium size machine parts. P.H. and John Turley in Chattanooga were expert tool makers as well as providing punches, throat plates and cutting grinders. During this time at Tennessee Textile Machinery, Albert Cobble was building both tufting or hosiery mill machines. His brother Joe was in business with George Muse of Sugar Valley at Cobble Brothers Machinery Company. They were building both single and multi-needle machines on a par with the 3115, and they had built a skip stitch machine for imitation hand work. This was in addition to operating a large hosiery mill business.

With the outbreak of World War II, the industries of Dalton were forced to convert to the production of essential wartime materials. Cabin Crafts produced shelter half tents, silk parachutes, field insect bars, navy mattress covers, chemical tank covers and airplane engine and wing covers. Redwine Strain Spread Company used its machines to make trench shell carriers and fragmentation bomb parachutes. G. H. Raushenberg produced olive drab handkerchiefs for the army while San-Ray made army towels and did dye work for both the army and navy. LaRose Bedspread produced insect bars, head nets, barracks bags and shelter half tents. Lawtex produced army uniforms, clothing for lend lease, and textiles used for mattresses and pillow cases. Smith Manufacturing and Blue Ridge Spread produced barracks bags, mosquito bars, sleeping bag covers, uniforms and bomb parachutes. Gordo Bedspread and King Cotton Chenilles made field bags and mosquito bars while Candlewick Yarns produced twine for the army and navy.

The machine shops in the area also were involved in the war effort. Cobble Brothers were allocated some of the smaller jobs that Wheland Foundries of Chattanooga did not have the personnel to do. They produced 50mm and 70 mm howitzers and anti-aircraft guns as well as other precision gun parts and munitions.

There was a continuing demand for tufted textiles, especially since the public had more money, but the government would not allocate the materials to plants that did not produce designated war materials. The woven industry could not meet the demand because all their looms had been taken to produce cotton duck. However, necessity was the mother of invention. LaRose Spread and others took material like mop yarn and coarse duck, whose quality was so poor that the government had refused it, and made rugs. At the time goods were not sold directly to the public, but to distributors, who acted as middle men to stores and chains. When word of the coarse rugs leaked out, distributors flocked into town and fought over what was available. Fred Rosen, Ira's younger brother, said that cases of rugs were sold as many as six times before they left town. He felt that this supply saved both the distributors and the mills from ruin.

Overall, the development of the tufted textile industry appeared to falter. To paraphrase the words of Franklin D. Roosevelt, "Dr. Win the War" took precedent over "Dr. Tufted Textiles." Yet the techniques and skills learned in producing machinery to win the war would later provide the basis for significant machinery development. Much of the manpower in the mills was drawn into some branch of the armed forces. Although the war put tufted textiles on hold, it proved to be a catalyst for the industry. The end of the war brought new technology, a pent-up consumer demand, and new ideas. The transition from spreads to rugs and then to carpet was beginning. The tufted carpet industry was poised to come of age.

## *Chapter Four*

# THE BIG MACHINES ARRIVE

Although World War II caused the production of tufting materials to nearly cease, it is considered the time of major transition for the industry. Some individuals returned to other industries with the feeling that the potentials for bedspreads had ended. John Frank Patterson produced spreads on single needle machines before the war. However, the cessation of demand during the war convinced him, Gordon Johns and Eddie Hall that money was to be made elsewhere and they left the bedspread industry. For others, the developments of new technology and better skills provided the avenue for a major leap in the industry—the yardage machine. Instead of using the 3115 gooseneck sewing-tufting machine, the yardage machine had a fixed support on each end and the sheeting or backing passed continuously under the needlebar. Lewis Card, a major producer of machinery in the industry, said that he believed the biggest development enroute to carpet production was the creation of the yardage machine, a forerunner of today's giant carpet tufting machine. Today's massive carpet industry bears out his belief.

**Henry C. Ball, Executive Vice-President of TTMA and mender**

The basic principle of tufting is the same whether done by a single needle sewing machine or a multi-needle yardage machine. The face yarn is inserted by needles into a pre-woven backing and the inserted tufts are held in place by the untwisting or blooming effect of the yarn and the addition of latex to the back of the carpet. A secondary or double backing, developed in the 1950s and 1960s, was frequently adhered to the back of the carpet to give additional "bond" and dimensional stability to the carpet.

By the early 1960's machines were producing rugs and carpet in widths ranging from 30 to 216 inches. The smaller widths were used as area rugs, runners, or sewed together to create wider rugs. In carpet manufacture the 120 inch yardage machine, producing nine foot carpet, the 180 inch, for twelve foot, and the 216 inch, for manufacturing fifteen foot wide carpet, predominated. The latter could also be used for tufting nine or twelve foot widths. The gauge of the machine, or the distance between the needles, determined the space between the lines of tufting. A major impetus for the industry was the use of finer gauges or closer rows. By the mid-1960's 1/8 and 5/32 inch gauge in loop pile and 3/16 inch gauge in cut pile were used most frequently. The yardage machines operated at the relatively high speed of 550 revolutions per minute and pile height variance was determined by raising or lowering the needle plates relative to the machine bed. Pattern attachments on either type of yardage machine made possible multiple pile heights. However, the tufting, at that time, could not match woven carpet in carpet density or clarity of pattern in the multi-colored variety.

Although most will agree that the yardage machine was a quantum leap, it is nearly impossible to agree as to who was responsible for its invention. R.E. Hamilton, a pioneer in the industry and head of the Tufted Textile Manufacturers Association, once said that if a newspaper announcement asked the man who invented the tufting machine to meet you on the courthouse steps in Dalton, it would be impossible to get up the steps because of the many claimants. Other accounts of his speech indicate there would be over 200 men. Even the conflict in his own story shows how difficult it would be to agree on any one significant person. However, there are several individuals who may be responsible.

Many accounts point to Albert and Joe Cobble as playing the most significant role at this junction. Their father had been a farmer in the Fort Payne, Alabama area. The family had moved to the Chattanooga area in 1896 in pursuit of work. At the age of 13, Albert began work in a hosiery mill for 45 cents a day. The family actually grew up in the hosiery business and, at one point, brothers Henry and Horace had two hosiery mills each. In 1936 Joe and Albert started Cobble Brothers Machinery as a machine shop to repair and rebuild hosiery equipment and make attachments. They borrowed $800 to start and worked for the first six months without making enough money to pay themselves. Albert recalled often having to divide a can of tuna fish for lunch.

They rented 1500 square feet at 230 East Main in Chattanooga and at the start they sought to increase business by delivering machines. It was a good business at the time and they entered the tufting business by accident. In 1937, the manager of Colonial Coverlets in Chattanooga, J. C. Wilson, brought them some parts to make for his adapted Singer 3115 bedspread machines. Slowly they began to expand their work in adapting the Singer machines to meet the demand. Joe developed a looper and cutting mechanism that worked very effectively. In the mid-1940's they expanded the number of needles on the machine by multiples of 2, to as many as 24. The bar had to have braces to hold the weight. They were unable to add more needles because of the limitations of the faceplate-looper-cutter needs. However, up until the war most of their business continued to be in hosiery.

In early May, 1940, the brothers had a major disagreement and Albert sold his interest in the business. It seems that they needed 10 cast arms for machines and Joe ordered 100. Albert got angry about it and sold his 50% to George Muse. Paul Jolley, who went to work with the Cobbles in 1937, remembers that although both were major contributors to the industry, their personalities caused conflicts. Albert was married with a son, while Joe was a bachelor and was the more demanding of the two. Paul said that if he had something that was not too good, he would take it to Albert who would say, "That'll do if it will work." However, if it was not exactly right, Joe would make Paul throw it away and do it again. They both were outstanding, but they have different temperaments and just could not work together.

Albert started the Tennessee Textile Machinery Company. He built his first complete tufting machine model in 1943-44; he built a complete head instead of using the old Singer head. In 1945, with the help of Bill Patey of Dalton, he built his first yardage machine. He delivered it to Judd Brooker at Brooker Spread in Dalton. Judd kept it a week or two and then sent it back stating that he could not afford the yarn to thread the needles. Albert then leased the machine to Ralph Rhodes of Georgia Rug Mill in Summerville. The machine was created to make chenille housecoats, but Albert believed that Rhodes made the first yardage cotton throw rugs on it. The term chenille, by this time, was used to distinguish machine-made spreads from hand-tufted or candlewicked. The machine was 3/8 gauge, 45" wide and had approximately 300 needles. The cost of the machine was $3,500 and Ralph more than paid for it in the first year of his lease. His commercial success led Ralph to buy it the next year and purchase another at the regular price. Albert felt that Ralph made a small fortune on the two machines.

In 1950, Albert sold Tennessee Textile to Hoot Gifford and, with $5,000, started Super Tufter in Ft. Oglethorpe, Georgia. He used some surplus machines and business expanded to the point that customers were willing to wait up to six months for their orders. (By 1950 nine and twelve-foot machines were being built by a number of people to tuft cotton pile rugs.) In 1958 Albert sold his operation back to Cobble Brothers which was then purchased by Singer. Albert designed most of the machines that he produced. In 1957 he held eight patents on tufting machines, and possibly the first pattern attachment on a yardage machine.

Paul Jolley felt that Albert's greatest contribution to the industry was the DT or dial attachment. Before this invention one had to change push-rods, eccentrics on the main shaft and other bushings and bearings to change the stroke on the needles. With the attachment the dial could be changed and the machine adjusted itself automatically to the demand. Albert's invention has outlived him and is still in use in the industry.

The role of Cobble Brothers was more significant. As mentioned earlier, on May 1, 1940, Albert sold his interest to George Muse of Sugar Valley, who already had a good deal of experience in tufting. At the age of eight, George was folding bedspreads after school for his father. In 1918, his father and B.J. Bandy had gone into business together in a farm supply store. When the boll weevil hit the area in 1920 they nearly went broke. With the help of Catherine Evans Whitener they went into the bedspread business in 1921. In 1936, his father bought 12 machines for about $10 each from J.C. Bandy who had gotten them from the Washington Manufacturing Company of Nashville. They were rebuilt 3115 Singer machines and their hacksaw cutting mechanism was inferior to the scissors cutter of the Consolidated Sewing Machine Company in New York, which had been improved by Cobble Brothers. Their adaptation by Cobble started an important relationship.

Initially, George was not going to follow in his father's business. He had signed a baseball contract with the Atlanta Crackers in the spring of 1936, but he was hurt in a car accident which ruined his pitching arm and ended his baseball career. George learned how to work on his father's machines by working with the mechanics at Muse Spread Company. As George bought hooks, knives and clutches from Cobble, he became good friends with Joe. When the falling out between the brothers occurred, he stepped in to buy out Albert. The price was $5,600. He had $3,500 and his father helped him raise the rest.

The year 1940 was a good time to be part of Cobble. Three months after the union of Muse and Cobble, the company created the first yardage machine. It could tuft bedspreads 108 inches wide with 99 needles on a 1 1/8 inch gauge. It was surrounded in secrecy and many who were active in the industry at the time find it hard to believe that it existed. Even though Paul Jolley was making parts for it, he did not know that it was being built. The old Lookout Mountain Hotel in Chattanooga was used as the factory; the first floor windows were blackened and the machine was built in the lobby. It was made of angle iron and channels. The machine was lubricated by grease on open connections rather than an enclosed oil-fed one. Therefore, it could not be run rapidly. Only five machines were built and one of these was taken to the old Velvetone Building in Calhoun. It was set up and run by the Muses who maintained the secrecy as

1940 Model Tufting Machine -- Open on top; cams and bearings exposed. Frame welded from standard steel material.

**Cobble machine, 1940**

noted by the fact that the windows were boarded up and the only entrance guarded. Who actually built the machine is unclear. Sid Manning was the shift manager and a good mechanic, Joe Cobble was also surely involved and George probably played some role. Cobble's major business continued to be hosiery so one might assume that George was at least a motivating force in the machine's creation. Actually, Paul pointed out that in the development of a new machine or attachment everybody worked together and, in a sense, the result was the work of a lot of the mechanics.

When World War II came, all work was directed toward meeting the designated needs of the country so developments in tufting naturally stopped. Over 90% of Cobble's production turned to defense work. Many of the workers fought in the war and co-owner George Muse joined the Coast Guard. After the war, Cobble returned to the hosiery and tufting business. George said that everyone in Chattanooga was trying to figure out how to get a closer gauge. George was driving to work one day in 1946, and the idea of boring a different set of holes for the cutters came to him. When he told Joe, Joe's response was, "Damn, I'm glad I thought of that!" In a week's time they had created a machine which tufted at a gauge of .625 (5/8) enabling them to make scatter rugs and carpets. Known as the Big Machine or B.M., it contained 185 needles

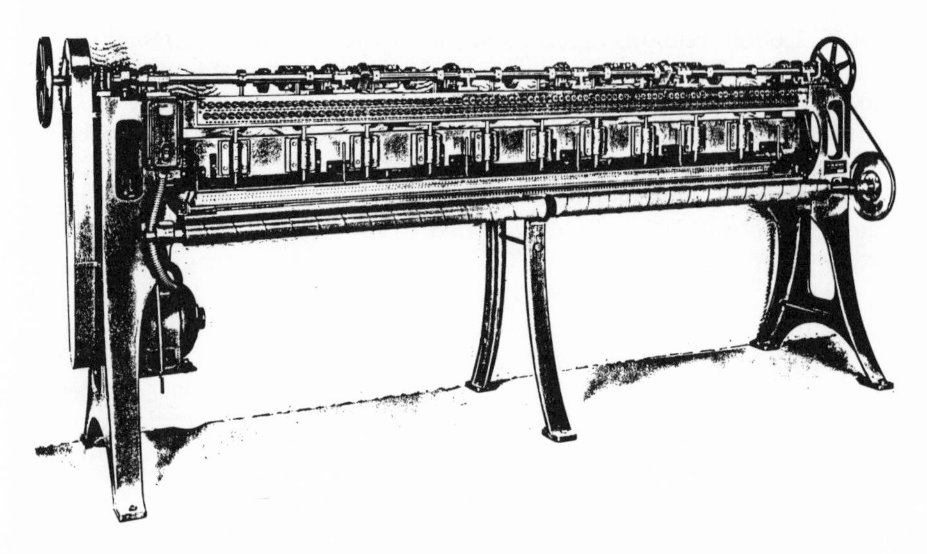

Approx. 1943 Model Tufting Machine. Drive mechanism still exposed, but castings begin to appear.

**Cobble machine, 1943**

and was the first cast frame machine built. Though called the Big Machine it weighed only 3,500 pounds; within ten years the machines weighed 10 times more. When asked if he felt that he had created the first carpet yardage machine, George said, "I can't say I was first, but there were none before me."

They continued to create machines for the industry. In 1949, they produced the first fully enclosed tufter, so oil rather than grease could be used on the working parts and the machine's speed increased accordingly. Bath mats were being produced with rugs and carpet soon to follow. In 1952, they introduced a twelve foot wide machine and added loop pile in .156 (5/32) gauge capabilities. The next year cut pile was added in .188 (3/16) gauge and an eighteen foot machine was created.

Foremost among the inventions in the 1950's were the pattern attachment devices. On a tufting machine this device permitted multiple pile heights and geometric and other patterns to be made in the same piece of carpet. Previously, this was only possible in woven carpet manufacture. In 1952, a roll pattern attachment was developed and in 1955, they introduced scroll and slat pattern attachments.

Cobble must be credited with many significant contributions in the field. It was the first to use frictionless bearings, introduced the cluster type creel, the tufting machine yarn feed, the waveline attachment, self-setting hooks, the roller-type pattern attachment, the Universal and Scroll attachments, the Controlled Needle principle and many other refinements.

In 1959, Cobble bought Super Tufter, a creation of Albert Cobble; Gowin Machinery Co.; and Southern Machines. In 1960, Singer bought out Cobble for $6,000,000. Joe and Albert repurchased Southern Machine in the early 1960s and built it up to the largest tufting machine manufacturer in the country before reselling it to Singer in 1969. In the early 1960s, of the estimated 1,400 machines being used, it was estimated that 85% had been made by Cobble-Singer. However, by the mid-1970s Singer decided to divest itself of certain product lines so that it could concentrate on the sewing machine market. In February, 1977, privately held Spencer H. Wright Industries bought the U.S. and overseas tufting operations of Singer which they continue to operate.

The sale to Singer led to the retirement of many pioneers. George Muse retired to Sugar Valley and the family business, while the Cobbles decided to enjoy life for a while. Their nephew, Lewis Card moved on, after a few years with Singer, to open with Grover Gowin Tuftco Machinery, and continued to build machinery even though Singer owned the Cobble patents. Lewis graduated from high school in Ft. Payne in May, 1939, and the next day went to work in Chattanooga for his uncles. The machines that he continued to develop were taking the basic tufting concept and expanding its abilities. This meant closer gauge, more needles, new shifting mechanisms, control panels, and various attachments. One of the basic ways that development took place was through experimentation or "good ole trial and error." Lewis remembers that the patent office told him that a particular machine design would not work, but it was already in operation. The machine industry also had to respond to developments in the yarn and backing industries. Tuftco has also gone through a series of changes and today is owned by a New York corporation.

George Hanson, who played a role in pre-war tufting development, made the transition from tinkering to inventing. In early 1940 George came to Dalton to work at Candlewick Yarn, and the next year started Dalton Welding and Machine Company with his welding instructor Mose Painter. Mills were making bedspreads with single needle machines, and he foresaw that bath mats would be a good addition to the marketplace. George started tufting small rugs—about 27 x 48 on a two-needle machine. By the end of World War II he had added needles to his tufting machine, and was making bedspreads, bath sets and robes with available materials. With the expansion of the post-war market he decided to create a 12- and 24-needle machine to make rugs. His mechanic, Gene Parker, was so sure it would not work that he would not build his design. "I can build it, but it won't run and you're just throwing away your money," said Parker. Finally, Gene did build it and when he started it, "it sewed right off." It was not built on a 3115 base, but on a steel base with a wide head. There was not enough room in the old flour mill for both the machine and the 36" duck backing, he cut a hole in the ceiling to the second floor, sewed the ends together with an offset and ran it. Then he sewed enough pieces together to create a 6 x 9, 9 x 12, or 12 x 15 rugs for two retailers in Washington and New York City.

Hanson's next goal was to create a yardage machine with 800 needles but could not figure out how to get the loopers to take the yarn off the needles at the same time. One night in a dream his mind worked it out and by daylight the next morning he had built a working model for his mechanics. Hanson's first yardage machine produced 4 feet wide tufting and later he expanded to 9 feet wide. He then turned his attention to creating a backing material to hold in the tufts and prevent rug slippage. Using talc from Chatsworth and latex and mixing it together in a 25 gallon barrel, created an acceptable backing. He developed a latex oven to cure the backing in 1947. In 1950 Hanson sold his company with its accompanying business headaches and became a consultant, which he continued to do into his 80s. The contributions of George Hanson are best described through the words of his contemporaries. Harry Saul of Queen Carpet, at one point, introduced him as "you're looking at the man who built the first carpet machine." While Frank Hawkins, who started out at Baldwin Sheet Metal building materials for homes, announced at an Elks Club dinner, "He made me a millionaire. He built the first latex oven and let me copy it."

One of the most colorful machine inventors was Mose Painter, mentioned earlier as George Hanson's partner in his welding firm. Mose's story is told in his book, *I Had a Millionaire's Fun.* He was not a millionaire when he died because as soon as he developed something new, he hurried down to the Elks Club to tell everybody what he had done. Others took the ideas and made fortunes, but Mose did have the thrill of creating some major innovations in the industry. He was a dreamer and, as frequently happens, dreamers do not grow rich. Mose, nicknamed that because he was such a scruffy little boy, started work at eleven carrying rail spikes. He was a hard worker, helping his father build grist mills as the family followed saw mills up and down the Greenbriar River in West Virginia. When his father moved to Conasauga, Tennessee, to work in logging, Mose began to run logging trains. Shortly before the Great Depression hit, he became shop foreman. Surrounded by lathes, milling machines, shapers and whatever, he discovered that he would have to learn on his own. "If you don't learn it, it's not our fault, it's 'your'n'," he was told. By 1940, the Georgia State Department of Education hired him to come to Dalton, an hour's drive, three nights a week to teach welding. They agreed to pay him six dollars a night, so he was soon putting in sixteen hours a day on the days he drove over from Conasauga just across the Georgia line.

In June 1941, Mose and one of his welding students, George Hanson, took $1,000 and opened a shop in the boiler room of an old flour mill building to work on heavy machinery. Each of them continued to work at their regular job and used any income from the shop to buy equipment and hire workers. Mose was making about $400 a month teaching, which was good money. Since war needs

*Diamond Horseshoe in New York (1945). Left to Right: Mr. Enoch Van, Herman Hirsch, Mose Painter, Tom Carmichael and Ervin Roach.*

**Mose Painter and friends**

depleted the best, most of the equipment was not "much account" and had to be rebuilt. Mose's first encounter with tufting dealt with trying to weld hooks on a hacksaw machine for LaRose Bedspread Company. His teaching of the mechanics there to braze hooks, instead of solder them, was soon followed by making the first hook for the five-sixteenth shag. This principle, which is used on every machine now built, was the start of all close gauge machines.

In 1943, Lou Goldberger persuaded George and Mose to go into business creating a machine to tuft long loop scatter rugs. They borrowed $1,000 from the bank, built five shag machines and with four two-needle loop machines, started making 24' x 36' scatter rugs. When they dyed their first batch at Green Wilkins' dye house, without latex backing, the loops pulled loose and they had a disaster on their hands. Fortunately, a Chicago retailer happened to show up looking for some seconds and George sold him all 1,000 for $2.35 each, five cents less than they had planned to sell them to Lou Goldberger. They were back in business. They solved those problems and were soon creating machines and rugs. They had so little space that each night after classes they had to cut, package and ship what they had made that day. Next, they turned to the Trust Company of Georgia to take on their factoring and improve their cash flow. Soon Stitt & Howell in New York and Sears were buying most of their product.

One of the major early breakthroughs came in 1943 with the aid of some "spirits". Tom Carmichael of Stitt & Howell sent his sales manager down to Dalton with a case of old Overholt Rye Whiskey, 100 proof, as a reward for the more than $100,000 worth of carpet they were producing monthly. About ten o'clock, after a full day of teaching, tufting, and packing, they were sitting around their small office talking about making carpet—real carpet. With the scissor-type machine there was not enough room on the attachment to make anything smaller than 7/16 gauge. The more they drank, the more they talked and dreamed, and Mose was definitely a dreamer. Mose created a sketch and assigned jobs. The mechanic Gene Parker was to make a hook out of a power hacksaw blade 62/1000 thick. Mose made a hook block 3/16 by one inch of cold rolled steel with a slot cut in it so that the hacksaw could go through and fasten around a half-inch shaft. George Hanson made a knife pin. Before morning they had created a 5/16 gauge which they fitted on a single needle machine. The next day they started building a twelve needle 5/16 gauge machine which produced a semi-shag carpet with a one inch pile height. Next, Mose talked Clarence Shaw, who was the head dyer at Dalton Bedspread Laundry, into dyeing it. Clarence was afraid that it would break his dye kettle but tried anyway. The finished apple green carpet was the first shag carpet made in the industry, but shag carpet did not reach popularity until 1960 when it was mass produced in broadloom.

In 1945, George and Mose dissolved their partnership. George took Hanson Painter Rug Company and Mose kept the welding business. He was doing the welding for many of the heavy equipment needs in town as well as the tufting business. The demand became so great that he sold that business and went solely into building tufting machines from single needle to twelve-needle, as well as all kinds of supplies through the Mose Painter Supply Company. After a brief partnership in Proffitt Textile in 1952, he went into business with Bill Bowen and Herbert Rogers as Painter Carpet Mills.

The height of the ceilings led to Mose's next major contribution to the industry. The building had a seven foot ceiling and creels could not be used. A creel is a large frame holding the bobbins which feed yarn to each needle in a tufting barb. A large amount of space was needed for the tubes that lifted the yarn from the creels up over the machine and down to the needles. Mose decided to try to run the yarn off beams which were huge wooden spools that feed yarn from a horizontal position to a machine. Something similar was being used in other industries, but everyone believed it could not be done for carpet machines. Since there were no geared motors in 1953, the machines were not strong enough to hold up all the tension, so the beams would not run continuously. His persistence paid off. Hugh Hamilton built a counter shaft that would pull the beams and Mose solved the gear problem. Shortly after that, other companies began to add beams to their operations. Beams tufting saved space and cut waste. Mose felt that this was his greatest contribution to tufting.

His last major contribution dealt with the problem of shrinkage. The finishing processes in Dalton were primitive at this time. After dyeing in a

First set of beams

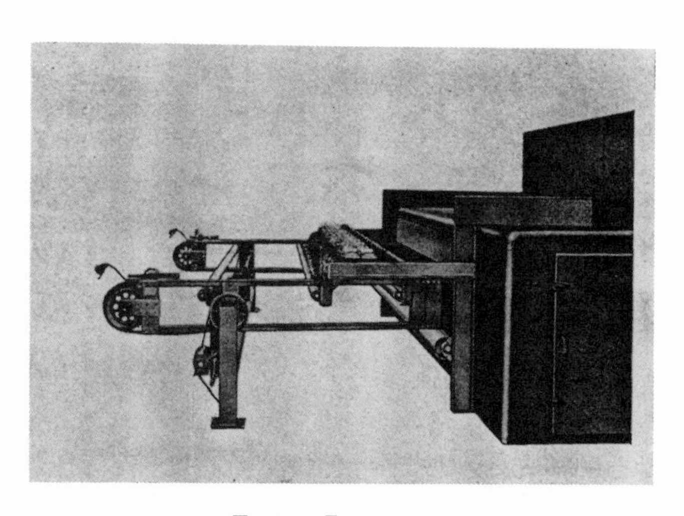

Tenter Frame

wooden dye beck and the extraction process to get out the water, the carpet's width could vary from 8' to 12'. Having seen the use of a tenter frame in a textile bleaching operation, Mose got the idea that it would work on carpet. In 1954 he bought an old frame in Chester, Pennsylvania, and altered it for his needs. Then he bought a bank of one thousand and eighty 500 watt plain bulbs with gold plated reflectors to dry the latex backing once it was put on the tenter frame mounted carpet. He persuaded V.D. Parrott, the Dalton Utility's manager, to wire up 440 power transformers to give him enough power. After ruining a number of rolls of carpet and not burning down the mill, they were able to dry the carpet at the rate of twelve feet a minute and it held its shape. Soon they were making bigger rolls of carpet; so big that they had to cut a hole in the ceiling to run the carpet in one end and out the other. When Gene Barwick saw it, he said, "Mose, if you had been my partner for the last four years we could have bought Dalton. The mistakes that we all made! Everybody was going to do this but no one ever did until you. This is IT!"

Mose went on to make numerous other mechanical inventions, but he never sought wealth. He built a machine to sew carpet together before it entered the tenter frame and oven. He designed the first carpet trimmers which were located on the exit side of the tenter frame. He even invented a device for inserting a frankfurter into a hot dog bun without breaking either side of the bun. Yet he tried to patent only one thing in his entire career and discovered that it had been patented in 1700 by an English shoe cobbler. He hated patents. "Patents are just lawsuits," he said, adding that he was "never meant to be a millionaire." Possibly it was just not his nature. He shared all his ideas with friends or moved on to other ideas and dreams before the dollars caught up with him. In 1960, he sold his one-third interest in Painter Carpet for $40,000, and five years later it was sold for $6,000,000 to become Collins & Aikman. Peter Spirer, who was intimately involved with Painter Carpet before going on to establish Horizon, possibly saw the true nature of this man. "He loved to invent and he shared with one and all his ideas without seeking financial return because he wanted to be recognized for his achievements by his peers. These considerations far outweighed the normal businessman's fervent pursuit of commercial advantage," Spirer said. Later in life, Mose generally played the role of consultant, but he seems to be one of the most admired contributors to the development of the industry. His gifts and spirit helped make the industry great.

The real story of the inventors of the industry probably will never be told adequately. Many of the breakthroughs came about as the result of mechanics or tinkers, as Mose loved to call himself, working with their simple tools and inventive minds. Artis Charles is representative of many unknown contributors. One of the youngest of fifteen children, Artis had a brief education before going to work for Carolyn Chenille in Sweetwater, Tennessee. He showed an aptitude for machines and in the mid-1940s in Dalton he developed a modification of a Cobble machine. His invention was designed to provide an auxiliary drive means for the feed shaft of a multiple needle bedspread machine. He was promised recognition and financial success for this as well as his 1960 invention of a Universal Multi-Needle Tufting Machine, but it never came. This was the case of many who made small, but significant contributions to the creation of the big machines. Yet it is upon the contributions of the Cobbles, George Hanson, Mose Painter and even the Artis Charles' that present day inventors have created the fast, wide machines of the future.

Dec. 9, 1947. A. E. CHARLES 2,432,469

TUFTING MACHINE

Filed March 10, 1947 2 Sheets-Sheet 1

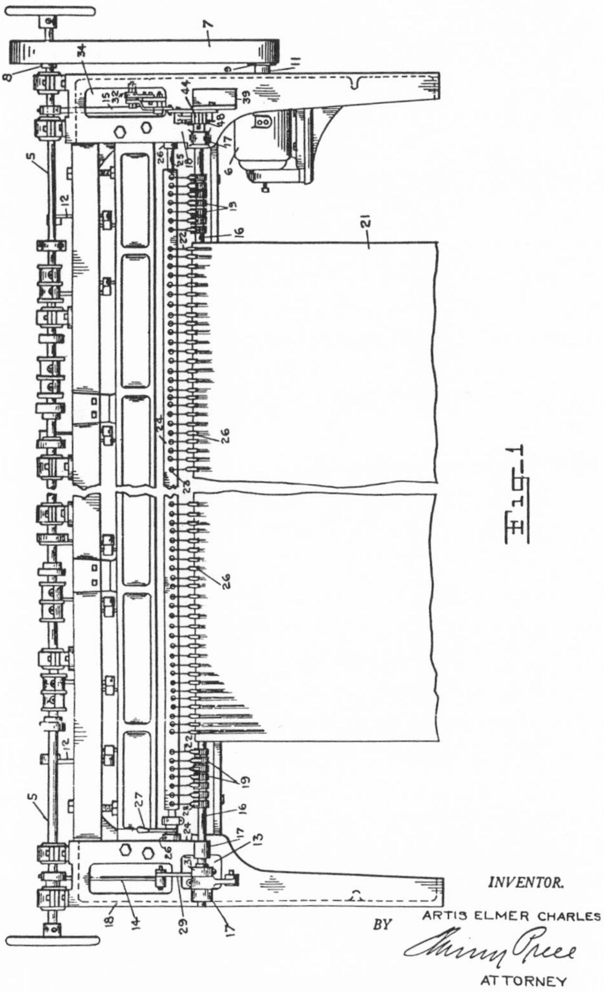

INVENTOR.

ARTIS ELMER CHARLES

BY

ATTORNEY

Artis Charles Machine

# *Chapter Five*

# COTTON, NYLON AND COLORS

Cotton had been used for the creation of clothing, slippers and floor covering for centuries. Although not in a major cotton producing area because of its hills, Dalton was in the cotton belt and had two cotton mills, Crown Cotton Mill and American Thread Mill. As the chenille industry developed, mills looked to areas as far away as Rhode Island to supply their needs. However, the demand was expected to spawn yarn producing plants.

Candlewick Yarns began in Cartersville, Georgia in June, 1937 to offer "consumer quality, American-made yarn for bedspreads." The four creators of the company were working at a Goodyear textile plant. Walter Slaughter had dropped out of school during 10th grade in North Carolina to play trumpet with a circus. He wound up in New England working for machinery manufacturers, where his job was to install textile machines and associated systems around the country. The Depression led to his being laid off when he completed installing machinery in the Cartersville plant. Walter was able to get a job running some of his machines where he met Jimmy Knight, a Georgia Tech graduate, and from one of the better families in town. Bob Dawson was also a Tech graduate, but had been hired because he had been a college baseball catcher; he played baseball for the Goodyear team in the summer and drove a truck in the winter. Rob Hamilton was from Dalton and the foreman in the card room where Walter was working.

They decided that the chenille industry needed a yarn mill. On the weekends they drove to bankrupt cotton mills around Georgia buying machinery at junk prices and placed them in a cotton warehouse. Since they had no money, the four persuaded the man who ran the warehouse to "transfer" bales of cotton and delay reporting it to management. They then borrowed money at the bank (which was owned by Jimmy Knight's parents) on the goods that "they had in process." They made the yarn, sold it and borrowed on the invoice. (This would later be called factoring.) They then allowed the original "transfer" at the warehouse to be issued and paid for it. They used this method week after week until they got on their feet financially. In late 1939 they opened a second mill in Dalton, using the Old Flour Mill. Each plant was making over 40,000 pounds a week. Hamilton and Dawson took over the running of the Dalton operation while the other two stayed in Cartersville.

The yarn that they were producing was seven different ply, from 3 ply to 12/5 made from 50% waste cotton and 50% virgin cotton. There are 32 upland grades of cotton and their virgin cotton was a very low quality, such as cotton stained or soiled when it fell on the ground. The waste cotton was 50% comber-noil and 50% strip waste. Noil is a short fiber which is combed out of good

**Stock bales being washed and sorted**

quality fiber. Strip waste also came from high quality cotton, but in the process of carding, short fibers are stripped off the card with a brush and this is strip waste.

In 1951 Dixie Mercerizing Company of Chattanooga bought Candlewick to expand its operation. Dixie was founded in 1919 by a group of men from a hosiery mill and in 1936 they began spinning mercerized cotton, which had a silk-like lustre. Their biggest customer was the Buster Brown Company who had been selling their comber-noil to Candlewick. However, cotton's difficulties forced Dixie Yarns to focus on non-tufting demands.

The use of natural fibers as the yarn for tufted carpet presented serious problems. Most tufted carpet in the post-World War II period was made with cotton fibers, but they soiled easily, matted down, and had problems with dyeing. Wool was much more resilient, but there were serious shortages after World War II, particularly in having to compete with woven carpet demands.

The American Viscose Company supplied a limited amount of rayon staple to the woven industry when their wool supplies were curtailed during the war. However, the return of foreign wool suppliers brought a sharp decline in demand for rayon. On the other hand, in 1947 tufted carpet used practically no man-made fibers. However, the growth of tufted carpet production and the problems with natural fibers brought a shift in yarn use. In 1954, 25 per cent of the total production of tufted carpet and rugs used rayon or nylon yarn and by 1958, 45.2 per cent. A better indication of fiber type may be seen with the decline of cotton fiber usage. According to a Census, in 1954 cotton comprised 75.3 per cent of the yarn, while by 1958 it had dropped to 13.0 per cent of the total. William A. Reynolds in his *Innovation in the United States Carpet Industry 1947-1963* noted that since the supply of natural fibers to the total carpet industry was inadequate, "Man-made fibers provided a necessary and alternative source of supply." His research denotes that "the early 1950s mark the beginning of the extensive use of these product innovations in the carpet industry."

Twisting Frame

Man-made fibers were first made from naturally-occurring substances such as wood or cotton linters which contained the long thread-like molecules supplied by nature. The filaments produced have the same fundamental chemical constitution, only in a different physical form. Viscose rayon, the first man-made fiber used in the carpet industry, is mainly manufactured from wood pulp obtained from Canadian or Norwegian spruce. The pulp is dried, pressed, and chemically changed into insoluble syrupy cellulose which is regenerated into a continuous strand of fiber or filament. Rayon was discovered through experiments conducted by Charles F. Cross and E.J. Bevan of Great Britain, who obtained patents on the process in 1892. After World War II, rayon staple was developed to compete with cotton and wool. Staple fibers are cut to a desired length, from eight inches down to one inch, so that they can be processed on cotton, woolen, or worsted yarn spinning systems. In this form rayon was introduced into carpet manufacture both as an all man-made fiber yarn and for blending with wool or cotton. The high point in rayon use in the industry was in 1957. Nylon was so rugged that it would ball or "pill up" and vacuum cleaners could not pick it up. Callaway Mills invented a machine with little clippers to cut the balls off, but other companies did not respond as quickly and went bankrupt.

Another type of fiber was produced by the Swiss Dreyfus brothers in 1921 from cellulose acetate solution. It was developed during World War I for varnishing fabric wings of aircraft. Because of its different properties it could not be dyed with the dyes used for cellulose fibers, but it had good heat setting properties. Both viscose rayon and acetate were difficult to dye and so brittle that they had a tendency to break over a period of time. When spilled on acetate, ladies' finger nail remover would solubilize the fiber. Almost any solvent would get the best of it and the fiber would not clean well.

Probably the most significant early development in man-made fibers was the invention of nylon by Dr. Wallace H. Carothers of Harvard. Doing pure research for DuPont he discovered, somewhat by accident, the combination of chemicals that made up the original nylon, polymer 66. The generic name "nylon" refers to a whole family of fibers that gets its raw material from petroleum or natural gas, nitrogen, oxygen and water. Chemical processes combine these elements to form long-chain molecules that constitute fiber-forming substances called polyamides. The fiber is noted for its great strength, quick resiliency from extensions, durability and water repellency. When nylon was first introduced in staple form in 1946, it made little impact.

However, in 1958 DuPont introduced a new filament nylon yarn, Type 501, which radically transformed the industry. By virtue of the bulk, texture and crimp added to the basic filament by DuPont it was also called bulked filament nylon (BFN) or bulked continuous filament (BCF). Its chief advantage was that no spinning was required so a manufacturer could purchase the yarn on bobbins for almost immediate use. It minimized pilling, shedding, and fuzzing; and carpets made from it could be piece dyed after weaving or tufting. This saved money since it eliminated the spinning process and reduced the amount of working capital needed in usual inventories of colored yarns and finished carpet. The innovation was provided with a two-year exclusive to the established firm of James Lees and Sons and the aggressive E. T. Barwick Mills. Most early tufted carpet pioneers feel that this caused Gene Barwick to surge past the rest of Dalton's mills.

A fourth of man-made fibers used in early carpet manufacture and the most wool-like in hand and general characteristics was acrylics. A chemical compound derived from coal, air, water, petroleum and limestone, acrylic was used in staple form and crimped before cutting. DuPont called it Orlon, while Chemistrand (owned by Monsanto and American Viscose) produced Acrilan. Established Firth Carpet Company and Dalton's Cabin Craft led in the use of the latter yarn. Professor Natta of Milan (Italy) Polytechnic Institute developed the last of the early fiber innovations, Polypropylene olefin, which was also used by Barwick and A.&M. Karagheusian.

Man-made fibers were the creation and development of firms outside the carpet industry. Motivated by the potential profits the suppliers of the industry contributed innovation and change which cut the cost of tufted carpet and increased its source of raw materials. The research, testing and development of the finished product is estimated to have cost the producers well over $60 million. Fortunately, the pricing of man-made yarns was kept low to make them competitive with wool. DuPont's 501 was introduced in 1958 and "experimentally priced at $1.47 per pound." In comparison the price of carpet wool averaged 73 cents per pound in 1959. When one considers that BCF eliminates spinning, reduces dyeing and bulks better, the price is competitive and the industry was able to keep the cost of tufted carpet low.

Dyeing has evolved from very primitive beginnings to complex chemical and equipment answers to synthetic yarns, intriguing designs and various sizes of companies. Early bedspread producers used white or predyed sheeting and colored yarn to create versatility and consumer demand. The first actual dye houses were the local laundries—Calhoun Spread Laundry, Dalton Spread Laundry and Star Laundry. The cotton spreads were thrown into the same rotary machines that washed men's shirts and were bleached or dyed. They would add a softener, fluff them up and send them back to each tufting house. Usually pre-dyed yarn had a faster dye and the chlorine bleach just brightened the colors. The dye used in the early days often was picked up from Fletcher Kiveller of Chattanooga, who was a pioneer dye salesman in the area. He would buy dyes, mix them up himself, put them in one pound sacks and sell them. Everybody in Dalton would have the same color brown or shade of pink. The rotary dryers were about ten feet in diameter and would hold 50 to 75 feet of carpet. After drying at 130 to 140 degrees it was pulled out manually. It was punishing work, but Charles Cofield, who was paid $.76 (a penny above minimum), remembers being told, "if you don't like this job, there is a barefoot boy at the gate waiting on it." Much of the dye work, he said, was "by guess and by golly."

The larger spread and rug companies began to built their own laundries and the need for more refined dyeing techniques appeared. DuPont had opened up a laboratory in Atlanta in 1948, to provide dyes for a need they felt was developing in North Georgia and East Tennessee—men's hosiery. Hugh Barrow, an Auburn graduate in Textile Chemistry and Dyeing, discovered primitive dyeing operations when he began to call on customers in 1951. Some designers dyed their preliminary designs in bathtubs while the more advanced used opened vats. The simplistic procedure involved throwing a paper sack of dye and salt, to set the dye, into a leaky wooden or stainless steel vat, bringing it to a boil in about 10 minutes and put in the spreads or rug for another 10 minutes. Sandrouge, later Rodgers Dye, and J & C Bedspread stirred the mix with wooden bats. Men in bathing suits or undershorts would then climb into the vat and drag out the goods. It was very unscientific and a number of employees were electrocuted as they stood ankle deep in the water. The wet goods were shoved into large centrifugal extractors to spin out as much water as possible and then dried in hot air tumblers. Hugh had difficulty in explaining to DuPont how Dalton dyers would shorten a three hour dye process to thirty minutes. On the other hand, he also had trouble explaining to the dyers the importance of following directions to get the desired results. One dyer put only half the necessary salt in the vats because a salesman had sold them 200% salt.

New fibers and larger rugs brought new challenges. Viscose rayon, acetate and cotton all dyed differently. I.V. Chandler at Patcraft decided that since the dye responded to different yarns in different ways that by blending the yarns you could create a tweed look. Hugh told I.V. that it was not tweed, but I.V. said it was tweed to him and became tweed to the industry.

Dye Beck

For the longer runs of tufted materials the dye becks were created. Tufted carpet was rotated through a steaming dye solution by an elevated turning beam, around which the front and rear ends had been sewed. Space dyeing created intriguing pattern combinations. It is a process whereby different colors are "printed" along the length of yarn before it is manufactured into carpet. When the yarn is tufted, the random pattern created offered the customer a customized look. Yarn might be stock dyed or the carpet was dyed one color and later other colors such as brown, yellow, red or white were added. Fiber companies came out with light dyeable yarns so that two-tone patterns were possible. In 1962 nylon fibers allowed a light, medium and deep coloration. In the early 1960's stock dyeing replaced piece dyeing as fibers like Acrilan required that approach.

However, with the arrival of 501 BCF nylon, technology began to assert itself. If a synthetic fiber were made to take color easily, then it would come out as easily. But a fiber which held its color also required trained technical people who knew what they were doing. Also the move toward wall-to-wall carpeting meant that the dye had to be uniform, or have good side and center side matches. Twelve foot wide carpet in fifteen foot wide rooms meant that color shades had to be strictly controlled to match. Carpet sent to the coasts of Florida, Texas and California developed what became known as "Florida Fade." Georgia Tech and Auburn graduates began to wrestle with these problems.

**Part of Kuster Dyeing Unit**

Dye becks gave way to the innovative solutions of Barwick's Zimmer printer or the Kuster machine which could dye carpet as fast as it could move.

Further developments initiated continuous operations involving roller printers, screen printing, printers with jets of color and stamp patterns with doctor blades to scrape off the excess dye. In the late 1950s a roller printing machine had a sponge-like roller which picked up color from a pan and applied it the carpet. It did not color well and one could not apply two colors at a time. It was later improved as the Stalwart roller printer.

J.B. Cleveland's Foremost generally is created with introducing the first wide screen printing machine. A silk screen printing machine placed specific amounts of color in specific places. In the process the material is placed under a screen, a color is rolled on, the screen is mechanically lifted and the material is pulled to another station. Each of three to six stations lays on a different color and it moved at a rate of about six feet a minute. In the early 1970s Peter Zimmer came out with a rotary screen printer, which used a screen on a beam to place color on the carpet moving beneath it in a continuous process. The beam was a big hollow tube, like an eight inch pipe, made out of monelle screen wire with areas blocked out with a lacquer in certain places. As the screen turned the areas not blocked received color. The designers could create a variety of designs with 6 different rotary screens at a much faster pace.

**Stalwart Embossed Printer**

In the late 1960s the Kuster dyeing machine used a flood application with a doctor blade to scrape off the excess and it could run at the rate of 35 feet a minute. Later Kuster came out with a tak unit. It dripped dye through little fingers onto the carpet to create a design and a doctor blade was used to cut off the droplets. The speed of the belt determine the drop size and if you put a patterning attachment on the machine you could make a multi-tak unit. Tak dyeing produced a random multi-color pattern which was usually less sharply defined than printed patterns. Kuster also came out with a double applicator which first put on a layer of gum in certain areas and then flooded color to the material. This produced a multi-colored effect which produced a light over dark appearance.

Tufting remains fairly basic in carpet production. It is color and its application, shades and style that sell the customer. Therefore, each company made machines that would create a slight difference and each company developed its own unique approach to give an advantage to their marketing division.

Tufting, backing, secondary backing, yarn, and color are all part of the package that developed in fits and starts over the period. The technology moved along at a very slow pace from 1965-70 and then an explosion in the early 1970s exhibited major changes that transformed cotton rugs and carpets into wall-to-wall, multi-color synthetic floor covering.

# *Chapter Six*

# JUTE, SYNTHETICS AND LATEX

By the late 1940s and early 1950s, the industry was just beginning to recover from World War II. There were terrific shortages of sheeting, yarn, and all materials used in the war effort. The development of large machines and movement away from bedspreads exclusively was just beginning. The industry's expansion into rugs of all shapes and sizes led to the explosion of other industries to solve the problems of holding the yarn in the backing, stabilizing its size, dyeing the material and drying the rugs. Since it was occurring in the hills of North Georgia, an area with only limited technical experience and that only in textiles, much of the response to the problems was haphazard experimentation.

One of the early problems that plagued carpet's development was the type and stability of the base fabric. The fledgling carpet industry first used woven cotton osnaburg, similar to what was used in bedspread tufting for backing. This flimsy fabric quickly proved its inadequacy, as did a heavier woven cotton duck. In order to produce cotton duck, it had to be woven double and this produced a very heavy ridge in the center of the fabric which was undesirable. Cotton also had a tendency to shrink in hot water and vary in size in its response to heating and dyeing. As long as tufted carpet was rather flimsy and unreliable, it could not gain any real acceptance.

The first alternative to the primary backing problem came in the early 1950s with the use of an all-jute woven product. Crude and uneven though it was, jute did provide a sturdier base suited to the coarse, early versions of cotton and rayon face yarns. Jute is an Asian plant fiber originally used for bagging and cord. It grows in the very hot, moist lands of India, Pakistan, Bangladesh, and the Philippines. India was initially the prime supplier with Pakistan later competing for the market. Jute grows very rapidly to twelve to fourteen feet in height and is cut into three foot lengths for use. Hard on the outside, it has a cellulose filling at the center. After prolonged soaking or wretting a laborer would peel the tough outer shell off and pull out the fibers. The fibers are 6 to 9 inches long, while in comparison, cotton fibers are 1 1/2 to 4 inches long and wool is 1 1/2 to 5 inches long. It would be baled up and shipped to mills in Scotland, Belgium and Germany to be transformed into yards of fabric. As the demand grew, India developed its own weaving industry.

The introduction of jute into the carpet industry parallels the role of Lindsey Dennard, known as the Jute King. On March 29, 1939 Lindsey spent the night in Dalton on the way to Little Rock, Arkansas, to go to work in dry cleaning industry. He had previously done that type of work in Milledgeville, Georgia. "I was so impressed with the bedspread business and all the laundries here that I thought there must be room for a dry cleaning plant, " Lindsey said. "I went on to Arkansas and bought some machinery and came back to Dalton and started one." Lindsey married Coy Watters, a dancing teacher, and she ran the dry cleaning plant for his five year stint in the army in World War II. In 1950 he sold his business and unhappily tried his hand at the used car business. "I started thinking there must be an easier way to make a living than dealing with the type of people you had to run into in the used car business."

Surrounded by the evolving tufting industry, he decided to look into its possibilities. The rug mills were using mainly cotton at the time so he decided to try to sell the mills on using wool. While Coy stayed home and taught dancing, Lindsey went to Philadelphia and started with the telephone book yellow pages. He spent the best part of three months there learning all he could about woolen yarns and trying to find a mill for which he could market. Their negative response was followed by "No one down there can pay their bills except Cabin Craft."

Lindsey finally became a sales agent for a small mill. He picked up two or three cones of yarn and returned to Dalton to sell them. He was making a living when a manufacturer called him with a contract order for a six months supply of one million pounds. The mill could not produce that much. On a suggestion, he went to Chattam Manufacturing Company, a woolen blanket manufacturer in North Carolina, and they adjusted their production and Lindsey was on his way.

Jute was just being introduced as a cheaper substitute to cotton duck in 1956 so, looking into other possibilities, Lindsey went to New York to talk with Jute Industries. They were importing jute in four foot widths made on looms in Dundee, Scotland. After a year and a half he was able to get the Dundee Mills to produce a 12-foot piece of experimental jute for tufting and have it tested by A. M. Kerr Goshen in Albany, Georgia. Lindsey became a manufacturing agent for Jute Industries, primarily in the Dalton area, as well as selling wool. Jute worked much better than cotton since it had little shrinkage and could withstand the heating, bleaching and dyeing; but most of all it was vastly cheaper.

Prior to this time, jute's primary use was in burlap bags, rope and netting for cotton bales. Lindsey and other early jute suppliers had to deal with numerous problems. They had to improve on the warp and weft of the weave. Being a natural fiber, the strands could not be too large or they might bend or break a needle. Neither could they be too tightly nor too loosely woven, so an evenness of thread quality and weave had to be developed. T.W. "Tanc" Lidderdale said the quality seemed to always be only fair to average.

Tanc, an Englishman, whose experience in India in banking and factoring with jute from 1939 gave him an insight into the product and the Indian mind. Acting as a go-between and trouble-shooter for companies expanding into jute's various uses, he ultimately joined forces with Lindsey. Previously, Lindsey was selling wool and jute all over the country and from time to time he had to travel to Scotland or even India to resolve product or delivery problems. He saw Tanc as a compliment to what he was doing and the right person in this time of huge possibilities. As Lindsey said, "He (Tanc) knew all the wheels of the Indian people. He knew just about everything. So, between he and I—well, that's how I got in the jute business."

Soon jute was not only being used as the primary backing, but it also was being used in a lighter form behind the latex as a secondary backing. The combined form gave carpet a stability and feel which added value to the product. After dealing with the early product and delivery problems in the later part of the 1950s, jute enjoyed its heyday from 1965 to 1975. Lindsey remembers shipping over 3,000 rolls a month and he was the largest of 12 to 15 suppliers.

Unfortunately for jute producers, many of the reasons for its decline was the result of their own actions. Being a natural fabric, water had an adverse effect on it. If a bale got wet during transfer from the mills to the port or slipped during transfer to ships and fell into the water, it would begin to deteriorate unless it was dried. Until shipping merchants finally sealed the product, jute would absorb moisture as the cargo sailed through the humid Gulf Stream air en route to the seaport of Savannah. Since it was a bother to dry it and they already had their letters of credit, suppliers shipped inferior or damaged fibers. Fibers sent to Western looms would have not only different weights but seemed never to arrive on schedule. A carpet manufacturer had to anticipate his need for backing six months in advance, since that was the time necessary to grow, weave and ship the product to the Dalton Mills. Supply was drastically affected in 1968 and 1970 when the producing areas were disturbed by a combination of crop damaging typhoons, a tidal wave, civil strife, and international warfare between the two major producing countries . Possibly one of the most crippling single blows to jute's use was the long U.S. port strike of 1982. Synthetic backing had improved and was more easily available and jute never regained its demand.

In addition, the Indian and Pakistan suppliers almost cut themselves out of the market by their actions. Once jute's value to the carpet industry was recognized, raw material suppliers tried any means to increase the price. Jute was definitely less expensive (about one-sixth the price) and lighter in weight. It was common knowledge among some agents, whether Tank, who bought out Lindsey after his heart by-pass surgery in 1974, or Mike Clark and Terry Jones of Patchogue Plymouth, that the jute producers could not be trusted. As one individual told Lindsey, "We have a different understanding of verbs. When they say, 'We have done it,' it means they are doing it now. When they say, 'We are doing it,' it means they will. When they say, 'We will do it,' it means they won't. And when they say, 'They won't,' it means they already have done it." Quality was uncertain, delivery open to variation, prices certain to fluctuation, and dealings unreliable. Synthetic backing had already made strong inroads into the primary area by 1982, and jute quickly lost much of its secondary demand.

Lou Meltzer came into the industry to sell jute and made the transition to synthetics. Educated as a textile converter at Columbia University in New York, Lou was with Pilot International, an exporting firm, when in 1954 they bought the small, floundering Patchogue Plymouth Company. Begun as a lace tablecloth and drapery manufacturer on Long Island, it also had a paper shade and fiber automobile seat cover facility. In Hazelhurst, Georgia, Patchogue Plymouth was producing summer rugs made of twisted paper. During spring cleaning in the South, Mom would roll up their woven rugs, sprinkle them with camphor and wrap them in tar paper until the fall. The twisted paper rugs would protect the hardwood floors during the summer. This small division was just beginning to create carpet backing out of 100% jute or jute and twisted paper.

Lou's task was to persuade the young carpet industry to use jute products in the place of cotton duck. When jute caught on in the mid-1950s and the Southeast Asia suppliers began to weave their own backing, Patchogue could not compete with the price. They then began to sell a laminated secondary backing. Carpet installers were beginning to criticize tufted products because they lacked stability once laid. If the area had high humidity, the carpet would crease and buckle. The repeated call backs for restretching made buyers shy away from it. Using a fabric, Craftcord, made of 100% paper, Lou started selling to Cabin Craft and slowly sold the idea to the total industry. The industry, however, had to develop a type of latex which would wed the secondary backing to the product. Frank DiGioia, a lab technician with General Latex, was able to develop a natural latex that dried almost instantly which worked in Dalton's three pass ovens that wedded both backings with the latex. Cabin Craft, under the direction of Harold Schwartz, pledged enough time and money to make the process succeed.

A cheaper jute product as secondary backing forced another innovation, a synthetic secondary product. Beset by shortages and only average quality jute, James Lees Company asked Patchogue Plymouth to develop a synthetic alternative. Darbin Brothers were extruding a ribbon material out of polyethylene, but it softened at about 240 degrees F. Polypropylene was tested, but when produced in a ribbon or slick film, the inherent structure caused it to fracture. Ultimately, based off James Lees' commitment to go with synthetics, they developed polypropylene as the alternative. Jute was a natural product that structurally had few problems, was inexpensive, but supply was uncertain. Individual selling and advertising of their new materials by both Lou and Patchogue won over the market over a period of six years. Synthetic backing resulted in new types of carpet construction, an impossibility with jute. The fine gauge led to a tighter, more plush feel to the carpet as well as insuring, that if the carpet got wet, it did not smell or rot as jute did.

Another of the early problems was how to hold the cotton stitching in the sheeting. The yarn in bedspreads was held in place by the shrinkage of the wash/dry process. That worked well for bedspreads because no one was running around on them, kicking out the loops. However, the tug of a boot or a ladies toe or high heel necessitated a firmer hold. First, they turned to heavier duck backing (16 oz.) and used heavier or coarser yarn. They would tuft in 2 or 2 1/2 inch cotton loops on machines with 4 to 64 needles, depending upon how much weight the machine arm could hold. If they were tufting throw rugs, they were often 36 inches wide, which could be sewed together to create wider rugs. If they were tufting a large piece of goods such as bedspreads or housecoats, the material would be passed under the needles as many times as necessary to tuft the width. Therefore, to tuft a 12 foot wide spread or rug would require 4 passes. Thus, they became known as pass machines.

**Pass machine**

Even with the heavier backing, the tufts continued to pull out. Manufacturers tried all types of stitching and cross stitching, but it proved to be very slow and expensive. All kinds of glues, adhesives, tire patching cement, shellacs, varnishes and other equally exotic concoctions were used to see which would perform best; none worked well.

Three early individuals who were instrumental in solving the problem of loose tufts in the backing were Doug Cochran, George Dees and Harvey Howalt. Doug came from a roofing background and worked with Wilt Moore, Pat Patterson and Berkhart Shure at Southern Latex in Austell, Georgia. George Dees was a colorful 60-year-old veteran of the shoe adhesive business in New England. He had been making compounds that would laminate together the various ply of cotton and fabrics for the shoe business. He became the senior spokesman for the latex business, and he was quite a character within the industry.

**Rolla Coater**

Harvey Howalt was a newcomer to latex when the backing demand appeared; but his story is indicative of the development of the solution. While in school in Boston Harvey worked in a latex factory where they dipped balloons, beach balls and cotton work gloves. The latex company bought their cotton shells from Reigel Mills, a manufacturer of cotton gloves in Summerville, Georgia. Harvey became friends with Roy Mann who came regularly from the plant to check out the quality of the gloves which had been shipped northward. After several years of swapping stories in the quality lab or over beers, Roy mentioned the problem that was occurring in the Dalton rug mills. Harvey got the approval of the latex company owner to experiment in the labs after work. The first quart of latex sent back with Roy clogged the spray gun and had to be applied with a paint brush. The rugs were then hug on a line to dry. Soon Roy was heading back to Georgia with a trunk full of gallon-filled containers. By the time Harvey was shipping 55-gallon drums to Roy, it became evident that he should quit his day job and pursue this emerging part-time job. Roy agreed to put up the money, Harvey would do all the work and they would share the profits. They rented the basement of an abandoned flour mill on East Waugh Street owned by Pete Sims. They worked in a small space, about 30-feet square. At first they mixed their batches with sticks in 5-gallon pails and later graduated to 55 gallon drums and a canoe paddle to stir. One of their early mechanical breakthroughs was buying a lightening mixer which was bolted to a post and the drums wheeled underneath.

The compounding of latex was uncertain. Natural latex came from trees in Liberia and Malaysia. It had many variations, depending on the rainfall of the area, its age, and the way it had been stabilized. Since each drum varied, it was necessary to compound it to create a uniform product. It then was adapted to fit the demands of their customers. Each morning Harvey would call on the mills and in the afternoon and evening he would try to create what he had promised for delivery the next morning. Harry Saul or Thurman Chitwood might want one type, while Gene Barwick wanted a green compound to distinguish his rugs. He often had to make numerous batches in an evening.

The developing process of latex application to the back of rugs to provide stitch control and non-skid qualities moved at an intermittent pace. The rugs were cut into various sizes and shapes, such as ovals, diamonds, hearts and circles. Rugs were placed on cotton duck conveyor belts which rode on wooden rollers through an oven with infra-red light bulbs. Using large amounts of soaps and lubricants in the latex, the mixture could be sprayed on the backing of the goods. It was very difficult to stabilize the latex to make it spray evenly, especially with lint from the cotton fibers getting into the mixture. They would spray a little, clean a little and spray a little more.

After latex was applied the application of heat was used to cure or harden the backing. Rubber latex consists of small particles of latex suspended in water, much like fat globules are suspended in milk. Curing involved the using of large amounts of heat to evaporate the water and harden the backing. Natural gas did not exist in the area, but TVA, just 30 miles to the north, could provide cheap electricity. Ovens were created with panels of infrared light bulbs and rugs moved through the ovens at a speed determined by the amount of latex on the materials and the curing rate of the latex. The bulbs would often expand and contract, causing them to break and hot filaments to fall on the latex. The filaments would ignite the flammable mixture of latex, and lint from the cotton or fuzz in the air would burst into explosive fire. Fire would cross the ceilings and walls in a matter of seconds causing everyone to run like the devil towards the doors or jump out of windows. The Dalton Fire Department was very inadequate at the time, resulting in the buildings burning down before they arrived. Each morning latex suppliers would call customers to see which ones had burned down the previous night. I. V. Chandler of Patcraft had to depend upon the generous support of Harry Saul at Queen Carpet to get his orders run when fire destroyed his plant. A couple of years later another fire allowed I.V. to return the favor. No one was exempt from the threat of fire. The conveyor belt was changed from cotton duck to metal mesh, but the fires continued to occur for another 5 years.

It was the conversion from electricity to natural gas that brought the fires to an end. At first manufactures tried butane gas, but it was too expensive and cumbersome. Dalton Sheet Metal was one of the pioneers in converting numerous ovens into gas heaters. This was the start of the modern process which blows hot air down on top of the latex and then takes the cooler exhaust air back from the bottom of the rugs. This conversion would not have been possible without the work of V. D. Parrott. As head of the local gas utility company, his vision and hard work helped bring natural gas to the town. The later development of heat sensitive fabrics and the zoning of ovens into cool and hot sections further solved the problem.

In the early days of latex application the person spraying would sit in a chair on a platform above the rugs or carpet and spray back and forth over the width. Gene Barwick remembered his black spray operator being white with latex by the end of the day. This changed with the introduction of a trough of latex over which the backing was drawn and is the basis for the current means of coating.

Another development in the use of latex was the application of foam latex to the backing, creating a foam pad. Foam latex was being used in pillows, mattresses, and various padding materials in the shoe and garment industry in the Northeast. This technology began to filter down to the carpet industry. One of the pioneers was Bud Callahan of Dalton Carpet Finishing Company, working with Doc Bolling and Iris Aker. They started one of the first latex ovens that applied foam directly as cushion and backing. Liquid latex was mixed with fillers, anti-oxidant ingredients, soap, and air in a foaming machine much like the Dairy Queen type of aerating mixer. When the process began, the first latex had a very low filler level with high quality and density. It worked so well as a backing and padding that many found it more acceptable and economical than separate carpet and pad. At one time as much as 37% of the total yards of manufactured carpet had this attached cushion. Unfortunately, the product deteriorated as the mills attempted to be price competitive with each other. Many carpet manufacturers would religiously guard the amount of yarn that was on the face of the carpeting but to lessen their cost they added more and more filler or air to reduce cost per pound. By the mid-1970s the attached foam, in many cases, was nearly junk. It would snap off the back under pressure and the cushioning effect was practically non-existent. Now only about 10-12% of carpet has a foam backing.

The role and scope of latex has gone through an interesting cycle. Born in the early 1950s, compounding grew with the emerging industry. It reached a peak in the period 1965-1970 where the latex compounder filler was necessary and the volume of latex-filler was high. Over fifteen companies employed several thousand people in compounding, chemical supply, trucking and oven building. In the early 1970s the industry began to consolidate and began to shrink as more and more big companies began to do their own chemical mixing and compounding to suit specific needs and reduce manufacturing costs. By the middle of the decade, some of the basic polymer producers were going directly to the mills reducing the supplier latex companies to less than a handful.

## *Chapter Seven*

# THE BARWICK PHENOMENON

"Innovator," "leader," "visionary," "pioneer," "demon," "crook"—these are all terms which have been used to describe Eugene T. Barwick. Tom Neal, financial consultant and former vice-president of Walter Heller (1960-64), said, "Members of the industry ought to get down on their knees and thank him. He and the industry remind me of the relationship between a shark and pilot fish. The pilot fish sticks to the underside of a shark, and then, after the kill, they race out to eat all the bits and pieces left. Gene was the shark that blazed the trail and the industry has benefited from his courage." *The Dalton Daily Citizen* (November 6, 1964), noting that Gene had received the first TTMA Distinguished Service Award, explained the award on the basis that he had "displayed a high degree of courage, determination, foresight, skill and drive."

His contributions to the industry are so numerous and his impact so significant that many speak of the Barwick Era and the Barwick Legend. Walter Guinan, whose many years span both woven and tufted textiles experience, explained the breadth of his contribution. "He put in a hell of a lot more in this industry in terms of personal effort not only for his company, but also for the welfare of the industry—more than many people ever realized." Yet not all is praise as recognized by the further words of Walter, who went on to say, "Any successful guy is envied, criticized, ridiculed and things like that." Neither saint nor demon, Gene Barwick played one of the more salient roles in the development of the tufted textile industry from a North Georgia craft business to a recognized international industry.

Coming from a modest family background, Gene went to the University of North Carolina on an athletic scholarship. He played end on the football team and made the Sports Illustrated All-American team. After graduation he went to work for Sears Roebuck in Jacksonville, Florida, and "by happenstance" ended up in the floor covering buying department. He advanced then to mail order sales manager in Chicago and then carpet buyer for the central office before being drawn into World War II. He spent much of his time thinking, rather than fighting, as a Navy officer in a remote outpost in the Alaskan Aleutians.

After release from the service in 1946, Gene returned to Sears and became the regional merchandise manager for floor coverings in Atlanta. Since most wool was allocated to the Northern states, he usually bought cotton rugs from the North Georgia mills. During this time, one of his sources, C. M. Jones, began to have delivery problems. Although Jones made one of the best throw rugs in the business, Gene discovered Jones' business operations were in disarray. A single trip to the mill to implement deliveries brought a broader vision for Gene of what could be done with this infant industry. As he later said, "If they can do that with one needle, why not 1500 needles?"

In 1948 Gene left Sears and became the sales manager for Ben Kahn, who owned a small rug tufting operation called Lawrence Products, Inc. in North Alabama. He was hired on a salary plus bonus and did an outstanding job, but friction developed over marketing and operations. When pay day came, Gene's bonus should have been $15,000, but Ben decided he was going to pay him only $7,500. When he gave Gene the bonus, Gene's response was, "This is not what my bonus should be." Ben remained firm in his decision. Whereupon, Ben said, "He took that check and shook it under my nose and said, 'You little son-of-a-bitch, I'm gonna take this and bust you.'" Ben told Tom Neal, "And he did." Whether the story is true or not, Tom feels that the story is typical of Gene Barwick's determination.

It was at that point that Gene met Frank McCarty and took another significant step toward the realization of his carpet empire. McCarty Chenille of Chatsworth, Georgia, was receiving factor financing through Bud Taylor of the Trust Company of Georgia. Bud lived in the same apartment building in Atlanta as Gene, and suggested that Frank and Gene get together. Frank's pilgrimage into the tufting industry is a representative story.

After graduation from the University of Georgia, Frank McCarty had given little thought to the emerging textile industry of his home area. Instead, he went into the wholesale grocery business in Louisville, Kentucky, but the 1929 crash dissolved his job and brought him back home to Dalton. He and a friend headed to California to seek their fortune. To make ends meet, they became the West Coast agents for Mrs. Blair Cannons' bedspread business. They even sold some spreads to Hollywood directors who had used the men as "extras" in a movie called "College Lovers." After that, Frank settled down to clerking in a grocery store and worked his way up through management, only to be stopped by favoritism. Resolving to work only for himself, he returned home and bought a North Georgia filling station and then an appliance business before giving the spread business a chance in 1939. In 1948 they began tufting cotton throw rugs with 12-and 24-needle machines and spraying the natural latex application for backing.

When Gene Barwick began selling rugs for McCarty Chenille, the firm was making cut pile and short loop rugs at plants in Tennga and Chatsworth. Soon he "had them covered up" with orders as well as demands to keep up with the industry. The development in South Carolina of a machine which sewed the loops down to keep them from pulling out forced a competitive response from McCarty.

Latex had been used to keep the rugs from skidding and hold the tufts in, but its application on rugs was a problem. At first, Frank recalled, they would pour it on the rugs and even it out with a grade school ruler. Then they developed a moving belt where Howell Brook, sitting in a chair on rollers, would move back and forth and spray the latex coating; by the end of the day Howell was covered with the latex. The latex was cured by infra-red lights, but this process did not work well. Young Charlie Bramlett, later Executive Vice President of Galaxy Carpet, had to pull the rugs apart in the dye house after they had stuck together. Frank Hawkins, who later began Dalton Sheet Metal, helped Frank McCarty build a trough through which a rolling drum drew up enough latex to coat the back of the rug which was rolling across the top of the same drum. There were a lot of problems, but after working on the process nightly for nearly a year the new procedure worked.

McCarty Chenille was operating two nine-foot machines built by Cobble Brothers, and Frank asked Albert Cobble, in 1949, to build them a twelve-foot low pile yardage machine. Albert said that he did not know whether he could make such a machine or whether it would sew. Frank said, "You make it, and we'll make it sew," since his mechanics could fix just about anything.

At this point, the tremendous marketing of Gene and the pressures of the business got to Frank. His doctor told him that his ulcer was getting worse. In August, 1949, in the offices of Fred Williamson at the Hardwick Bank and Trust Company, the sale of McCarty Chenille was concluded. McCarty Chenille was renamed E. T. Barwick Industries and moved from Chatsworth to the King Cotton Mill building in downtown Dalton. With $4,500 down Gene Barwick owned his first carpet mill.

Interestingly enough, Frank McCarty's involvement with Gene did not end at this point. After a few months in retirement, Bob McCamy invited Frank to Cabin Craft to help Bob Hackney develop a twelve-foot wide loop machine. After a year, Frank was helping Gene in operations and stayed for three or four years more. Frank later sold latex for a period before he went into business with two of Gene's salesmen, Eddie Evans and Art Black, to form E & B Carpet Company. Later, after Evans and Black sold out to Armstrong, Gene brought Frank out of retirement to help straighten out problems in his English and Dutch plants.

Soon after acquiring McCarty Chenille, Gene bought a small Dalton rug company, Morrill Manufacturing, and then, in 1951, he purchased from the Fortune family the old Walker County Hosiery Mill in LaFayette and turned both mills into tufting plants. His first major acquisition took place in 1954 when he bought Monarch Mills from Ira and Howard Nochumson. Before Gene was through, he had built Barnwell Spinning Mill; bought Jefferson Woolen Mills (Knoxville, Tennessee); several plants in Dalton; Cavalier Bag Company (Lumberton, N.C.), and Georgia Furniture Company (Dublin, GA). The bag company manufactured synthetic carpet backings, and the furniture company produced solid wood bedroom suites and case goods (bedroom, coffee, end and occasional tables), which later changed to less expensive mass market furniture. In 1964, he built the mammoth Archer plant in Kensington, Georgia,

(19 acres under one roof), and later opened mills in Bolton, England, and Oss, Netherlands,

Acquiring and building plants was not what made Gene Barwick have such an impact on the industry. The words of his contemporaries explain much of his influence; some referred to his charisma and others spoke of his sales ability. Walter Guinan pointed out Gene's magnificent build, his dynamic presence—appearance, dress, and driving personality. Gene was a super salesman. Tom Neal said distributors begged the Walter Heller Company not to increase their borrowing level because Gene would sell them more. Whether a dealer was inclined to buy or not, he would create such a deal with low prices and advertising perks that the buyer would be foolish to say no. One of his accountants recalled that when the bills began to pile up and the business office staff worried where the money would come from to pay them, Gene would grab his samples, leave and return in several days with orders ranging from $2 to $3,000,000 worth of carpet.

There were two ways to run a company—for bottom line or for cash flow. Gene always ran the company for cash flow. When you deal with a factor, you go out and sell and present the invoice to the factor and then you can draw. Depending on reserve, you can draw up to 80% to 90% down immediately, but pay "hellish interest." The factor made money by touching the same dollar as many as five times and the company had money to keep going. Gene wasn't worried about the interest, with the demand there was plenty of money to be made. Possibly, Gene's biggest mistake may have been that when he hit $100 to $150 million that he "didn't bring in a pencil pusher that would have held onto the profits better," offered Don Browen, one of his key managers. But Gene use to say, "You're only spending fifty cents of every dollar, the government's taking the rest, 'cause we're making so damn much money."

Others attributed Gene's impact to his leadership in the industry. Tom Neal said, "Gene Barwick was always two years ahead of the industry because he had the vision and he had guts. Those are the two things that you need to be successful.... Gene Barwick was 'the identification' that took us out of the 'in-house' business to that of a recognized industry." Buford Talley, first president of Barwick Industries, said in 1981, "Mr. Barwick was a hell of an innovator. He probably did as much, if not more, for this industry that any other individual.... He had more guts—he'd take chances that nobody would or could afford to take, and he could not afford to take them. Most all of the chances he took worked. He made them work because he was a hell of an aggressive man. Hours didn't mean anything to him. He worked seven days a week." In *What You Should Know About Carpet,* Annette Stramesi said, "'Innovation' was a byword in the Monarch tufting empire. The company was the first to use jute as a primary backing on carpet..., first to promote 100% nylon carpet, first to manufacture 100% polypropylene carpet and first to roller-coat and vulcanize the back of carpet to lock in the pile and make it stand well on the floor." Gene's contributions go on and on.

One of his plant managers said that if Mr. Barwick heard that a mechanic was working on something with merit, he would build a separate area complete with tools and materials to work on the project. Sometimes these gambles paid off and sometimes it was an expensive dryhole. It was easy to get into the business at that time, it did not take millions of dollars. You could make as good a piece of carpet in a chicken house as you could in a nineteen acre mill. Gene had invested $4,500 to get started and felt he had little to lose. He said, "The more shit you throw against the wall, the more will stick."

Many others attributed Gene's tremendous contributions to the technology of the industry and his attendant economic windfall from two major developments—the DuPont 501 nylon yarn and the Zimmer printer. Cotton was being used in the industry when Gene bought out Frank McCarty in 1949. Cotton made a beautiful carpet, the carpet could be washed, but it was not acceptable for heavy traffic because it matted and soiled quickly. Cabin Craft was working with rayon, and, although it looked good, rayon had little resistance to crushing. Some tried viscose with similar results. In one year Gene paid over a million dollars in claims and nearly broke the company. Wool was not any better since it was expensive and matted.

Experimentation with nylon began in 1953-54. Nylon wore well and was easily cleaned. The only nylon available was type 101 which was a staple-making the weight heavy, heavier, and heaviest. They had such good response from it that Gene began to worry about the supplier, Dupont. Anticipating World War II, Dupont had begun developing continuous filament nylon. With the end of the war, the carpet industry flocked back to wool and cotton, leaving Dupont "high and dry with several million dollars in development costs," said Gene.

According to Gene, he played a major role in getting Dupont to develop Dupont 501 for the industry. He said that he filled his DC-3 with all his colors and samples and flew to Dupont's home offices in Wilmington, Delaware. He covered the auditorium stage completely with the entire line and impressed the technicians and Andy Buchanan. "Andy Buchanan was what you would call the father or developer of man-made fibers at Dupont." Gene remembered, "He came in and talked a while and looked at it and said, I think you have a real program. Dupont will support you and will start work again in developing for this industry."

Others remember Dupont being the one who developed 501 with the intention of selling it to the industry. In 1955-56 Dupont offered the new 501 BFN (Bulked Filament Nylon) exclusively to Lees, an old-line carpet company, and Barwick's Dalton plant. It had superior resilience, good texture retention and better appearance. The original fibers had major problems with pilling, shedding and streaking. Streaking would result from yarn differences that would show as tension lines after dyeing. Pilling, shedding and fuzzing also threatened early production. Soon after installation, the traffic lanes would look like a cheap sweater—knots and balls on it. They developed shearing machines to try to cut the pilling and fuzzing away, but they had to replace a lot of carpet. If Dupont had not stood behind it, as far as the replacement of the carpet and even paying labor at times, Barwick quite possibly would have gone under.

However, once the problems were solved, the profits made it worthwhile. With the Dupont 501, Lees and Barwick had a $2.65 cost and they developed a gentlemen's agreement that they would not sell for less than $6.50 a roll or $7.35 a cut. When business began booming they agreed that they would not sell rolls, but just cuts at $7.35. The exclusive use of 501 nylon along with the Zimmer printer created huge profits and catapulted Barwick far into the lead in the tufted carpet industry.

The Zimmer printer brought color to the market. Prior to this development, the industry worked with certain basic colors and piece-dyed it in a dye beck. Gene was constantly looking for new ideas. In 1960, on one of his periodic trips to Paris where he felt all color began, he saw a window design with material which had six different colors. He recalled, "I said to myself, 'You wouldn't have to touch it at all if you could just put it onto a carpet'... So I went in the shop and started looking at it; and I thought, 'Hell, this is not woven, this is printed.'" He then tracked down the originator, Peter Zimmer in Gustan, Austria. Others doubt the story, suggesting that Zimmer hunted Gene down and Gene, being a gambler, tried it. Either way Gene helped introduce the Zimmer printer to the industry.

There were numerous problems to be solved. The widest Peter had printed was thirty-six inches, far from fifteen feet. The printing could not be topical, but had to be fully saturated to the backing of the yarn. Even after the print was developed, the one million dollar investment sat idle because of the kinks in it. This development was too far ahead of the materials. The jute backing lacked stability and pulled badly under tension throwing off the pattern. It was three or four years before Dupont developed a spun-bonded, wide-width replacement called typar for jute that gave dimensional stability. Even the dye processing required innovation. The top of the machine was a simple printer compared to the tremendous lattice of magnetic attraction underneath. The dyes were premetalized and literally drawn through the carpet. The impact on printing was fantastic, but the cost was twice as high.

Barwick Industries also installed the first Kuster machine which was so massive that one could dye twelve thousand square yards of one color. The machine could take the place of twenty-five dye becks when run wide open. Again the story was the same, with Gene hearing of the printer in Europe and advancing him money for development.

In the Zimmer flat bed printer the carpet moved up three feet, a screen came down; the applicator rolled across applying the dye. Then the carpet moved to the next screen for the next color with as many as four different colors possible. In the Kuster, the carpet is dyed as fast as it moves. The Kuster follows a three-step technique of impregnation with chemicals in a trough, padding with a swimming roller, and controlled application of dyestuff on carpet pile by means of a doctor blade. The swimming roller in the padding mangle guarantees perfectly even impregnation and squeezing effect regardless of carpet width. Dyestuff is then applied to the pile of the carpet by a dip roller and a doctor blade, providing absolute control. Penetration was perfect for all pile heights. The dyestuff was fixed in a saturated steam inside the loop steam ager. The ager was designed to avoid contact with the carpet face to prevent any pile distortion. Next, the carpet moved into the Kuster rotor-washers with a swimming roller mangle on the final washer. Buford Talley later described the new process as a "hell of a breakthrough" in dyeing.

Interestingly enough, Mr. Barwick was not a believer in patents. He felt that patents led to lawsuits, and he was not in the business of hiring lawyers and spending time in court. He believed that if a person was the first to come out with an idea, that it would take the competition one to three years to copy the idea. By then, the inventor would have developed further advances.

There were a lot of innovations and breakthroughs, along with a number of costly flops. The attempt to develop a flocked piece of carpet is a good example. Instead of using continuous nylon and tufting it, nylon was cut into predetermined lengths, specially washed and electrostatically charged so that the pieces would hold in an upright position and stick to an adhesive-type backing. There were something like 80,000 ends per square foot, and close matting gave a smooth velvet look to the carpet. Flocking could have been a technological breakthrough, using almost any type quality of yarn which could be dyed without streaking or matting. It was so highly secretive that only six or seven persons were permitted in the area, but they could never solve the problem of "walking" or shedding. It was more expensive than it was worth so it was abandoned by Barwick.

Gene was also the first to use computers, but it was so premature it nearly wrecked his business. In 1955, a dealer oversold Gene into using its system in the Dalton plant at a cost savings. It ultimately took so many programmers, planners, and systems people that in March, 1956, Gene simply moved the equipment out into the storage area and sent the vendor a certified letter to come get it. Later, in Atlanta, he tried again with a different company and spent over three quarters of a million dollars on a building alone. A distributor was supposed to be able to call in at anytime and determine the status of his order. The programmers got so far behind in putting the orders into the computer that they got lost. That system did not last twelve months. Sandy Sobelman, Mr. Barwick's son-in-law, remembers how Gene flew in his distributors to pick out their lines so that they would not be hurt by the foul-up. That year Gene took a full page ad in *Home Furnishings Daily* which read "Barwick sales in excess of $150,000,000 in spite of the computer."

Yet equally important in Gene Barwick's success, if not more so, was his ability to sell not just yards of carpet but the whole tufted industry. He was "Mr. Carpet" or the "Carpet King" to many people. He was such a good salesman that Buford Talley said the greatest problem the company had "was building and expanding manufacturing to keep up with sales. He was a master salesman." Gene could so impress distributors that they had to have the Barwick line of carpet. He used the government's Buying Power Index (BPI) effectively with the dealers. He would point out that the BPI in their part of the country was four percent but they were only doing one to one and a half percent. Then he'd sell the carpet to them, help them finance it, advertise it, and move it.

Gene Barwick, master showman

Another innovation he developed was the Road Shows. Only seven percent of the buyers came to the regional carpet markets so he put together twelve to fifteen major and junior road shows. He would completely cover a large ballroom in virginal white carpet and then put the displays on top of that. In addition, he would offer clinics on merchandising developments, complaints, sales examples, market approach, and other ideas. The Road Show took knowledge and personal attention to the local representative, making each feel proud of his company and personally important.

Airplanes also helped sell his carpet as well as better penetrate the market area. Here again he was a pioneer. He would use his three million dollar BAC-111 to fly as many as four hundred retailers a year to his offices and plants. The experience, the tour of a plant, and the VIP treatment was a tremendous incentive. At one time it took a million dollar-plus budget to maintain his four planes and support people. Starting in 1953, he used planes to fulfill a very demanding schedule. He might have a sales meeting in Denver in the morning, Salt Lake City in the afternoon, and Seattle that night. If time was too short, he would have distributors come to the airport and see the samples displayed in the BAC-111. Many have criticized his use of planes and apartments (New York, Chicago, and Atlanta), but he used them to stimulate sales and care for company people. Even his yacht Marco Polo in the Caribbean was used as a motivator and reward to successful individuals. It is possible that it was used more personally, because when the company went public in 1969, he personally bought the ship.

Gene was also the first to use models in his showrooms at the regular carpet markets to attract customers. Distributors came to see the models but stayed to see the new lines. He also maintained two different product lines complete with different sales organizations - the Barwick line and the Monarch line. That way he could have two competing lines in the same area with high quality but different looks. They were their own best competitors.

Bryan Gibson, Vice President of Industrial Relations (1969-1980), pointed out that possibly one of the hallmarks of the company was the high degree of loyalty. From the beginning Gene never lost concern for the people who helped him build E.T. Barwick Industries. He wanted to make sure that all were treated fairly with industry-leading wages and benefits. When a pension plan was instituted in 1975, Gene put in enough money from the company to take care of service back to 1955. Even when the company ceased to exist, he kept the pension fund intact. His people responded in kind with strong loyalty. They worked for Mr. Barwick, not just a company. In 1976 when things got real bad, Howell Brooks, who had moved from latex sprayer to Fifth Avenue (Dalton) plant manager, had a number of employees who said that they would donate two weeks work, if it would help save the company. There are those still who would go back to work for him if he could start up again. Gene was loyal to them and they returned the feeling.

Gene Barwick also sold the benefit of Barwick companies to the local communities. He paid well, possibly too well, including a profit sharing plan for all employees. Janie Giddens, secretary of the company, is still amazed at the amounts she wrote in checks for him to help build things like the LaFayette airport, hospitals, schools, public services in Walker, Whitfield, and Murray counties. The weight of this impact can be seen in the remarks of LaFayette Chamber of Commerce President, Bernard Wheeler, at a luncheon honoring Gene on October 10, 1978. "As Barwick grew, LaFayette grew with you. You were a part of that growth because you encouraged us to build some things. You helped us to build and some things you just built and gave us. You have been and are today and you'll continue to be a very important person in LaFayette."

An impressive example of this assistance which would be later emulated by other companies was the Barwick scholarship program. If an employee or his parents had worked for a Barwick company for at least one year, a scholarship was available. As a renewable scholarship for four years, it did not require a specific scholastic average, only that the student pass. Over 2,600 persons took advantage of the opportunity. The company attempted to hire as many students as possible each summer to further defray their college costs. Each year Gene would bring the students and a school representative to Atlanta for dinner and a speech by the governor.

Much of Gene's success must be attributed to his executive team. First, and most influential, was Charlie Goodwin. Starting as a salesman in Alabama, Florida, and Georgia, Charlie ultimately controlled the whole operation as executive vice president. Tom Neal said of Charlie that he "was a very honorable man... a man who would control expenses and look after details." Others pointed out that it was his firm hand and wise direction that kept everything moving well. Janie Giddens, secretary to the company, spoke of how Charlie worked between all the divisions. "He okayed everything,... had Mr. Barwick's approval. He treated Mr. Barwick's money like it was his own." When Charlie retired, he was impossible to replace.

The second of the four who directed the company during this period was Mel Keller. Working with the CPA firm of W.W. Stribling in Dalton, Mel helped work out the purchase of Monarch Mills, and came to Barwick at that time. As treasurer, he had to find enough money to meet the bills. When there was trouble, he would call suppliers and tell them when the money would be coming. Janie remembers that their cash flow kept them hopping, but Barwick never failed to meet a payroll. A number felt that the company was financially healthy as long as Mel was there. He carefully watched the balance sheet, as one said, "If you wanted to show him the pencil, then you'd better show him the short pencil." When Mel left it became more difficult to control the rapidly expanding company. At one time the company had forty-eight different bank accounts and Buford Talley recalls going quarterly to their creditors and talking with them face-to-face about the progress of the company and its loans.

Joe Nix started early with Barwick and was in charge of manufacturing. He was the one who led Barwick to build the Archer plant in Kensington, Georgia. The initial building covered nineteen acres and, although an expansion of his existing plants, it was larger in area than 90 percent of the carpet manufacturers at that time. Finally, Phil Stillman moved up through sales to become vice president of sales. Later, as these men left, Buford Talley moved up to fill the void. Beginning as a mail clerk in October, 1955, his knowledge and practical experience helped him move up through the accounting department. In 1965, Talley became the secretary of the corporation, then vice president in 1966, and the first president other than Mr. Barwick in late 1969. Under his leadership Barwick Industries expanded into synthetic backing, furniture, carpet tile, and needle punch work. Talley left in August, 1971, to begin his own company and develop his own share of the yarn industry. The third and last president of Barwick Industries was Jack Paton.

The growth of the Barwick company was phenomenal. From his first sale ($1,800 worth of rugs) in 1949 to Rich's basement store in Atlanta, the company grew rapidly. Sales were $2.7 million in 1950 and doubled a year later. By 1953 Barwick sales reached $14 million. In 1954 he bought Monarch Mills and continued to grow. When the organization went public in 1968, sales had reached $134 million. It was the largest tufted carpet manufacturer in the country and accounted for about nine percent of all carpeting produced in the USA. By 1969 the publicly-held corporation boosted sales to $142 million.

Unfortunately, the next decade was one of depressions and inflationary periods. As Paul Troop of the Atlanta *Journal* pointed out, "In 1975, the company was reeling from twin effects of wage-price controls that had allowed raw-material suppliers to raise prices but restricted big manufacturers like Barwick from passing them on. The deep recession in housing and the oil embargo, which quadrupled the price of synthetic yarns, hit the carpet business."

In 1973, the company reported to its stockholders a $27 million loss. The banks, led by the Bankers Trust Company of New York, began to involve themselves more and more in an effort to protect their interests. First, the planes were sold, then the furniture operation was sold in 1975 and the overseas carpet mills and the Dalton plant quickly followed suit. In 1975, Gene asked banks for a one-year moratorium on the $5 million a year in interest payments on the company's debt. He pointed out that the company was not behind in any of the payments on the $28 million he said the company then owed. The banks instead brought in a new Chief Executive Officer, Charles Selecman, a Dallas business consultant and one-time president of the U.S. Industries conglomerate. Gene remained for one year as chairman of the board and then, due to friction between the two of them, Gene was forced to leave the company completely, turning over voting rights to his stock while retaining their ownership. Selecman and Robert Schultz, formerly of Colt Industries, then tried to run the company on a classic accounting basis rather than as a typical carpet company.

In 1974, the company with revenue at $211 million, and in 1975 at $169 million continued to decline. In 1976 while other companies were coming out of the economic slump, Barwick Industries dropped to $150 million and by 1978 only $100 million. A positive net worth had been changed to a negative. In late September, 1978, the banks decided to get out, and using $17.5 million borrowed from Walter E, Heller & Co., Gene was able to regain his company.

Being the innovator he was, Gene went to the Chicago market in January, 1979, with 42 new carpet styles. His theory was to not go for quick profit, but break even and saturate the market with Barwick and Monarch carpet. He cut prices on certain lines and the old Monarch and Barwick distributors came back and bought at a bargain level. Unfortunately, he did not sell enough at regular prices. Just before Gene bought back Barwick, a "cheater" cut loop called Pecant had been developed for the Monarch division which could be offered with terms at $6.05 to distributors with about 6% to cover fixed costs. To the big distributors in New York, he offered to deliver it there for $3.95 including $.15 or $.20 freight. It was as though he was selling back in the glory days of 501 Vega when you could count on a $2.65 base. But times had changed. By April he was in a serious cash flow situation. The economy was suffering; the housing and automobile companies were sagging badly, and credit was tight. Things went from bad to worse as Barwick Industries curtailed, did commission work for other companies and finally closed in 1980.

With anything as large as the Barwick empire, there were problems, particularly in an undercapitalized industry. Numerous reasons have been pointed to for the problems of the 1970s: the tremendous cost and time of starting up the Archer plant, loss of key executive personnel due to firings and retirement, the loss of morale, Gene's temper, heavy expenses, lack of internal leadership, a large number of bad or questionable receivables and problems with company owned distributorships.

By the mid-1970s the incredible demand for carpet by the home building public had slowed down and the free-wheeling style of Gene Barwick started to catch up with him. Spending money like water overwhelmed the company. The BAC-111 cost a minimum of $3,000 per hour in the air and it was too impractical for Gene to use for his family's needs. His three apartments and the "models" which stayed in them to provide him with an escort when he was in town was part of his image, but too expensive. He continued to offer $50,000 to $100,000 in advertising to those who bought heavily. Gene had originated the "spiff." However, now his dealers bought only the spiff with its extra financial bonus for extra sales. They ceased to sell the regular line which was the heart of the profit. In August, 1974, Jack Paton and Gene tried to gain control by slashing thirty vice presidents to thirteen, but it was too late.

Once the company went public, financial statements had to show growth and profit, even if there was none. It was a joke around Dalton that when the independent auditors came to town, Barwick's inventory was on wheels. With a fleet of 50 or 60 trucks you could take the inventory from one mill after the accountants left, and move it to another mill with new tags on the rolls. Finally, the Securities and Exchange Commission caught up with the practice and six of the top officials, including Gene, signed consent statements that they "had fraudulently inflated earnings reports, destroyed documents and concealed loan defaults." Each month or two the Atlanta *Constitution* revealed defaults on more loans, millions in quarterly losses, and suits brought by companies, such as Cavalier Bag, that the stock they had been offered was misrepresented. Once they started moving the inventory, they could not even tell whether they were making a profit—much less gain control of the company.

In April, 1976, Gene tried to sell his 83% share of the stock and get out, but the deal fell through in the face of, as the *Constitution* said, "staggering losses, heavy debt and court suits." The unfortunate part about the growing worthlessness of the stock was that the employees' pension had been tied to it. Once the books were altered, it was easy for those in power and whosoever desired, to overuse credit cards, misuse purchasing orders and take profit.

In summary, Bryan Gibson, who in 1968 came to Barwick to take charge of industrial relations, saw four basic problems that brought down the Barwick empire. The industry had caught up with demand by 1973 as newcomers poured into the field for the quick money, and the successful had to adjust. Second, Barwick had overexpanded into capital-draining, non-productive areas. The ventures into carpet tile, needle punch and synthetic backing were particularly disastrous. Third, Gene tended to put too much trust in people on "face value." Bad advice on crucial ventures and not keeping a close eye on the cash flow or the stock offering package severely hurt the financial structure of the company. Finally, the recession of 1974-75 depleted his ability to sell his way out of the crisis. In other words, he could not use his greatest strength just when he needed it most. Which of these reasons is correct? Some critics blame one or all.

There is no doubt that Gene made a tremendous impact on the industry. His courage and foresight brought explosive powers to bear on style, design, manufacturing, and sales. Unfortunately, some of his bad practices also have been emulated. Practically anywhere a person turns in the industry today, he will find executives, owners, and innovators who began with E. T. Barwick. Gene Barwick's impact makes it certain that no history of the tufted carpet industry can be written without his name being underlined.

On July 7, 1993 E.T. (Gene) Barwick died in Atlanta, Georgia.

# *Chapter Eight*

# THE CORONET STORY

The Coronet Story is the success story of three totally different but achievement-oriented individuals—M.B. (Bud) Seretean, B.J. Bandy Jr., and Guy Henley. Their background, previous experience, and temperament were quite different, but they blended their individualities to produce one of the largest carpet companies by 1980.

Born as a dream around the kitchen table of Mrs. B.J. Bandy, the aggressive New Yorker Bud Seretean, the production-wise Vanderbilt-educated Guy Henley, and the economic-expert Jack Bandy, created a well-balanced floor covering conglomerate. Coronet far exceeded its original goal of $5,000,000 in sales and providing each a modest income. To understand Coronet and its success one must first understand the three who crafted its structure from the beginning.

In 1927, Frank Guy Henley Jr. was born in Chattanooga; his father was in the knitting business at the time. Guy's aggressiveness demonstrated itself at Baylor Military School in Chattanooga, there he lettered in football, wrestling and boxing. In the Navy he boxed and played football. One season he played for the Great Lakes Navy football team earning the nicknames "Gus" and "Big 8", the latter because he wore a size 8 helmet. When he returned to Vanderbilt after his two years in the service, he lettered four years in football while majoring in business administration.

Although Guy's father influenced him toward a business major, Guy had a even broader aptitude. Some hint that his later success in working with people at Coronet might be foreseen as his degree (1949) showed he had minored in English, History, and Psychology. After a brief, lucrative but unhappy sojourn into life insurance, Guy settled with Dixie Mercerizing Company (later Dixie Yarns) in yarn production control. At Dixie E. H. Hill gave him some very valuable lessons in attitude which he felt proved invaluable in later years. He also spent a short time as production manager at Katherine Rug Mills in Dalton. There he met Seretean and then went to manage Lawtex's newly purchased carpet mill in Chickamauga. After a year or so, Seretean and Bandy asked Henley to take charge of production at the newly established Coronet.

Leonard Lorberbaum of Lawtex recalled, "I told him that he was crazy to leave a $10,000 a year job for a company that might not make it, since the times were so tough then." Henley told Lorberbaum that he had been offered a piece of the company, and he had to take the chance or he might regret it later in life. Leonard added, "I should have gone and let him stay."

As earlier stated, much of the success in production must be attributed to Guy's attitudes toward the importance of company growth and the quality production of people. In the early days when the plant was operating six days a week, Henley was there, doing whatever jobs had to be done. Henley also had a selective bent which influenced expansion. He did not feel a machine should be purchased until it was running efficiently, used to its fullest extent, and with enough demand to support it. This same demand often forced Coronet to move ahead faster than he wanted.

Guy learned at Dixie that his greatest responsibility was creating the right atmosphere for the job. Many of Coronet's employees were small farmers or sawmill workers whose jobs were fading out, but whose work ethics knew how to produce. Guy explained, "If you ever worked in a sawmill, having to get up early and try to get the saw working in the cold, you'd know how to work and would do good." Henley felt much of company leadership should be developed from within. "We picked some good people," said Henley, drawing an analogy with a harvest. "And they grew, often picked them green, but they ripened in the sun—we were growing so fast that some had to be green."

Henley felt that the attitude and motivation of people were the key. "Good people can turn out good products on a mediocre machine, but skilled people who have a bad attitude will turn out a mediocre product on good machines. Morale and attitude are more important than the skill," shared Guy. Coronet understood management techniques and computer aids, but people produced the results. He liked to tell his fellow workers, "We are trying to get up a ladder, and there will always be someone above another. If you step on the hands below, they will pull at your ankles. But if I reach back to help you and you give me a little shove, we will get up and enjoy the fruits of getting there."

Some of the fruits Coronet provided was its incentives: profit sharing, better wages, good work environment, and access to management. Supervisors, who worked with 15 to 25 people, were taught to lead their personnel, to know who to lead and who to push. Guy said that he always told his supervisors, "I can make you the supervisors, but those people will keep you there. They must look to you to protect their interests. You treat folks right, show interest in them, let them know why their job is important, and that their job is needed and appreciated."

In 1972, two years after Coronet was bought by RCA, Guy retired. The company had gotten so large that he was spending his time reading computer print-outs and not meeting people. His job had ceased to be fun. In his early years of retirement in Dalton, he spent much of his time aboard his sixty-four-foot sport fishing boat in the Bahamas, often searching for sunken treasures.

When Jack Bandy was born in 1926, his parents were already heavily involved in the bedspread business. His earliest memories were of diving into the yarn bins and crawling across sheeting. B.J. Bandy's business was carried on just as much at home as in his office. He owned hotels, drug stores, spread houses and a large farm. Jack grew up in a home that was constantly filled with his parents' business associates and business seemed like fun. His father gave J & C Bedspread Company to his children: Christine (who was married to

Joe McCutchen) and Jack, and although it was run by Joe and Christine, Jack had a stake in it.

Jack traveled a great deal with his father to the Gastonia and Cartersville operations and he worked in the plants washing, folding, carrying, and inspecting spreads. World War II and the Army shortened his study and football playing days at Georgia Tech. After his discharge he began a business education at Bowling Green (KY) Business University, but he returned home in 1947 shortly before graduation to help his father temporarily deal with some problems concerning the Internal Revenue Service.

He and his wife, Aggie, settled in Rome, Georgia near the family's Southern Craft plant. It was one of the most up-to-date plants in the industry with its own laundry, dye operations, and drying ovens. Their mechanics were even developing machinery which could produce 9 x 12 rugs. It was an incredibly enjoyable learning experience since the industry was evolving so rapidly.

In December, 1948 B.J. Bandy Sr. died intestate and Jack had to work out all the problems. The interests included a hotel, several drug stores, three manufacturing plants and a large farm with more than 500 head of cattle. It took five years before the estate was settled.

When the estate was settled in 1953 to the satisfaction of the family and the government, Jack began to work with John Carter, a "jack-leg" engineer who owned Specialty Machine Company. John could build anything the industry demanded and he was especially intrigued by the development of pattern configuration used in tufting.

Jack began selling his equipment to different manufacturers and learning the supply side of textiles. During this time of rapid tufted growth, each machine varied from its predecessor due to continuous innovations.

In 1953 Said Shaheen of Katherine Rug Mills called Jack's mother to see if she would rent a room to "a fine young man" who was coming to Dalton as his national sales manager. Dalton had only one rundown hotel, no motels or boarding houses. The only hotel was adjacent to the L & N Railroad line and salesmen experienced two hours sleep, a train and then two more hours before the next train. Some widows in town had taken in boarders to help with costs and to fix maintenance problems around the house, so Dicksie agreed to rent a room to Bud Seretean, Shaheen's new sales manager.

Jack and his beautiful wife lived in a small house out back and they often ate with Dicksie and Bud. During the next three years Jack and Bud got to know each other very well and often shared their dreams of starting their own company. The industry was still in its infant stages with machines developing both width and design capabilities.

Synthetic fibers were starting to move into demand under the innovative leadership of Gene Barwick. Jack had studied the industry very carefully over the years. He noticed that a manufacturer, a salesman, or a financial expert could start a company, but when it reached approximately $5,000,000 in annual sales, his leadership became so thin that the company would fall back or fold.

In the spring of 1956 Bud came by Specialty one day and stated that he was ready to get started in his own business. That night in the Bandy kitchen Jack and Bud planned the company. Jack's knowledge of financing, the Dalton labor market and administrative structure and Bud's sales experience and leadership fitted well into their plans. Bud recommended Guy Henley as the third member of the triumvirate since they had worked together at Katherine.

**Coronet's First Building**

Since Bud was still employed, Jack did all the leg work. He convinced Guy of the merits of the new company, leased the old "King Cotton" building near the railroad track from John McCloud, ran off the first samples of tufted carpet at Singer-Cobble in Chattanooga and set up their office. The original office of Coronet was a small room in Mrs. Bandy's home where the three founders and their office staff, Barbara Bremner, worked. They inspected the small 18 inch wide samples on the front porch.

Jack also arranged the financing. Although the partners put up a total of $40,000, Jack had to secure about $300,000 in credit guarantees. At the start Bud stayed on the road selling continuously, Guy kept the plant operations moving and Jack tried to control the exploding money management demands. But as time passed Bud stayed in the office more and became a strong administrator.

M.B. (Bud) Seretean, who was the driving force behind the origin and explosive growth of Coronet, came from an entirely different background. Born and raised in New York City of Rumanian immigrant parents, he was known as a scrambler and a hustler from the start. In 1976 he told a *Modern Floor Covering's* writer, "It's the challenge that intrigues me, playing a long shot and winning." At age 7 he took on a route for the sale of *Liberty* magazine, but gave it up in 24 hours because selling 50 magazines to earn a jackknife "did not add up." He progressed to shining shoes, working for a tailor, working in his parents' grocery, and delivering for other shopkeepers.

At an early age he was aggressive and resourceful. If the grocery store did not have what was needed, he'd sneak out the back door to the nearby A & P and bring the product back. But much of this attitude came from his parents who had Bud and his three sisters pile up the canned goods in the window so that it looked like the store was well-stocked. His mother pawned her $150 engagement ring time and again to keep the store in supplies. At the age of thirteen, Bud convinced the supervisor of New York's three stadiums that he was fifteen so he could sell soda pop and hot dogs. Unfortunately, he ate most of his profit.

He was goal-oriented and one of his goals was to play the trumpet. He told Furman Bisher of the *Atlanta Journal-Constitutional*, "More than anything else, I wanted to play in a band. I played hookey from school 25 times to go to the Paramount and hear the big bands, like Harry James." He took lessons for 50 cents a week and rented a horn for 50 cents. He finally got to play with a band two or three times a week as well as at parties. With this kind of devotion his grades naturally suffered. He barely graduated from high school and did equally dismal at City College of New York.

At this point his life underwent a dramatic change. "I was averaging about zero, going nowhere, nothing in mind beyond blowing a trumpet the rest of my life," Bud recalled. He heard that if one enlisted in the service to fight in the war (1942), one would get a passing grade in all the subjects he was currently taking. So with no professed patriotism, he entered a new phase of his life, which profoundly changed his directions. Starting in the Air Corps he switched to the Engineer Corps and finished the war as a field artillery officer in the 77th Division in Italy. (He said that he changed positions, so much because nobody wanted him.)

One of the first significant decisions occurred while he was stationed in Little Rock, Arkansas, in 1943. He had a date arranged with a local girl who was going to pick him up in her car. But he had gotten into military trouble and ended up on kitchen duty. He was peeling potatoes in front of the mess hall when she drove up to pick up her new date, Bud's company commander, "and she saw me as they drove away." He vividly remembered that "suddenly the whole situation made me very angry, and I made up my mind that from then on I was going to make something of myself." The next day he applied for Officer

Candidate School and was accepted. He was discharged as a First Lieutenant in 1946.

While in the Mediterranean Theater, another salient event occurred. The captain in charge of the post exchange was ordered back to the States and Bud was offered the job. He told a *Chattanooga Times* reporter, "Running the PX was the most enjoyable business management experience I had ever had." Looking back he saw a definite shift in goals. "I now knew what I wanted to do, where I wanted to go—retailing and marketing."

On discharge, the aggressive New Yorker took his G.I. Bill and went to Oklahoma State University, but not for its academic offerings. He had grown to 6'4" in the service and turned out to be a fairly good service basketball player. One of his fellow officers convinced him that he'd like Oklahoma State, particularly since he might be able to play on one of their many championship teams. After three or four days of practice, "I knew I was out of my league. I liked the place by that time, though, so I stayed," said Bud.

His desire to achieve, which he gained in the service, had not cooled. He graduated in the top five percent of the class and he was president of a number of service organizations. He moved on to N.Y.U. and received a Master's Degree with honors in Retailing. While working on his degree, he served as a student trainee at Stern Brothers and again committed himself to a goal. "I wanted to be the president of a department store by the time I was 45," said Bud. However, jobs were scarce and his applications to Macy's, Bloomingdale's and Allied Stores were all turned down.

"Rejection," Bud felt, "becomes a force that drives me to do better." When he was made part of the executive training group at Abraham & Straus in Brooklyn, he discovered his $45 a week salary did not match well against the $75 that others in the program were drawing. To prove that they had underestimated his potential he worked 15 hours a day, six or seven days a week.

At this time the crucial break came. Bud felt that the careers that most people enter were determined by 90 percent luck and 10 percent design. Bud used another set of figures from Thomas Edison who said that genius is 10 percent inspiration and 90 percent perspiration. At this point Bud's 90 percent of hard work and perspiration met his 10 percent luck.

After two months in the management training program Mel Pollock sent for a temporary replacement for the assistant buyer in floor coverings. It was just prior to the Labor Day promotions and Mel simply asked for "the biggest and strongest," caring less about the intelligence. Bud fit the job description, and that was how he got into the carpet business.

He was liked by the buyer and within two months he was awarded the job permanently. Approximately six or seven months later he was attending a trainee seminar conducted by the vice president in charge of training. During the question period Bud asked how long an assistant buyer had to stay at that level before he could be considered for a buyership. Usually a minimum of two years was the answer he was given. Bud responded by asking if it would make any difference if he had a particularly talented assistant buyer.

The answer was an adamant NO. The next day Bud began looking for his next job. He left the store 30 days later to become the buyer of floor coverings at Allied Stores, a chain of 80 to 90 stores. Again he attacked his job ferociously, even spending time in Europe trying to develop an import carpet business there. After eighteen months Allied was showing its biggest increases ever in floor coverings, and again Bud set his goals: merchandise manager as soon as possible; store president at 40; government service at 50, and a college professorship at 60. His boss agreed that Bud was ideally suited for his next step but needed to be placed with "the right opportunity." After being denied several openings because they were "not the right one for him," Bud left to become the sales manager with Katherine Rug Mills, a small company from whom he had been buying carpet.

Actually, the tufted carpet business had been exciting his attention for the past several years. While still at Abraham & Straus two significant introductions had grabbed his interest. First, shag carpet in 36-inch rolls made of cotton yarn to retail at $8.95 a square yard, was introduced by Wunda Weve. "It proved that carpet fibers other than wool could be sold. It proved customers would accept new and interesting textures. It also proved sales training and sales promotion would work in our industry," Bud said.

Secondly, Gene Barwick tufted loop cotton and Bud felt that it was a fantastic value at $6.95 retail compared with everything offered on their sales floor at that time. "I ran to the workroom to see this new breed of carpet." A new era was dawning for Bud.

In 1953 when Bud came to Dalton, Katherine had sold $2,000,000 in scatter and room size rugs the previous year, and it was expanding its business into broadloom. In three years time he tripled its sales volume. Bud then attempted to buy a small equity in the company owned by Said Shaheen and his brothers. They did not want to bring any outsiders into their business thus forcing Bud to leave to follow his dream.

During his three years in Dalton Bud's friendship with Jack Bandy had bloomed in the home of Mrs. B.J. Bandy. Not only did she include a room in the price of the rent, but she also provided an occasional meal, good solid advice, her personal interest, and lots of stories of the early days in the bedspread industry. Bud's appreciation of the knowledge and help of Mrs. Bandy remains to the present. Built in this type of surroundings, Coronet became the fulfillment of their dream.

It was not the best time to be starting a new company. The tufted carpet industry was in the 1953-54 recession at the time and all the Dalton mills were in keen competition in the low price merchandise field. Bud decided that they

**Coronet's first six employees: M.B. Seretean, Guy Henley, Harold Langham, Jay Jordan, Ervin Sexton, and Jack Bandy**

needed an exclusive niche. The industry was a morass of highly competitive cotton and rayon products. Manufacturers could not make it cheap enough. Yet at the time the woven industry was producing 80% of all carpet sold to the public. About 85% of the fibers that they used were wool. During the Korean War wool had shot up to over $2.00 a pound. As a result wool woven products were costly. Coronet might be able to fill this opening and become the only all-wool tufted carpet supplier.

Bud developed a sales brochure out of construction paper and other companies' advertisements which emphasized Coronet's distinctiveness: all-wool carpets only, middle price bracket only, proven best sellers in loop textures only, only carefully selected colors, only durable construction, a bonded guarantee and concentration on point of sales merchandising aids. Actually, most of the distinctiveness was a composite of the best in the industry with the exception of the all wool, the heart of the price brackets, and a selling brochure, "Selling the Coronet Line." The initial sales brochure used hand drawn graphs and construction paper to prove points. Their two carpet colors were determined by picking the best colors from Bigelow and Mohawk and the bonded guarantee was the expansion of an idea from a cotton carpet firm.

Using samples from test machines in Chattanooga, with yarns they were not sure they were going to use and colors from competitors' lines, they attempted to present a professional picture of a stable and experienced firm. As Bud later said, "We had to look old and experienced in a hurry."

In August, 1956, Bud went north on a three-week sales trip to see if he could pick up enough orders to pay for the yarn and the machine on which they had an option. He first went to a friend who was a buyer at an Allied store in Boston. Business was terrible, but he called a carpet distributor Ben Elfman & Sons, for a visit. His response was, "Business is lousy and we are overstocked." He finally allowed Bud a fifteen minute visit that turned into a four hour sale and an $90,000 order for 160 rolls. Bud immediately called Jack to buy the machine and start running because he had made the impossible promise of early fall delivery. He picked up eight more accounts from eight more visits in upstate New York. Coronet was off and running.

Its first plant was a dilapidated metal-and-wood warehouse next to railroad tracks. The small front office leaked, and next to it was a larger area whose rotting floors were home to a local rodent colony. An inventory at the end of the first month led to the discovery that 10 of their 50 roll wool inventory had provided dinner for rats. The back of the building was the only place that they could put their tufting machine since it had a concrete floor. The building shook so badly when trains came by that they had to check each time to see if the machine was out of balance. If any buyer wanted to come to Dalton to see the plant, it was always going to be closed at that time due to some distinctive Southern holiday, such as Jefferson Davis Day or the opening of squirrel hunting season.

Finally, Charles Snyder, owner of Hollywood Carpets in Bradenburg, Maryland, showed up to see the plant. They had planned to show anybody who got to Dalton one of the better carpet mills from a distance and claim it for their own, but here he was at the door. Bud assigned Guy to show him around. Both men were rather heavy-set and as they walked through the middle section, the timbers gave way. They rushed the buyer to the primitive Dalton hospital with a fractured leg. Incidentally, he remained a buyer with Coronet.

In the early days Coronet could not afford a showroom at the Chicago Merchandise Mart so they rented a hotel suite at the Morrison Hotel, about 15 blocks away. The parlor was converted into a showroom and the bedroom into a dormitory for Bud and the four salesmen. They would entice buyers to leave the market and come over to look at their products and munch on sandwiches and drinks of their choice. In January, 1957, Bud came down with a high fever from having to walk back to the hotel in a blizzard. He was forced to turn his early morning interview of a prospective regional salesman over to one of the others. The prospect saw the small line but would not give up his connection with a certain Patcraft line unless he could "meet the guy who runs the company." The company representative opened the door to reveal Bud covered with head towels and surrounded by the whiskey bottles which had earlier been shoved out of the showroom. The prospect who had been offered parts of the Midwest said, "I'll take the job. This is my kind of customers."

Always a strong believer in goals and planning to meet those objectives, Bud set the goal of $1,500,000 for the first full year (1957) and Coronet reached $1,745,000. The *New York Herald Tribune* in April 1964 documented their rapid growth. Their 1958 sales of $2.6 million netted the company $124,000; 1960 sales of $8.9 million yielded $311,000, and the 1963 $21 million netted $1.25 million. They had planned for moderate growth with a $5,000,000 goal, but within seven months they had to build their first plant, since the original building was inadequate. Actually, the founders could not remember whether the first building was condemned or just falling apart. They built a brick building on Jack's father's old airstrip just north of town and added a second machine to the flat loop machine they already had.

In late 1963 due to heavy borrowing and a cash flow problem, the leaders found themselves in difficult straits. They tried to sell the company which looked so good with good profits, but no one was interested. At this crucial point Bud decided that the only answer was to go public. Because the market was in the doldrums, Coronet had to agree to very tight conditions, including a very low multiple and Bud's selling each institutional house around the country on the worth and potential of the tufting industry. It went public in January, 1964 for $14.25 Bid and it's success led to its listing on the New York Stock Exchange on July 20, 1966. Coronet became the first tufting company to be publicly-held.

**Coronet Industries, Inc., 1963**

On October 12, 1970, the *Wall Street Journal* reported that on the basis of a one-for-one stock exchange R.C.A. had purchased Coronet for approximately $147.9 million, making Bud Seretean the largest single stockholder in the conglomerate. In 1973 Bud was the last of the three founders to retire from active involvement with the company.

Coronet's amazing growth must be credited to a number of factors. Bud told a *Chattanooga Times* reporter, "Our strength has always been in selecting the best people available and then in providing the best possible environment composed of the best facilities, advancement opportunities and, above all, enjoyment in what they are doing." The strengths of the management team insured a "tight ship," while a good working relationship under Bud's leadership moved steadily toward specific goals.

At the beginning of March, 1971, *Floor Covering Weekly* noted that the company had, from its initial beginnings, expanded from floor coverings to commercial furniture, metal chairs, vinyl wall coverings, dual sleeping units and convertible sofas, and urethane foam and cotton batting for furniture. Besides plants in Dalton and California, it had operations in Canada and Belgium.

**Coronet Industries, Inc., Board of Directors, April 26, 1968: Thor W. Kolle, Jr. Louis Regen Stein, B. Jackson Bandy, M.B. Seretean, Frank G. Henley, Jr., Herman W. Lay, and Rankin M. Smith**

Having started in retail sales before making his way up through the ranks, Bud brought to marketing a unique vantage point. His educational majors in accounting and marketing coupled with his experience led to his very aggressive and intuitive approach to sales. The Coronet Carpet Caravan program was a pioneering approach to using covered buses and trailers as educational showrooms on wheels. They toured the United States and Canada on a year round basis touting the Coronet, Riviera and Heritage lines as well as training future sales representatives who were the driver/hosts.

Coronet led in the use of computers, data-phone systems and state-of-the-art machinery. In 1966, Sentry Industries which was automated in dying and finishing was added to its integrated package. It was the first to introduce the Honesty tufting machine by Singer-Cobble which used hollow tubes and air pressure instead of needles. In 1976 Coronet brought the first multi-TAK dye machine into the United States, introducing a revolution in styling and dyeing of carpets. Coupled with its commitment to the latest hardware was its management development program. Committed to a policy of "promotion from within," a generous profit sharing program for executives rewarded excellence in marketing and performance.

Finally, a major degree of success must be credited to the management team of Seretean, Bandy and Henley. Each understood their role and worked toward a common goal. Yet the drive and goal-orientation of Bud Seretean was at the core of their success and unity. Interestingly enough, Bud was attempting to overcome two perceptions which he felt people saw as his limitations—his age and his religion. He was rejected by Macy's and others because he was entering the field at the mature age of 25. At Oklahoma State he was rejected by several fraternities because he was Jewish. Rather than rebelling, he determined to "fight three times as hard as anybody else to prove that he was at least the equal of most other people." He was a leader on campus and resolved to be recognized one day as OSU's most outstanding graduate. By 1979 Bud was the president of the Board of Trustees at Oklahoma State and a member of its Business Hall of Fame. The M. B. Seretean Center for the Performing Arts now graces the university's campus. It is interesting that he does not consider his growing up in a poor Rumanian immigrant family as an obstacle, but as a building stone. One theme seems to run throughout any interview or talk which Bud has given—his commitment to goals. This is seen in the fact that when he was working at Coronet he kept three legal pads with him all the time. One pad was used to keep track of responsibilities on which he used a series of stars to indicate the urgency of tasks to be completed. The second pad was to keep track of earnings and projections. And the third pad listed board meetings, travels and other fixed appointments. His actions were the logical extension of a vision that he had for himself and his company. Dreams provided the motivation of his life. As reported in *Women's Wear Daily,* Bud's favorite quote is from Robert Browning, "A man's reach should exceed his grasp or what's a heaven for."

After a series of ownership changes, Coronet was purchased by Carl Bouckaert and Ed Ralston and became part of the Beaulieu Group of America. Coronet is known for its broad line of popular and medium priced broadloom saxony carpets for the residential market. Tapis Coronet Carpets, its smaller

Canadian division, is one of that country's premier producers of high end saxonies. In 1992 Interloom, with its finely-styled, high-end line of Berber products, was merged into Coronet. The Coronet name continues to set the pace in fine styling and quality products.

## *Chapter Nine*

# THE WORLD STORY

Big oaks from small acorns grow. This is the story of one of the largest privately owned carpet manufacturing facility in the United States. A careful mix of ground floor experience, academic preparation and strong personal values yielded this pacesetting company. Even in World's modest beginnings there was the guiding determination to certain basic principles of its founder, Shaheen Shaheen.

Shaheen was in high school when his uncle Said Shaheen first came to Dalton. The family was in the jobbing business for imported goods from Italy, Belgium and France. World War II cut off the sources and the twenty-eight-year-old Said came south to buy scatter rugs, bath mats, and bedspreads. After several years the climate, the small community, and a friendly church all appealed to him.

Shaheen and Piera Shaheen

Literally, one day Said walked out of Dalton's favorite Oakwood Cafe and saw a picture of deep snow drifts from a storm in Chicago paraded across the pages of a newspaper. He called his older brothers; Awad and Azeez, father of Shaheen Shaheen; and suggested that they join him in Dalton. In 1945 the partnership bought the Hanson Painter Rug Company. At first called Katherine Chenilles, it produced chenille spreads and scatter rugs. Shortly afterwards, following the advice of their accountant Melvin Keller they concentrated totally on rugs and carpets.

Initially, Katherine rugs were made on a single needle machine, but by 1948 they were using narrow broadloom machines to make the rugs.

In 1947 nineteen-year-old Shaheen Shaheen spent the summer working in the mill and two years later he began selling for them in the Midwest. He had just graduated from Illinois Institute of Technology with a B.S. in Industrial Engineering (Business Management). Fortunately, his program offered training in plant layouts, time and motion studies, cost accounting, marketing, labor relations, management and administration. It provided him with a good background for his future in Dalton. At first, he traveled about a thousand miles a week over six Midwestern states, primarily selling scatter rugs. In February, 1952 he came to Dalton to manage manufacturing and the office of Katherine's growing operation. Demand and developments were spurring the industry forward. Actually, everything was growing so fast that Shaheen helped in the design of a new plant to fulfill Katherine's needs.

However, Katherine Chenilles moved to a downtown location on February 1, 1954, but Shaheen Shaheen stayed. Said implied that they had different ideas about how to run the business which would seem natural considering their different educational backgrounds and experiences. Shaheen decided to take his 15% share in the family business in the form of the old building on Green Street and start his own business. In June 1951 he had married very talented Piera Barbaglia, and they founded a new company with their total life savings of $3,500. Their assets included a 15,000 square foot building, one twelve-foot level loop tufting machine and a twenty-foot infrared-light latex coater. The work force consisted of five male employees and a secretary to handle billing and shipping. It took all six men, including Shaheen, to run the latex coater and without an expensive forklift everybody was needed to load and unload rolls at the shipping dock.

A name for the new company offered a challenge. Shaheen believed that tufted carpet would dramatically change the homes of America. In honor of their first son John, who was born on July 4, 1953, the name American seemed appropriate, but the postmaster said it was already claimed. While reading the Bible Shaheen found the words, "The scene of the world is changing," in a translation of I Corinthians 7:31. Like lightning the word "world" stood out in bold relief. The company had a name.

In getting the company moving, Shaheen scavenged north Georgia for used sewing tables, fringing machines, typewriters and even paid $10 to $12 for large wooden laundry buggies to move the rugs about the plant. Using an 8/6 ply cotton yarn at 54 cents a pound World's first carpet created was called Xanadu and was offered during the January 1954 Chicago market at $3.00 a square yard. Eight commission salesmen across the country agreed to represent the new company after its initial showing. World was up and going.

Representative Bill Anderson had an order from Southwest Wholesale Floor Covering in Dallas, but a problem developed immediately. Bibb Manufacturing decided that cash rather than the promised credit was the only conditions for yarn delivery. Rather than jeopardize his product by using a different yarn than his samples, all the cash was used on the C.O.D. order on Monday, February 1. By Tuesday the yarn had been creeled and tufted. It was latex coated by Wednesday, dyed at Dalton Spread Laundry on Thursday and by Friday it had been inspected and shipped. Using James Talcott as a factor this process was repeated week after week in the early days.

With growth Shaheen tried to secure a loan from local banks. Both First National and Hardwick Banks suggested Shaheen instead go to the Small Business Administration. This new agency agreed to go along on 80% of a $20,000 loan, providing the bank would support it with 20% of the total loan commitment. Both banks refused this loan of $4,000. Shaheen has kept these letters through the years as a motivation and remembrance. "It taught financial self-reliance," recalled Shaheen. A $20,000 loan was arranged with Bob Mathis who had just sold Dalton Rug Company and the $7,000 balance in the principal three-year loan was paid off after two years.

Determination and self-reliance keyed World's early growth. During the first month in 1954, sales at World were $16,000. By April, sales more than doubled to $38,000. During the summer production expanded to two shifts and in September they went to 35 employees on three shifts. A cut pile machine was installed next to the loop production. World was profitable and on its way.

In the early days of tufting the demand for carpet was great and World benefited. Later, due to his training, his philosophy, and his experience Shaheen developed the basics of a totally integrated company. In those days it was still common to buy yarn, job-out dyeing and finishing, rather than integrating it altogether under one company. Years later in talking about his continuing success he commented, "Unless you are a pioneer in technology, product, equipment and concepts of distribution and service you can not survive." He is an excellent example of Thomas Edison's statement that genius is "when preparation meets opportunity." Good habits and techniques yielded positive growth for World.

From the start Shaheen developed strong work and people skills. Although owner and chief executive officer, Shaheen helped train the workers on the machinery. In the absence of a hyster in the early days he also helped muscle

**World Carpet and Waterfall**

the rolls from the machines to the dyeing operation to the docks. When a fifteen foot wide high-low pattern machine was ordered from Cobble Brothers, Shaheen spent two days in Chattanooga learning the principles of the machine's operation so that he could teach the operators. Often he trained the operators by having them put the machinery together upon its arrival in the plant. They would not only be able to operate it, but also fix it if the need occurred. (He had to be an expert teacher considering the fact that the operators might have good practical skills, but most had barely a grade school education.)

For sales World began by using already successful carpet salesmen who added World lines to their repertoire. As the demand forced them to represent the company exclusively, they were backed by innovative warehousing, production and styling. By the mid-1950s the concept of regional sales managers in the field replaced the older plan of a plant-directed sales force. Using commissions, management overrides and even a share in the warehousing profits World tried to hold onto its most successful salesmen. A rather innovative method of motivation involved paying commissions in large denomination bills. The payment of commissions in bills as large as $10,000 created an indelible impression on the sales force. They say imitation is the sincerest form of flattery and World's success led to numerous companies trying to copy their sales field tactics. In management, World tended to develop techniques that others would follow. Shaheen said, "We tried to hire self-starters who do not need much supervision and we'd work with them. We let them learn our policies" or "what we wanted to do in product and style and let them use their ability" to get the job done.

As a further motivation, a profit-sharing program was developed to inspire hard work and loyalty. In 1957 a profit-sharing retirement plan was inaugurated. Cash bonuses at Christmas and July vacation time were later added. There are annually over one hundred full education scholarships for employee children, an active in-plant GED program and a tuition reimbursement program for employees who pursue a college program in World-related fields. Shaheen personally is very active in speaking to high school students trying to influence them to finish their high school education. At one time Mountain Lakes Golf and Country Club at nearby Spring Place, Georgia, was purchased to provide recreation for World employees. Approximately 35% of the company profits before taxes go back to those who create the success of World Carpet. The success of the company is certainly measured in the success and happiness of its people.

In the mechanics of distribution Shaheen feels he led the way. When it became apparent that the color demands of the West Coast were different than those of the Mid-West and the East, a unique approach developed. In 1955 Bill Green, World's western regional sales manager, suggested sending greige goods which were then dyed to suit the brighter California customer demands. Sometimes entire rooms of carpet were sewn together before dyeing so that seams would match. A commercial dye house allowed World to store undyed goods for free. Later the dyeing out west was phased out, but this was the first of the regional warehouses. Through the years World has serviced the nation with as many as 14 regional warehouses, which were continually expanded, as sales increased.

Distributing the product to the market place also proved a major challenge. Before the age of interstates, it took 75 hours for a trucker to pull his load to the West Coast. Railroad boxcars took a long time in transit and were difficult to load. The main local trucker disliked competition and used the Interstate Commerce Commission to harass World for using private truckers. Finally, in 1957 at the suggestion of an I.C.C. investigator, World developed its own trucking fleet to ship to the West Coast, Dallas, the Northern states and Florida. Soon other companies were following their lead. In the early 1970s the strengthening of the Teamster's Union increased World's dependence on distributors and warehousing and caused the addition of piggyback freight with the railroads.

As sales demands grew, it forced production facilities to expand to the demand. Shaheen tended to let the demand force World's expansion and often it was paid for out of immediate profits. In 1957 the original 15,000 square foot building added 10,000 square feet. The demands for new space for production, inspection, shipping, storage and office led to additions of 15,000 (1958), 20,000 (1959), 25,000 (1960), a small addition in 1961, 40,000 (1962), 100,000 (1964), and 160,000 (1966) square feet. As addition followed addition contract labor proved to be slow and not cost efficient. Therefore, a construction crew was formed at World and stayed continuously busy from 1960 to 1975. By 1985 World Carpet was the largest privately owned carpet manufacturing facility in the United States and one of the largest privately owned carpet manufacturing companies in dollar volume in the world.

**Modern Broadloom Tufting machine**

Because the city would not expand its limits, including its utilities and fire and police protection, World had to expand in its original immediate area. A major obstacle was one of the highest hills in the area, one of Dalton's Civil War defense positions, which was immediately behind the plant. Soon Shaheen found himself in the earth moving business with a fleet of dump trucks. In the course of 20 years over 2,000,000 cubic yards of earth were removed from the site. In 1968 an additional World facility south of town began to be built to its current one million and a quarter square foot capacity. It was totally integrated with a large yarn mill, yarn storage area, tufting, five continuous carpet dye lines and two backing ranges.

Extensive construction was also necessary in the development over a period of years of a totally integrated production facility. In 1959, five years after World began, Shaheen Shaheen and his brothers Shouky and Tawfeek began a wool yarn spinning business in Cartersville. In 1967 Shaheen took total control and changed it into a nylon spinning operation. In 1975 he bought Jordan Yarns, a yarn spinning company in Columbus, Georgia. In the fall of 1978 Charles Whitener approached Shaheen and his wife Piera at lunch in the local Oakwood Cafe. He asked if they would be interested in his filament twisting and heatsetting operation in nearby Spring Place, which they bought. Spinning and filament heat setting additions were made at the New World plant over the years. In mid-1985 the old Trend spinning facility in Rome, owned by Integrated Yarns, was acquired by World.

Initially, World used local dye companies such as the Dalton Carpet Finishing Company. In 1960 Shaheen Shaheen, his brother Tawfeek Shaheen, who had joined the company, and J.B. Cleveland began Foremost Carpet Dyeing. World's demands increased so rapidly that Shaheen sold his interests in 1962 and began his own operation, installing four dye becks and a 30,000 pound steam boiler. Previously they had used pre-colored yarn (stock dyed) and solution-dyed rayon.

In 1968, World became the first in the industry to put into use a Kuster continuous dyeing range—first in solid and then in TAK multi-color. World had to develop new dyes and new styles and with time and experience was able to make it cost competitive with beck dyeing. Later in dyeing polyester Kodel carpeting, World became so efficient that Eastman Kodak sent its engineers and technicians to learn from them. In 1971 World purchased the first complete TAK dye line from Germany, flying it to the U.S. on a Lufstansa Jet. In one month World had it assembled and in operation. A sophisticated refinement using air nozzles and jets which produced greater color possibilities was the first in operation in the United States.

Through the years World had to compete with carpet companies who produced inferior products. Cheapening production in the bedspread industry had resulted in lint that would easily shed off on other materials and Shaheen foresaw that lowered standards would create similar problems for the image of tufted carpet. The FHA certification standards worked on an honor system and often weight and other standards were ignored. Prior to 1967 the FHA would not include carpet or its cost in a mortgage. Once it was accepted, certain companies used lighter weight carpet than the minimum 20 ounce specification face weight that the government initially required. Some manufacturers were as much as 30% below, but would give their dealers letters certifying "full weight." World maintained its standards, but lost valuable business to the dishonest producers.

For seven years (1967-74) World led a frustrating, but successful fight to get an administrative agency to require the fulfillment of industry-wide standards. Finally, with the threat to remove all carpet from inclusion in government mortgages, an agreement was reached and the standards pushed so consistently by Shaheen saved the industry from FHA exclusion. The consumer was the ultimate winner.

In an industry where pressure to go to public financing, World has remained private. Coming out of a family background tradition it was common for businesses to develop and stay within the family. In the early years the demand for growth and their commitment to their dream caused the Shaheens to continuously reinvest their profit back into the company to the point that at times they were personally strapped for cash. By not going public, the benefits to the employees were retained, contrary to many acquired companies who look to maximize profit statements.

The total Shaheen family became involved in the company's growth. "I started working in a mill on rainy days when I was nine years old," recalled John Shaheen who became president of World Carpet in 1985. "Mom wouldn't let me work on sunny days because she wanted me to go out and play." His brother David, who also served as president, pointed out, "Meal time easily becomes a board meeting." Currently, Shaheen and Piera are enjoying retirement, while John is Chairman of the Board and David is vice chairman and CEO. The day-to-day operations are in the capable hands of President David Polley, Vice President of Operations Charles Mitchell, Vice President of Manufacturing Charles Parham, and Vice President of Marketing Bill Waters.

Many in the industry consider the quiet, but firm power within this family to be Piera Shaheen. Before marrying Shaheen her life experiences created a very strong and capable lady. Though born in Iowa, she lived in Italy for twenty-one years. During World War II she was in charge of keeping the finances for the underground movement against Mussolini's Fascists and the Nazis. Living with the constant threat of death, injury, or the terrors of capture, she developed a strong character. She witnessed the cruelty of Nazi firing squads killing young boys, she hid alone in a dark tomb for twenty-four hours and risked even a personal firing squad by carrying underground documents with her. In the early days of World she played a major role and still is active in the areas of color, styling and finance. To sum up the family's role Shaheen said, "We're all extremely interested in innovative techniques and often are firm believers in expressing our opinions."

The success of World must be attributed to several areas. Gene Barwick and Bud Seretean were primarily salesmen while Shaheen was totally involved in training and production. He trained leaders and then made it financially attractive to keep them with bonuses and profit sharing. He had a vision of what he wanted in the future and made sure than the plans were not just for the immediate, but also long range. Their strong marketing support for their salespersons is coupled with a predominant distribution to the "working man" sector. They have developed a reputation of providing good, up-to-date stylish products, often before the rest of the industry. The horizontal integration of all facets of the business as well as developing their own trucking and construction units has paid valuable dividends. "Being a privately-owned company gives us flexibility that publicly-owned companies don't have," added John. They have created a strong loyalty within management and plant employees with profit-sharing, educational benefits and personal attention.

# *Chapter Ten*

## THE INDUSTRY COMES OF AGE

The five-year period from 1955 to 1960 is considered to be the Golden Age of Development, setting the stage for a new "breed" of leaders. Virtually, all technology which lifted products out of the category of washable cut rugs into a viable and cheaper alternative to woven carpet was put into place. The conversion to synthetic yarns, the development of basic printing techniques, the addition of backing and new machines evolved onto the scene. Floor covering engineers, chemists and machinists made all sorts of efforts to make manufacturing "cleaner and quicker" so that carpet has become an affordable luxury product, but the basics for future design were in place by 1960.

Also five different markets began to develop. Residential became about one-half the total market, followed by the institutional sector which reached approximately twenty-five percent. The remainder was divided between other commercial sectors, outdoor carpeting and, finally, the automotive market. This diversity provided a new group of entrepreneurs the opportunity to build significant companies.

A challenging second wave of industrial change swept through the industry in the late 1950s and was precipitated by a serious national economic recession by 1958. A number of small, underfinanced tufting mills had such a low profit margin that even a slight decrease in payment on outstanding bills threatened their existence. The typical old-style manufacturer usually ran their business "out of their back pocket." They did very little planning, little or no forecasting and little budgeting. Often their creditors or factors arranged the transfers of management from the old pioneering people to a new breed of professionals. Although, in spite of this, the period of the early 1960s have been referred to as the "Golden Age of Tufting." New, somewhat better educated, more experienced operators assumed control of some companies and other old-line companies adopted better methods in their efforts to survive.

One of the new companies which evolved out of these challenging times was Horizon Industries, the creation of Peter Spirer. Peter was born in New York City in 1931. Over the years his father owned several businesses, including manufacturing fur coats and leather sporting goods. Peter went to the University of Miami, intending to become a lawyer and possibly enter politics. However, fascinated by some business courses he was taking, he switched majors and graduated with honors and a degree in Business Administration. He then joined R.H. Macy and Co. New York as an Executive Trainee. In two years

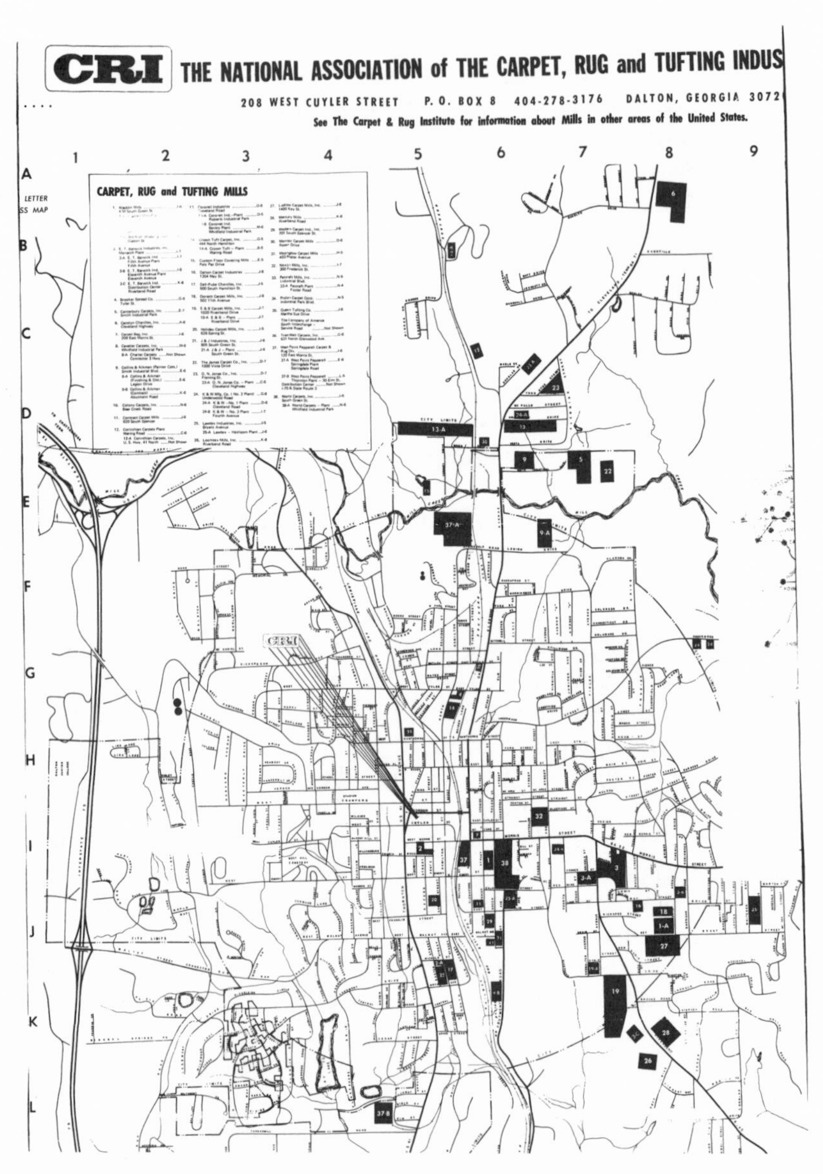


Map of rug and tufting mills

he had acquired valuable lessons in retailing and business management as well as a wife.

The latter development led him, in 1955, to join Stitt and Howell, a New York floor covering distributor, owned by his father-in-law, Tom Carmichael. Stitt, Howell were prominent distributors of Roxbury and other fine woven carpets. Mr. Carmichael correctly concluded that woven carpet was a luxury item available mainly to the rich, and was impressed with the economic possibilities of the emerging tufted technology. He envisioned it as "every man's floor covering" and saw himself as a discoverer of a diamond in the rough. Many have claimed responsibility for the first 9 x 12 foot tufted rug. Tom was firmly convinced that "Mose Painter made it and Tom Carmichael bought it." Tom painted a picture to Peter of Mose as the mythical mountain man with the wonderfully inventive mind. Dalton was a magical place, a small town nested in the mountains of north Georgia whose energetic citizens were creating a whole new industry. In 1956 Peter paid his first visit to Dalton and to Painter Carpet Mills. It was even more exciting than what he had expected and he determined that "this is where I will come to seek my fortune." Having sold some tufted carpet Peter knew that there were numerous problems such as streaking, unproven new synthetic fibers, flimsy backing materials, and fading dyestuffs, but he was convinced that it had exciting possibilities. He later said, "Dalton seemed like the 1956 version of the Gold Rush. For me this was the last frontier. It was where the entrepreneur could really identify with the future trend line."

The more he visited Dalton, where he spent a lot of time with Mose Painter, the more his desire grew to return permanently. In 1958 he resigned his position as vice president of Stiff and Howell, and set up his own sales agency, Loom Trends. It was natural that he would represent Painter Carpet in the northeast and he was soon accounting for two-thirds of their national sales. The recession of 1958 put serious strains on the mill, and Mose and his partner, Herbert Rogers, began having difficult administrative and financial problems. Tom Neal, who headed the factoring division of Walter Heller Company, (Painter Carpet's financial backer) ultimately arranged a buyout of the partners and assembled a management team headed by Bill Glasscock.

From the very start Glasscock and Spirer had serious differences. Glasscock, a former Dun and Bradstreet credit man, was certain that the mill was losing money because of low prices to dealers and distributors. He even went to the extreme of sending Spirer a collection letter billing him for what he claimed was the difference between the cost and selling price, while at the same time withholding commissions due on sales. Peter's response in an angry phone call to Dalton, was that if Glasscock wanted higher prices to let him know, but "don't expect me to work for nothing." He observed that "slaves were set free in 1865" so "send me my commission check."

Painter's Sales Manager, Lou Trousdale, was dispatched to New York to fire Spirer, but once there, he found that the pricing was in fact equal to competitive product lines. Instead Peter was invited to Dalton in hopes that he and Bill Glasscock could work out their differences. When Peter arrived, he recalled that "it was raining a real frog-choker, and the office building floor was a mass of puddles. Water was splattering down on Bill Glasscock's desk and the guest armchair had a big spring sticking through the leather right in the middle of the seat." Noting the scene, Peter broke into laughter, telling Bill that "I'd be depressed too if I had to sit in this environment and write silly letters." The meeting broke the ice between the two, and soon they became good friends. In eight months time Bill invited Peter to become a partner and vice president of marketing. By 1965, Peter had become a major stockholder and his initial investment of $10,000 multiplied when Collins and Aikman, a large textile company, bought out Painter Carpet Mills for $7,500,000 in October of that year.

Following the purchase Peter became the president of the Painter Carpet division. During the following years the company entered the commercial carpet market with the invention and introduction of "Powerbond," a vinyl backed commercial carpet which, more than twenty-five years later, is still a major product in the commercial marketplace. In 1968 Spirer left Collins and Aikman to form Tile Company of America, launching America's first carpet tile company. In 1972 when his non-compete clause expired, he founded Horizon Industries which soon set the industry standard for beautiful, uniquely styled carpet for the medium and higher priced residential market. Horizon became known for its high profile, creative marketing style, as well as for a seemingly endless parade of industry best-sellers. Color and style were the drivers at Horizon, and the company grew rapidly based upon its willingness to take risks in introducing new looks and its skill at employing unique marketing techniques. Its Harbinger subsidiary, begun in 1979, achieved success by concentrating on fashion styling for the designer specified commercial market, while its Helios division made exquisite carpets and rugs for the residential design trade.

Following the sluggish recession of the early 1980's, Horizon's sales climbed from $184 million in 1985 to $274 million in 1988. In 1984 Ralph Boe, a veteran DuPont manager, joined Horizon as C.E.O., and the combined leadership team vaulted the company from 14th to 6th in industry rankings by 1990 with sales topping $300 million.

In July, 1992, the industry was stunned by the announcement that Mohawk Industry and Horizon had agreed upon a merger, in which Mohawk would purchase the company for $87 million. By October, the deal was done, making the combined entity the third largest in the U.S. carpet industry.

While Horizon's success is often attributed to high fashion marketing and innovative styling, J & J Industries' growth is the result of the management philosophy of Tom Jones and Rollins Jolly.

Tom Jones was educated at Georgia Tech in Industrial Management and after a short stint in sales with Coca Cola, he served in World War II. He was part of the officer pool which worked with an experimental all-negro anti-aircraft unit. Tom considered it the "greatest learning experience of his life." He learned many lessons from supposedly uneducated troops. Tom entered the military as a private and emerged, at war's end, as a major. He returned home to Dalton, where his father was both an attorney and a car dealer, and Tom worked in a number of vehicular-related businesses. While selling a truck to odd-lot yarn dealer, Rollins Jolly, he was persuaded to join him in business.

The partnership bought a tufting machine from Cobble Industries and expanded into level-loop residential carpet. Rollins was a silent partner in J & J while he continued to run Jolly Textile Sales Co. However, from time to time, Tom would come by the Jolly office to inform him of their progress. Occasionally, he would add, "We need to go see Uncle George." (George Rice was president of the First National Bank of Dalton.) They'd proceed to borrow more money for J & J's growth. It was a relationship of trust between the two.

In late 1967 J & J began to phase out selling odd-lot yarn and residential carpet. The company began to concentrate on commercial tufted carpet and Tom persuaded Rollins' son, Jim Jolly, to join the company. Having graduated from Georgia Tech, Jim really did not want to work for his father, but Tom persisted that Jim would work for him, since his father had not been told about the offer yet.

At the time J & J's only competition was the old-line woven carpet manufacturers, Bigelow and Mohawk. Although J & J led in the commercial field, its success is more attributed to its management style. Tom Jones explained it well when he said, "We are primarily in the people business, we incidentally make carpet."

In 1982 J & J received the first Lamar Westcott Industry Appreciation Award for exemplifying "all that is good in a local manufacturer." Chamber President Joe Sheppard noted, "They have low employee turnover, and a people-oriented management style. They know their employees well and have demonstrated a sincere interest in employee well-being."

In 1982 the industry was in the doldrums. When asked why J & J was doing so well, Tom's immediate answer was "the people," as he led the listener to his famous "Wall of Fame" (photographs of long-term employees cover the wall.) He constantly ascribed the company's success to the hard work, positive attitude and studious concern for excellent carpet to his employees. He claimed that it was the result of "good Christian folks who work together to make it possible." Tom nurtured this philosophy through a significant profit sharing program, aid to education advancement and health care, which in the early 1980s was a novel idea. Also there were programs in which people in the plant and in the office swapped jobs so that they would appreciate each other and his general supportive attitude. He knew everyone by name and spoke to them all. Tom is remembered as always having a kind word and a smile, and he would often write words of support and encouragement on their weekly paychecks. At the annual company June picnic he was always at the end of the line offering a coke and handing out potato chips. After Tom's death, Jim Jolly, who had succeeded his father as partner, took Tom's place at the end of the line and continued the focus of J & J's success on its people. Tom Jones once commented, "We are in a business in which the carpet has to meet exact specifications for major buildings, we cannot be approximate. We are exact and people who are appreciated will do the job right the first time." In the institutional market, or corporate selling to office buildings, churches and airports, it may take months for J & J's salesmen to know the right people before getting a chance to bid on a project. But J & J will support them during that time, knowing that exacting quality demands of the company, its ability to make custom orders (where often big companies cannot do economically) and its low cost base produce repeated customers. J & J was one of the first carpet manufacturers to specialize totally in the commercial part of the business.

Jolly says that the three keys for J & J's future are education throughout the organization, a total commitment to customer satisfaction and an ongoing quality improvement process. Much of the success of a company is in the creation of the proper chemistry in sales, service and manufacturing. Tom Jones and Jim Jolly found the means of success in appreciating, rewarding and letting the employees know their value. It works for J & J.

Queen Carpet is the successful development of a father and son team, Harry and Julian Saul. Harry came to Dalton in 1939, and was in the retail clothing business until 1946 when he lost the lease on his building. The tufting business was just getting started after the war and in 1946 Harry decided to give it a chance. Using $1,750 of his savings, he bought from C.T. Pratt Chenille Co. 7 single-needle machines, 3 eight-needle machines, tables, chairs and other chenille-production materials to get started. Harry and his wife started with children's robes, then added bedspreads and by 1951 had expanded into rugs. They began in a small concrete block building next to Dorsey Buick on Thornton Ave., and then moved next to W & W Laundry to make transportation easier for dyeing. As Harry's business grew, he was approached by machinist-inventor George Hanson to go into the carpet business with him. (George had built a nine-foot yardage machine which could tuft cotton carpet.) Harry told him, "George, you're crazy. It costs too much." (At the time it would have cost about $5,000 to go into the carpet business the right way.) However, they did progress into broadloom by 1969.

Queen actually got into the carpet business by accident. A friend of the Sauls had some odd lots of yarn and, as Julian said, "We got to fiddling with it." At the time Gene Barwick was doing "fantastically" and they were drawn toward the possible wealth.

In the early days, financing was difficult. The banks felt that they were ready and willing to help the fledgling business, but Harry remembers it was never enough. "When we first started this business, we always needed another hundred dollars. Then it became a thousand, then ten thousand. Later it became fifty thousand, then a 100 thousand, a million and now another ten million." He felt that if there had not been factors like Textile Banking Company, a part of Commercial Credit, and Citizens And Southern Financial Corporation since 1964, they would have never made it.

While other companies rose very rapidly only to decline as quickly, Queen grew slowly, being profitable and meeting demands. At one point they made 7,000,000 waxing pads for Johnson Wax. The profit on each item was not even in pennies, but in mills, but it was profit. Finally, they divested themselves of the small rug division and concentrated on carpet. In the early days carpet and rugs had a seasonal demand—through the fall and up until Christmas. They would work two 12-hour shifts with Harry sometimes working 22 hours at a stretch. Then the slow time of the spring and summer would bring very lean financial times.

During the 1980s, with Harry's son Julian joining him, Queen established itself as an aggressive producer with a modern, well integrated manufacturing operation. Julian had grown up working in the plant, doing whatever had to be done. After gaining an industrial management degree from Georgia Tech, Julian returned and helped in the tremendous growth the company enjoyed in the 1980s. Julian attributes their rapid growth in the early 1980s, while the industry was in the doldrums, to finding a niche with five exciting styles.

During that time Queen expanded from a concentration on BCF nylon to developing its own spinning capacity. The firm's medium priced product range was not particularly broad, but styles seemed to be chosen for maximum sales appeal. In early 1990 Queen purchased Patcraft Mills, which made some well-designed patterned commercial carpets for the custom-designed markets as well as medium and higher priced residential carpets. This acquisition introduced Queen into the more profitable and less price sensitive commercial market. Four months after Queen bought Patcraft, the firm acquired a $15 million spinning mill from BASF. Two months later, it added Crown America's Valdosta, Georgia BCF yarn processing plant. Much of Queen's growth in the early 1990s has been on the West Coast and coupled with its new market focus, the company needed to expand its spinning and yarn processing capacity.

One of the early pioneers was a teacher-principal who decided to try his hand at the bedspread business. As an educator, I.V. Chandler learned that life is filled with lessons of success. While majoring in agricultural education at the University of Georgia, he sold Bibles door-to-door to pay his tuition and learned "what it is to live hard." His second teaching job ended with his firing, teaching him that "no job is safe." He came to Whitfield County as an agriculture teacher and ultimately, became the principal of Valley Point

J. C. Brooker
*Brooker Spread Co.,*
*Dalton, Ga.*
*President*

R. E. Hamilton
*Dalton, Ga.*
*Executive Vice President*

Russell C. Gebert
*James Lees & Sons Co.,*
*Bridgeport, Penn., Vice*
*President*

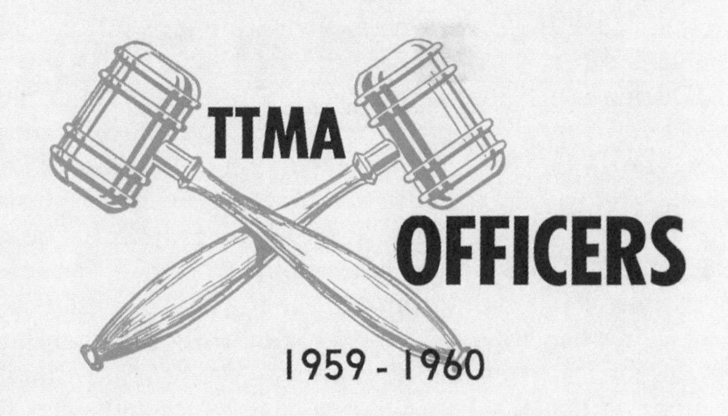

A. L. Zachry, Jr.
*G. H. Rauschenberg Co.,*
*Dalton, Ga., Vice*
*President*

Arthur N. Richman
*Art-Rich Mfg. Co.,*
*Dalton, Ga., Vice*
*President*

James T. Porter
*Tifton Rug Mills,*
*East Point, Ga., Vice*
*President*

M. E. Kellar
*E. T. Barwick Mills,*
*Dalton, Ga.,*
*Treasurer*

**W. H. Sparks**
*Mayfair Division,*
*Collins-Aikman Corp.*

**Leon A. Lee**
*L. A. Lee Company,*
*Dalton, Ga.*

**I. V. Chandler**
*Patcraft, Inc.,*
*Dalton, Ga.*

**J. L. Knight**
*J. L. Knight & Co.,*
*Dalton, Ga.*

**G. D. Wright**
*Crown Lau. & Dye Co.,*
*Dalton, Ga.*

**W. V. Williams**
*Modern Tufting Co.,*
*Dalton, Ga.*

**G. Richard Keim**
*C. H. Masland & Sons,*
*Carlisle, Penn.*

**L. P. "Mose" Painter**
*Painter Carpet Mills, Inc.,*
*Dalton, Ga.*

# and Board of DIRECTORS

**Sam H. Hodges, Jr.**
*Alabama Bedspread Co.,*
*Scottsboro, Ala.*

**J. W. Bryson**
*Tex-Tuft Products, Inc.,*
*Rome, Ga.*

**Nathan B. Levine**
*Carolyn Chenilles,*
*Dalton, Ga.*

**Leonard Lorberbaum**
*Lawtex Corp.,*
*Dalton, Ga.*

**Harry I. Saul**
*Queen Chenilles,*
*Dalton, Ga.*

**Nathan Snow**
*Dixie Belle Mills,*
*Calhoun, Ga.*

R. Carter Pittman
*Attorney*
1945-1947

O. R. Strain
*Cabin Crafts, Inc.*
1947-1948

Thomas J. Brown
*Georgia Textile Corp.*
1948-1949

J. K. McCutchen
*J & C Bedspread Co.*
1949-1950

A. B. Tenenbaum
*Blue Ridge Spread Co.*
1950-1951

## Honorary
## BOARD OF GOVERNORS

. . . composed of the immediate and past presidents of TTMA

E. J. Moench
*Tennessee Tufting Co.*
1951-1952

Ira N. Nochumson
*Noxon Rug Mills*
1953-1954

R. E. Hamilton
*Tufted Textile Mfrs. Assn.*
1954-1955

E. T. Barwick
*E. T. Barwick Mills*
1955-1956

M. W. Wiesen
*Lawtex Corporation*
1956-1957

W. H. Sparks
*Collins-Aikman Corp., Mayfair Division*
1957-1958

E. D. Lacey
*Russell-Lacey Mfg. Co. Inc.*
1958-1959

J. C. Brooker
*Brooker Spread Co.*
1959-1960

G. H. Rauschenberg
*G. H. Rauschenberg Co.*
*(Now deceased)*
1952-1953

School. He lived in the county, four miles north of the school on Highway 41. In 1945 one of his school bus drivers and a friend decided to go into the "spread business" and thought that I.V.'s garage would make an excellent tufting plant.

I.V. had been in education for 20 years and he saw the chance to make some supplemental cash. Instead of selling them his garage he offered to be their partner, and Star Chenille came into existence.

The next year he resigned from teaching, due to growth of the business and two years later he bought out his partners. He renamed the company Patcraft, in honor of his daughter Patsy, and began to expand into scatter rugs. In those early years he used Singer sewing machines with extra needles added to the bar. At this point another one of his lessons of life occurred. On March 5, 1952, right after he bought his first twelve foot tufting machine and a new oven, the plant burned to the ground when lint and latex exploded in a vent. He found himself with no building, equipment or money and $15,000 in debt.

At this point, the camaraderie of the tufting business was demonstrated. Suppliers started sending word not to worry about what he owed, but to pay when he could. The laundry which handled his outside finishing told him to get back in business first, pay his current bills and take care of the old ones later, when he could. Odell Edwards, whose Del Rube Chenille was in direct competition with I.V., ran enough yardage to fill Patcraft's orders, cut and shipped them to his customers. (Several years later when a fire hit Del Rube, I.V. returned the favor.) With their help and a government loan, I.V. was able to get the business going again. Within 15 days, Patcraft was making scatter rugs again and within a year they were paying their bills on a fairly regular basis. I.V. felt that so many people helped him get started that he should give something back and he has done it generously. As evidence of his gifts Valley Point's football field is named after him, as is the local Junior Achievement Center and one of the buildings at Truett-McConnell College in Cleveland, Georgia. At one time he also carpeted the University of Georgia athletic offices and dorms.

Within two years after the fire Patcraft expanded into rugs and then in 1956 they began manufacturing carpet. While others in the chenille and scatter rug business stayed within that area, he learned from an old company, Furness Carpet, who helped him after the fire, that carpet was more profitable. He also noticed that the home bedspread and chenille business kept the price of those goods extremely low.

Patcraft's success is attributed to some basic principles. In 1916 I.V.'s father put his arm around the teenager and shared a piece of wisdom. "What you do speaks so loud that I can't hear what you say." I.V. took this advice to heart. Some companies in the early years "showed good goods, but delivered poorer quality," I.V. always took pride in giving good quality goods and shared with other companies and people in need.

I.V. learned very early to manufacture anything his customers wanted. When he was making spreads, he got so tired of seeing peacock bedspreads on the lines on Highway 41 that he decided that he'd "never have a peacock on any of the spreads I made." However, when he received an order for 24 peacock bedspreads "at the tremendous amount of $8.00 each," he changed his tune. It turned out to be the most popular spread that he produced. Cecil N. Smith, who succeeded to the presidency when I.V. retired, felt that one of their biggest assets was "service." "We have a commitment to our customers. Anything they want, we'll try to supply." However, maybe I.V.'s answer to his personal and business success was the best response. "Hard work, dedication, Georgia 'Bulldog' excitement, plus a little Jack Daniels Black. That's real living."

Diamond Rug & Carpet is an example of a company that was begun over 20 years ago, but has experiencing rapid growth in the last five years. Ed Weaver began selling remnants in his hometown of Eton, but in 1969 he bought three tufting machines and started making broadloom carpets. In the early days Weaver helped his 12 employees with everything from running machines to sweeping floors. Diamond grew at a measured pace to $100 million by 1982, then it began explosive growth to $290 million in 1992.

Its growth surge has been attributed to its carefully engineered direct sales force, its entrance into the higher end market in 1984 and its integration of production. About two thirds of its product line goes to the residential market with the remainder to the commercial market. Its early commitment to low end cut/loops and cut pile carpet has expanded to a broad line of tufted broadloom carpet, synthetic turf and indoor/outdoor carpet at popular price points. Diamond has systematically acquired tufting, dyeing, and extruding facilities. It is thought to be the second largest polypropylene fiber extruder in the carpet industry. Its recently acquired inhouse yarn making and processing capabilities make Diamond one of the world's most fully integrated carpet and yarn manufacturers.

The architect of this expanding company, Ed Weaver, is a flamboyant entrepreneur in his early 40s who is noted for impressive collection of cars. He has every Corvette since Chevrolet first introduced them in 1953 as well as Mercedes, Jaguars, Ferraris, Lamborborghinis, and Rolls Royces. In 1986 his collection, which is carefully housed, numbered more than 175. To aid in his growth in January, 1993 Ralph Boe was named president and COO of Weaver's company. In March, 1993 they weathered a devastating snow storm followed by a fire which destroyed 15% of the company's total plant sites.

There are a number of developing companies which are surging forward to claim their share of the market, developing unique retail programs and carve their niche in the field. Their star is on the rise as they learn the lesson of low cost manufacturing and sophisticated marketing.

Dalton Mini-Market

## *Chapter Eleven*

# WOVEN CARPET RESPONDS

Somewhere in ancient history the art of carpet making emerged. Babylonians were skillful carpet weavers and hieroglyphic representations of carpets and weavers were found in the pyramids. Myth tells of Cleopatra wrapping herself in a carpet to insure her safe delivery to Caesar. Carpets were woven according to tradition in homes by domestic labor. Dyes were made from roots, seeds, berries and even the famous purple dye made from Mediterranean shellfish. The fibers were stoutly woven flax or hemp as well as wool and cotton.

Rome's expansion, the Crusader's return from the Holy Land, Marco Polo's Oriental travels and the Moslem advance helped move the knowledge and artisans toward Western Europe. The French expulsion of Protestant weavers in 1685 spread the techniques to the Low Countries and England. As early as 1701 English weavers in Axminster and Wilton were given a protective charter by William III. Both these towns gave their names to distinctive fabrics in which American weavers concentrated into the 20th Century.

Carpet manufacture in the New World started about the time of the Revolutionary War. It was done on hand looms and some person in the village acted as the village weaver. The early carpets were either rag or wool yarn produced in New England or the Philadelphia area. The first Ingrain carpets were manufactured by William Calverly in Philadelphia as early as 1775. Ingrain carpet is made in two or three plies, the warp being worsted or cotton, with a wool filling. William Peter Sprague set up a small plant in the same city in 1791 for the manufacture of Turkish and Axminster carpets. By 1811 Philadelphia boasted of four thousand hand looms and similar production was occurring throughout the Middle Atlantic and New England states. Three of the early important mills were the Thompsonville Carpet Manufacturing Company in Enfield, Connecticut; the Lowell Manufacturing Company in Lowell, Massachusetts; and the Saxon Mill in Saxonville, Massachusetts.

The expansion and sudden growth of the American industry is attributed both to economic and technical developments. The increased wealth of the Eastern seaboard cities and the introduction of tariff duties in the 1820's and 1830's were significant factors. The former created a demand for the luxury product and the latter protected it against a well-developed English enterprise. The English had an advantage of a finer product at cheaper prices as the result of their numerous textile inventions, including Edmund Cartwright's invention of the power loom. The invention of the Ingrain power loom by Erastus Bigelow in 1837 transformed the American woven carpet industry.

Bigelow's early aspirations were medical rather than mechanical. He pursued a variety of careers to earn money for medical studies. He fiddled for a town band, wrote and peddled a book on shorthand, and taught penmanship. Still in need of funds he produced a model of a counterpane loom and invented a power loom for the manufacture of coach lace. His later work ended his medical career and brought a commission from Lowell Manufacturing Company to build a power loom for Ingrain carpet. While his invention produced an operating profit of about $1,000 per loom for the first year he received no more than $18 a week. When his successful invention of a power loom for weaving Brussels and Wilton carpet proved to be too costly for Lowell, he and his brother found their own company, Bigelow Carpet Company. In 1929 in an attempt to position themselves to expand into broadlooms, Bigelow merged with Sanford and Sons of New York. Sanford already had a few broadlooms available and had made in 1897 the first wide Axminster (9 feet wide) ever made.

Broadlooms were just becoming important in the late 1920s with American woven carpet companies. Prior to that time all American carpets were in narrow widths (27 inches) and they were drawn together by sewing. The finest wide carpets were made in Europe, primarily on chenille looms in Scotland, on fabric which was 24 to 28 feet wide. The American market became enchanted with this type look and started to develop broadloom. At this time Wilton, Velvet, and Axminster were the principal weaves which produced a luxurious and expensive carpet. As the broadlooms developed, Bigelow found itself making broadloom carpets in seven widths—from 27 inches to 18 feet. Production was very slow. A twelve foot machine would average about 1,000 square yards a week on a two-shift basis.

The second major woven carpet company in America in 1950, the time that Dalton's tufted carpet industry emerged, was Alexander Smith. To Smith goes the credit for the Axminster power loom developed in his plant by Halcyon Skinner in 1856. Whereas Bigelow's invention had duplicated by mechanical means the action of the hands or feet of a weaver, the Skinner loom employed entirely new principles. Smith purchased his first rug mill in 1845 and despite numerous adversities, including the total destruction of his plant in 1857 and again in 1858, he utilized his creative powers and extensive marketing philosophy to develop a solid company. With continuing adaptation and managerial changes Alexander Smith was challenging Bigelow for national leadership in 1950. In 1956 the company became a division of Mohasco Industries, Inc.

According to carpet historian John Ewing in his *Broadlooms and Businessmen* James Lees and Sons and Mohawk were close behind the leaders in 1950. James Lees, a textile engineer from England, had founded a small textile company in Bridgeport, Pennsylvania in 1846. However, its surprising growth came as the result of a bold step in 1938 to move to Glasgow, Virginia. Its low-cost labor supply, accessibility to some raw materials and to markets, and good managerial decisions made Lees the most profitable company in the business in the early fifties. Another reason for Lee's growth was the progressive leadership of Joe Eastwick. He was an aggressive marketer, who recognized that market demands dictated production innovations, and tufting was indeed the greatest innovation since Erastus Bigelow hooked the waterwheel to the loom. James Lees was chosen in 1956 by DuPont to have a two-year-exclusive use of DuPont 501 nylon, along with Barwick Industries.

Mohawk Carpet Mills began in 1878 when four Shuttleworth brothers brought fourteen second-hand looms from England to Amsterdam, New York and set up the Shuttleworth Brothers Company in the basement of a mill. About 1908 the company introduced a new carpet, Karnack, and its success was phenomenal. Expansion followed quickly. Weavers worked for four and five years without changing the color or pattern on their looms. In 1920 the company merged with McCleary, Wallin and Crouse to form Mohawk Carpet Mills, Inc. The new firm became the only mill in the United States to produce all domestic weaves of carpet. In January, 1956 Mohawk and Alexander Smith merged to form Mohasco.

Mohawk was, perhaps, the first old line weaver to take the step into new production methods when, in the early 1950s, they surprised the market with an all new knitted carpet called Trendtex. Introduced into major department stores through their distributors, the style had instant appeal. The market was searching for a "new look" in home fashions similar to what was occurring in women's fashions. Trendtex had a warm generous loop texture that stood up to foot traffic and because of its random texture it showed little degradation in traffic lanes.

This further opened the eyes of the management to the power of innovation in post-war markets and interest swelled in tufting as well as knitting. In response to tufting's growth Mohawk built a state-of-the-art tufting facility in Laurenbury, South Carolina. In 1988, Mohawk Industries emerged as a private firm in a leveraged buyout which purchased the carpet operations from Mohasco.

As tufted carpet seized greater portions of the floor covering market share, the 1950s became a Decade for Decision for the old-line companies. Vast amounts of capital were tied up in inefficient multi-level plants and obsolescent equipment. Their preoccupation with wool lingered. Wool was a commodity and carpets and blankets were what you did with the commodity after your fortunes were boosted by trading and hedging. The advent of man-made fibers erased this dimension of profitability and eroded the buying power in wool markets.

With the advent of synthetic carpet yarns in the post-war period it was only a question of time before the appeal of lower priced, more durable carpets would relegate the higher cost, more finicky woven woolen products to minor yardage in the market. The chemical giants: DuPont, Monsanto, Allied, Dow, Uniroyal, Cortauldi, Exxon, Celenese, and Eastman, could see tremendous poundage in the production of carpet with their various fibers. The old-line companies had to adapt or decline.

The collision between these old-line woven companies and the emerging tufted textile carpet industry perhaps can be seen best through the eyes of woven carpet's own leaders such as Walter Guinan. Walter worked for 26 years with Bigelow-Sanford, then went with Karastan in 1954 and retired as president of it and Laurelcrest in 1973. As chairman of the board of the American Carpet Institute (woven carpet) he was a principal mover in the merger with the Tufted Textile Manufacturing Association to create the Carpet and Rug Institute.

Bored with public school Walter dropped out in 1928 to begin work as a sample boy for Bigelow at a salary of $10 a week. This son of a warehouse manager for National Casket Company felt that only then did he begin to learn. "It was the best education I could ask for. I worked Saturdays and Sundays learning all I could," he remembered. As a sample boy he often had to lay out samples for buyers, but he learned styles by interacting with customers. Guinan continued with Bigelow until 1954, studying management at night at New York University and style by day -period as well as personal style.

Walter was trained through Bigelow's "on the job program" as well as selling on the road. Salesman, contract specialist, assistant district manager of the Chicago office, line organizer and analyst in the styling department were the stepping stones to the executive job of stylist in 1949. His background prepared him well. One associate in 1973 said, "He's the best versed man in the business. Styling, management, selling, production, new technology—he's on top of them all." Yet it was his styling ability that catapulted him forward. Clem Stein, president of the International Academy of Merchandising & Design of the Chicago Merchandise Mart, said that Walter was the best style designer the industry has had. Walter could convince salesmen and management that pattern and color were the only important factors—not price at all.

In 1954 Guinan moved to Karastan as sales manager and then within six months he became a vice president. His modification of Karastan's Karaloc loom was only the beginning to his major styling coups which revolutionized Karastan. Guinan's philosophy has always been to sell "quality and style at a profit." At the age of 60 Walter retired as president of the company to pursue his life-long dream of travel.

Walter was one of the leaders of the woven industry who helped his company respond to tufted carpet. In the late 1940s and early 1950s he was attracted by two new Southern products, Wunda Weve and Nobility. Wunda Weve was a woven carpet made by Bell Rug Mills in Greenville, South Carolina. Prior to this time inexpensive carpet was characterized by either poor styling or poor construction. Wunda Weve was a cotton carpet woven in narrow widths on an old W-2 loom, but it had beautiful colors and beautiful textures. It was a success overnight and Bell Rug Mills was distributing it to the pace-setting stores, rather than low price distributors. (Woven carpet was sold to distributors who then sold to department stores, chain stores, furniture dealers and specialty stores.)

Nobility was a tufted carpet by Cabin Craft made out of viscose (a thick, golden-brown viscous solution derived from cellulose). The style had the look, the colors, the texture, and it sold for $9.95 a square yard which gave the consumer a beautiful style at a moderate price. It had a flimsy cotton backing and was coated with an inferior type of latex, but its styling brought acceptance.

While visiting Bigelow's largest buyer in California in July, 1950 Walter was impressed with the retailer's prediction. He predicted, on the basis of Nobility's preformance, that tufting would gain 50% of the industry volume. About one month later Walter visited Ralph Rhodes at the Georgia Rug Mills in Summerville, Georgia. His machine was nine feet wide, but he could make carpet only four feet wide because his laundry dyeing tubs were that wide. It was the first time that Walter had been exposed to high speed carpet making and he "was completely carried away with it."

Based on these two experiences Guinan returned to Bigelow and began to pressure management to get into tufting. Clem Stein remembered that Walter was treated with disdain for his suggestion. His insistence occurred at the same time that Gene Barwick's showy salesman was beginning to rock the floor covering industry. In December, 1950 Bigelow bought Georgia Rug Mills and poured in its money and technology. By 1952 Bigelow was the biggest tufter in the world and then the management "fell asleep" and starting ignoring tufting.

This was indicative of the major mills who were reluctant to accept tufting and man-made fibers. The woven industry was related to wool and its control of the wool market gave it power and dependence that it was not eager to relinquish. The industry leaders felt that tufting lacked credibility. In a speech in Philadelphia in 1952 an old-line carpet man referred to tufted carpet as "glorified bedspreads." In 1956 *Newsweek* quoted another as saying that the tufted industry had finally peaked out.

Walter Guinan points to five major factors which catapulted tufted carpet into dominance. The introduction of man-made fibers, particularly Dupont's 501 nylon, provided a quality fiber which gave good styling at a practical price. Then the development of cross dyeing, differential dyeing and space dyeing gave the industry colors that it never had before. Next the advancement in printing as initiated by the courageous vision of Barwick with the Zimmer Printer opened amazing pattern potentials. The production of a handmade Persian rug of good quality required 15,554 man-hours or 7 1/2 years of work. With the printer that Barwick introduced to the industry a 9 x 12 rug of good quality, good style and excellent consumer satisfaction could be made in 30 seconds.

Guinan also pointed to the continuous decrease in the price of synthetic yarns while the cost of wool yarns soared. The aid and assistance of chemical companies solved the problems of the limitations of beck dyeing and chemical compatibility. Finally, Walter felt that the industry became successful because it stood on the shoulders of Fred Westcott, Gene Barwick, Bud Seretean and other legends.

**Painter carpet Mill bought by Collins and Aikman**

Another facet of woven carpet's involvement in the industry can be seen in Collins and Aikman's purchase of Painter Carpet Mills in 1965. In the 1920's a group of the mainline carpet people from Philadelphia and Greenwich, Connecticut had created Collins & Aikman. At the time they were perceptive enough to see the opportunity for the use of fabric in the new automobile industry. The use of leather seats in cars was proving to be expensive and impractical and they offered to General Motors the option of fabric seats and cloth headliners. Later, they developed little woven mats for the floorboards. In the early 1960's Collins & Aikman's president, Donald McCullough, decided that the returns on tufting were very good and they should be involved. They originally tried to buy Coronet, but when the price was too high they bought Painter for $7,500,000. It was a small tufting plant whose product line lacked depth, if not originality, and it had a new building.

Working in another plant in Dalton Collins & Aikman developed the first formed carpet for automobiles. They tufted the carpet and treated the back of it with a heat-sensitive compound. Then they put it in a heated mold and molded it to a specified shape so that the Chevrolet division could use it in their assembly-line method. General Motors loved the idea and Collins & Aikman was in the automotive carpet business. However, C & A wanted to keep the idea to themselves so they moved its production to the Anen Plant in Ablemarle, North Carolina. This action left them with property in Dalton that was tufting headliners with a reduced output which was unproductive.

At this point they hired Bill Wiegard to do "something" with their investment. Bill had a variety of experience in both woven and tufted carpet and seemed like a reasonable choice. He had graduated from Loyola College in Baltimore in 1947 with a degree in philosophy, but, since jobs were scarce, he went to work for J.J. Haynes, a carpet distributor. They sold Armstrong hard surface floor covering, Deltox craft paper rugs, and Mohawk carpets. When Mohawk moved to consolidate their distributors in 1955, Bill went to work with Gulistan Carpets, the upscale carpet producer of A.M. Karagheusian, Inc. Gulistan produced both high end woven and moderately priced tufted carpet.

The company had invested a fortune in a state-of-the-art stock-dyeing plant in Statesville, Georgia to dye woolen staple and produce woolen yarns. Its' tufting plant in Albany, Georgia was still trying to beck dye wool carpet, with no streaks, and dry it in time for the next order. Guilstan tried to change its production facilities and its marketing structure to deal with the demand. By the early 1960s Guilstan was on the block to be sold.

Wiegand was approached in 1965 by Rudy Geofsic,a former A. & M. Karagheusian employee, to become the Regional Manager for the contract sales for Barwick Mills. The company had recently purchased print dyeing equipment which was designed for the contract market. They did well in developing contract lines for both the Monarch and Barwick lines, but the big markets were dominated by mills which specialized in product and sales persons for that market. Barwick sold only pre-determined styles and colors, and tended to deal around their distributors. Tensions arose and Barwick was already under financial pressures.

By 1967 Barwick's empire was coming apart and Bill accepted the challenge of doing something with Collins & Aikman's Dalton operation. Bill is fond of saying that desperation makes you do things which sometimes are creative. The Painter plant's tufting machines were small and inadequate.

When the carpet came off the end of the line, the jute would fall on the floor and the carpet would roll up on the roller. His first task was to create a specialized floor covering on a narrow face, 54 inches wide with filament nylon. Problems seemed to plague his early endeavors. The rubber backings put on by a finishing company was a disaster. The surfactant, which was like a green soap, tended to foam up when it got wet. His major problem was finding an adequate backing. Believing that a closed-cell foam would solve his problem Bill finally found a Lowell, Massachusetts manufacturer of inner soles for shoes. By modifying this product they were able to produce what became one of Collins & Aikman's most successful running style—Powerbond.

Another contribution to the industry also was the result of necessity. In 1970 Bill was looking for something that could be used on gym floors. Many schools were having difficult finding funds for renovation. Working with his research staff they came up with the idea of creating modules with hard vinyl backings that would be stable and provide a variety of applications. Prior to this time all soft floor covering, even in elevators, was carpet which was installed as a unit. These modules opened the possibilities not only for basketball courts, but also offices, airports and buildings.

The size of the modules, 18 x 18 inches, demonstrates his feeling that "little inventions come about because of necessity." Their premier salesman was Harry Borperian, a bald, five foot six inches tall dynamo whose personality and knowledge made him successful. A box of 18 inch squares could fit easily under Harry's short arms and the number of squares in a box were just enough for an installer to carry. Necessity, not extensive research, decreed the module size.

The invention of the modules demonstrate another of Bill's tips of success—"Figure out which direction everyone is going and go the other way." Everyone was going in the direction of wall-to-wall carpet, but module tiles are now a major field in floor covering. In 1985 Bill Wiegand stepped down as the president of the Floor Covering Division of Collins & Aikman.

In 1987 it was discovered that test results were being altered and that led to the disclosure of serious management irregularities. The company went into a financial tailspin, losing millions of dollars and the company's integrity was seriously challenged. To turn the company around the top management was fired and Charlie Eitel was recruited as president of the floor coverings division.

Although only 38 years old Charlie Eitel had a very successful background in the carpet industry. When Bud Seretean was visiting Oklahoma State University to endow the Seretean Center for the Performing Arts, he was hosted by Charlie and his fiancee, Cindy, who was Miss Oklahoma State University. Bud persuaded Charlie to be the first management trainee at Coronet. When Charlie arrived in Dalton in 1971, they had to track Bud down in Las Vegas to find where to start Charlie and what to pay him. Charlie had acted on trust in Bud, rather than specifics. He started in the order department at $7,500, which was less than the $13,000 other companies had offered. Cindy had to go to work to help pay the bills, but Charlie worked his way up through the corporation to become president in 1980 of the $200 million business at the age of 31.

**Collins and Aikman Plant**

The following year Charlie left Coronet to become president, Chief Operating Officer and part owner of Carriage Carpets, which was losing money. Under his leadership from 1981-1986, Carriage's sales grew from $6 million to $75 million; it led the industry in profitability and went public. At this point his differences with the other major partner led him to sell out. He attempted to buy Coronet which had been sold by RCA to General Electric. The employees wrote hundreds of letters in his behalf, but General Electric chose the bid by Joe Moffatt.

He was then recruited by Collins & Aikman to restore their troubled floor covering division's profitability and integrity. Today, this division is the top performing division of the corporation and leads the industry in profitability.

the anatomy of
POWERBOND RS

For more information on Powerbond RS
contact your Collins & Aikman contract specialist
or call 1-800-241-4085.

7

Figure 1
Detail: Powerbond RS
A. Super dense face constructed of 100% continuous filament nylon.
B. 100% woven synthetic stabilizer.
C. Encapsulating vinyl sealant coat.
D. Closed-cell cushion vinyl polymer.
E. Micro-encapsulated tackifier.
F. Protective plastic membrane.
8

Some tough decisions had to be made, but they have paid off. The $25-30 million broadloom business was considered to be in conflict with the heart of their focus, commercial carpet in modular tile and six foot vinyl backed roll goods for corporate and institutional applications. Charlie feels that if given two days he can demonstrate to distributors or technicians that their carpet with *Powerback RS.* is the best in the industry. Most carpet is tufted into a primary backing, sealed with latex and stabilized with a secondary backing, but susceptible to water damage. Powerbond uses super dense constructed continuous filament nylon tufted into a woven synthetic stabilizer and vinyl sealant coat which is welded to the closed cell Powerbond. The Vinyl sealant allows water cleaning of the carpet without any penetration. Most commercial carpet is laid down with tack stripes or wet adhesives, which are unsatisfactory. A micro-encapsulated tackifier on the bottom of the Powerbond seals the carpet to the floor without harmful gases being released and holds it firm. The carpet is in six foot sections and welded together so that there are no seams and no leakage.

Under Charlie Eitel's leadership the company has become technologically-driven, but customer focused. With Source One they offer a total package of product, installation and even maintenance directly to the end-user. Also its environmental focus has led to recognition by the Georgia Department of Natural Resources and the *Wall Street Journal.* They are the only company which can totally recycle its product back in its pure form into a component of their product. They call it Cradle to Cradle. Collins & Aikman takes the product and slits it, grinds it, fluffs it, extrudes it, molds it and calendars it back into backing. Finally, these commitments to a quality product, customer focused, environmentally friendly, and open door policy to employees has brought success and integrity to C & A. "Integrity is one of our major selling points," adds Charlie Eitel.

Masland Carpet has evolved from a woven background to total involvement in tufted carpet. Born into a family rich with a tradition of English weavers and knitters, it was natural for Charles Masland to be involved in textiles. In 1866 he founded in Philadelphia one of the carpet industry's oldest continuous companies, C. H. Masland & Sons. Beginning as a carpet yarn dyeing business, he expanded into the carpet business in 1886. Although at the turn of the century the company was devoted to the manufacture of Ingrain carpet, Charles anticipated the change in styles and was already developing tapestry and velvet production. His ability to foresee trends led him to begin printing yarn at this time. Later, he introduced the printing of carpet with a roller printing machine.

During World War II Masland's Carlisle, Pennsylvania plant became the largest producer and fabricator of canvas in the world. Tarpaulins, bomber hangars, Red Cross markers, bunk bottoms, tents, all types of truck covers and foul-weather clothing for the U.S. Navy issued from its plant. By 1950

Masland's line included Wilton, Velvet, Tufted and Knitted Broadloom carpets which were available in colors, construction, texture, fibers and patterns to suit all decors and prices to suit all pocketbooks.

In 1960 the company went public and in 1966 it was determined that the Carlisle plant would concentrated on automotive carpet while a new plant in Atmore, Alabama would focus on specialty carpet. When the Carlisle plant began in 1919, it was producing woven carpet for Ford Model A's. Interestingly enough, the office began in an old chicken coop.

Masland Carpets, lead by Ed Peach, Vice President of Floor Covering, determined in the 1970's that the Alabama plant could not compete against the low pricing of the larger tufted corporations and had to focus on a niche. It was decided that high end carpet and rugs with distinctive styling for specialty stores was an area of growth. Then as the market changed, they added contract carpet.

In 1987 Burlington, who had gained control of the company, sold off both divisions. The Carlisle division continued its automotive focus as Masland Industries. The Atmore operation was controlled by five management investors, but Dixie Yarns had control of 49 percent of the company. Dixie did not purchase more for fear that it might discourage the purchase of yarn by other carpet companies. In 1993 Dixie gained the total control of Masland Carpets.

In his thirty-one years with the company, Stan Albright, vice president of Masland Carpets, has witnessed and participated in their growth and response to the challenges of the mega-corporations. In 1962, on the day he finished his military commitment, Stan went to work applying latex backing on carpet in Carlisle. He worked his way up through the departments: auto manufacturing, creel operator in tufting, automotive product development, accounting, manager of accounting, manager of product development to vice president.

At Masland product development is a team effort in which stylists, colorists, technicians, machine operators, and marketeers are involved, but Stan's background provides the bridge to blend them all. His background in accounting makes him aware of the bottom line costs, while his manufacturing experience leads him to involve the operators who know the capabilities of their machines. Rather than an autocratic approach to management Stan sees leadership orchestrating the finished product. One might create a product like an atom bomb, but without the input of marketing it would not be sold.

This interactive style can lead to innovative and creative leaps in development. Ed Peach brought to his attention an entire page advertisement on sisal in the *New York Times.* Later, at the plant in Atmore Stan noticed how that the backing of their carpet looked like sisal. He had the backing operator latex the carpet upside down and they sold it successfully as Sawgrass. When asked by his competitors how this new product that looked like sisal was made, he would brush off the question with a suggestion that it was by a special process.

Finally, Stan's style has been shaped by his personal background. Working with his mechanic father he learned about complex machines as well as the lessons of hard work, long hours on a job, and honesty with all men. His father always pushed him to set goals and excel. Stan is representative of many in the industry who entered his first plant as an hourly employee and now is mixing his education, his experiences, and creative intelligence to lead his company.

## *Chapter Twelve*

# SHAW BUILDS AN EMPIRE

Undoubtedly, the most amazing story of the 1980s is the growth and impact of Shaw Industries. During the decade Shaw surged on sales from number six ($213,000,000) to an overwhelming number one ($1.6 billion). Chuck Reece of *Georgia Trend* (August, 1990) speaks of Shaw as being "the undisputed ruler of the carpet world." Frank O'Neill of *Carpet & Rug Industry* (June, 1990) pointed out that Shaw's 656% sales increase during the decade has made its output more than four times larger than number two Burlington. At the very center of this transformation is the direction and leadership of Bob Shaw.

Robert E. Shaw grew up immersed in the developing tufting industry. His father Clarence Shaw was in Dalton textiles before tufting machines began to appear. He was the dyer for Lamar Westcott at Westcott Hosiery Mills until it was sold to Real Silk in 1928. When the company went into full-fashion hosiery, there was no further need for a dyer, so Clarence went to work for Washington Hosiery Mills in Nashville, Tennessee. When Cabin Crafts was begun, Lamar called Clarence to come back as the dyer at Dalton Spread Laundry, which was the commission dyer for Cabin Crafts. In 1945 he and John McCarty purchased a commission dye house, and the new Star Dye concentrated on spreads, scatter rugs, and robes for a number of local manufacturers. After high school graduation Bob majored in business at the small Episcopal liberal arts University of the South at Sewanee, Tennessee. After three years of college he began to sell yarn for Bibb Manufacturing Company of Macon, Georgia, whose biggest customer was the carpet industry. From 1952 to 1956 he lived in Chicago and sold string to meat packers as well as other textiles throughout the Midwest. After four years with Bibb, Bob decided to leave the harsher climates for friendlier, warmer Southern options. As a chemical salesman for F. H. Ross, a supplier of wet goods processing, he began to travel the Southeast.

In 1959 his father's serious illness forced him to take a leave of absence to return to Dalton to sell off the family business. It took him only three weeks to realize that the family business offered him more than his sales position, and then another week to write his resignation to Ross. Prior to this time Bob had been labeled as a playboy. He described himself as "young, footloose and fancy free." However, a combination of factors forced him to settle down. He got married, had a child and in 1960 his father died.

At this point Bob began a careful, progressive growth in business, always guided by the principle of being the low-cost producer. When Bob began, Star Dye was a little $300,000-a-year business, dyeing scatter rugs. Working with his older brother J.C. (Bud), Bob pooled their money and experience with the

**Star Finishing Company**

help of Marion Manufacturing interests and John McCarty to create Star Finishing Company in August, 1960. (Star Finishing Company soon became the largest commission finisher of tufted carpet in the world.) The brothers, Star Dye and Marion Manufacturing provided a $100,000 capitalization. The new enterprise expanded to the areas of printing and applying backings to carpet. Their primary customers were Barwick, Coronet, Patcraft, Columbus Mills, Evans & Black, and a number of others.

Bud Shaw had already been fully prepared by schooling and experience for their paced growth. Bud also had grown up in the industry, but he was a graduate of Georgia Tech in textiles. Upon graduation he came back to Dalton to work for Crown Mills. "I saw in the carpet industry," he said, "a chance to own your own company. Or part of one." At Crown he had success in originating a program with solution dyed rayon. As one of the owners of Rocky Creek Mills, along with Marion Manufacturing Company, Bud was among the first to start producing nylon yarns. Rocky Creek Mills was sold to J. P. Stevens in 1963. His first experience at a carpet mill was as vice president of Dan River Carpets in 1965. In two years he was able to help turn around a losing operation through upgrading the product, re-organization of marketing, and broadening of the retail base. Bud learned early that planning and a strong follow-through was essential.

The year 1967 was the first of three pivotal years in Shaw's growth. In February, Bud, George Lane, a former Barwick executive, and long-time friend Warren Sims formed Sabre Carpets in Cartersville. In their first year with one machine they did $4.7 million in sales. Furthermore, the Shaws sold the Star Dye plant and equipment to Aladdin Industries as part of a process of moving totally out of scatter rugs into carpet. In line with this in December, 1967, they purchased an old line woven carpet company, Philadelphia Carpet Company of Cartersville, Georgia. Philadelphia was founded in Pennsylvania in 1846 and had concentrated on woven lines until it opened a tufting plant in Cartersville in 1958.

In 1963 Philadelphia transferred their headquarters out of their namesake city to the warmer climate of Bartow County. By 1967 it had become apparent to the Doerr family that as owners they would have to insert a significant amount of funds or sell their holdings. Bob points out that their purchase was not part of any grand design. "The reason we got involved in Philadelphia was that they were going bankrupt. They owed us $500,000 and our net worth was $700,000 and so we had to take it over. It was not a planned move, it was a forced decision," said Bob. In order to raise the $3.2 million purchase price Philadelphia Holding Company was created, merging Star Finishing, Sabre Carpets, Star Dye, and Rocky Creek Mills. The latter two firms were actually dormant companies. With Bud in charge of carpet production and Bob directing finishing, they moved to add a broad based carpet marketing program to support the manufacturing.

The 1970s were a time of transition and formation. Shaw had entered the business from the supply side (yarn and dyeing) and had to integrate forward into marketing to be a complete business. Also many companies had depended too much on factoring, which meant borrowing large sums for a short term. Faced by the need to expand, Bob acknowledged that the developing company was "not able to create enough capital internally to expand." In 1971 Philadelphia Holding Company went public as Shaw Industries at 20 times earnings at $36,000,000. With $7,000,000 from the offering, Shaw concentrated first on yarn supply. It purchased New Found Industries, a spinner of fine gauge carpet yarns and started up a heat-set and twisting operation as part of its new Yarn Division. Because of the more aggressive West Coast market a finishing plant was opened in Cucamonga, California to provide manufacturers services in carpet dyeing, shearing, jute and rubber secondary backing.

**Bud Shaw**

A second pivotal year in the growth of Shaw's move toward dominance was 1977. By 1975 the operations had grown so much that it was evident that organization was the next priority. Bud was running the woven and tufting parts of Philadelphia and Bob controlled Star Finishing. They had two giants going in different directions. Bud became the chairman of the board and "Mr. Outside," while Bob took the title of president and the running of the inside operation. Warren Sims, their childhood friend and associate since the formation of Sabre Carpet in 1967, began to commute in 1976 between

Cartersville and Dalton to pull things together in the new Dalton national headquarters. Warren's twelve years experience at First National Bank in Dalton prior to 1967 made him a logical bridge for people in both communities. In 1977 the preparation came together in a series of rapid moves. The Annual Report of that year noted that all "dyeing, printing and tufting" would be used exclusively to manufacture carpet "solely for Shaw." (A small amount of commission carpet finishing was still done in California.) Yarn sales to other companies were discontinued as the company's needs were greater than its own yarn producer's output. In July, 1977 they acquired the inventory, accounts and trade style names of The Magee Carpet Company, one of their better finishing customers. They expanded four other operations and acquired a heat-set filament plant in Decatur, Tennessee.

Since they were advancing into the market place, they began to sell carpet products to distributors such as L.D. Brinkman & Co., which was the largest wholesaler in the Southwest. To supplement this they created major marketing programs in media packages for radio, TV and newspapers. Shaw had concentrated upon manufacturing and one of its persistent themes at that time - low-cost production. In this pivotal year Shaw integrated forward into marketing, as opposed to Coronet which had to integrate backward into finishing as it grew. This solid growth through the years, excellent profitability, and careful financing enabled Shaw to take the next step.

As the decade of the 1980s opened, it brought the Reagan Recession of 1981-82. The carpet industry called it "a soft economy." However, it brought Shaw Industries to its third pivotal move.

In 1983 under the marketing leadership of Bob, Bill Lusk, senior vice president and treasurer and Vance Bell, vice president of marketing, Shaw Industries took a dramatic leap forward. Vance was a graduate of Georgia Tech in marketing and had previously been with West Point Pepperell before he became the first of many college-trained graduates who came to Shaw. This broke with the traditional way of selling carpet and was a calculated risk. Shaw began to sell to whoever wanted to buy from them and to only a limited number of wholesale distributors. During the previous years, the normal sales sequence had been for carpet mills to either sell their products in bulk to wholesalers like L.D. Brinkman & Co. of Dallas, who in turn would mark up prices between 18 to 22 percent and sell carpet to retailers, or to sell direct to large department store chains like Sears, Roebuck & Co. This bold, new strategy caused many to question Shaw's and Bell's judgment. "The others kept waiting for him to fall on his ass," said Reg Burnett, president of RBI International Carpet Consultants in Dalton. They believed that he was so big that he'd "have to sell through distributors."

This leadership group recognized a new trend that was taking place in the market and chose to make a drastic move. The fastest-growing segment in the market was small specialty carpet retailers. There were about 30,000 of them with sales under $2 million a year. Department stores, meanwhile, had been losing their market share. Secondly, most consumers were shopping three or four places before buying, looking for the best deal. More placements of Shaw products gave them a greater chance to sell the cautious buyer. By dealing directly with the small retailer, Shaw's salesmen could undercut wholesalers' marked-up prices. The year before the move, fifty-five percent of the company's sales were to distributors, national accounts and overseas. The remaining forty-five percent was direct to retailers. In a few short years retailers accounted for eighty percent of the company's sales. In 1983 Shaw had 70 salespersons and by 1990 they had over 700. At the time of the change there were only three warehouses outside of Dalton, but by 1990 there were 14 distribution centers with a combined floor space of 2,500,000 square feet carefully covering the needs of the continental U.S.

**President-Elect Bud Shaw at 1st Annual Meeting of CRI—1969**

In 1980 the company had $213 million in sales and a 9% market share; in 1990 Shaw was selling $1.48 billion with a 22% share. While 28% of the industry's output is sold through wholesalers, only 4% of Shaw's goes that route. It cost more money to provide the inventory, more distribution centers and personnel, but they staggered the expansion on a staged basis. The rest is sold by salespersons who work basically on salaries, with some incentive compensation. Bob feels that commission selling does not fit with the goal of Shaw Industries becoming a world class corporation. "We had to make them a part of our managerial team rather than just entrepreneurs out selling for themselves. They had to see farther in this company than just being territorial salespeople. They have got to see an opportunity to go from a salesperson to a vice president," said Bob.

In 1987, Shaw pulled out of the annual National Floor Covering Market at the Atlanta Merchandise Mart. Now, year round, at its Shaw Design Center in Dalton the company can set the trend for the market without its competitors getting to see its designs and colors. The Center has become a mecca which draws the retailers from Atlanta northward in chartered busses to their Dalton showrooms. Shaw also moved ahead by a combination punch of modernization and acquisition. As Kerry Hannon in *Forbes* pointed out, it "spent $200 million over the next five years to modernize its mills." This enabled it to absorb the fiber breakthrough in stain resistant yarn and change its machinery quickly to gain in the market share. Then in 1987 Shaw bought WestPoint-Pepperell Carpet and Rug Division for $126 million and two years later the carpet divisions of Armstrong World Industries for $129 million. The WestPoint acquisition with a sales volume of approximately one half that of Shaw's made it a billion dollar corporation in sales. Interestingly enough, WestPoint had gotten into the tufting business in 1946 with the acquisition of Cabin Crafts, a company whose founders had been family acquaintances of the younger Shaws. In 1980 WestPoint Pepperell was the nation's leading carpet maker with Armstrong World as number three, while Shaw was only number six. Cabin Crafts was allowed to retain its individuality as a marketing entity, under the Shaw umbrella. The Armstrong purchase was also a friendly purchase. Armstrong got out of a very competitive field and fortified itself against a hostile takeover attempt. Shaw likewise benefitted. Frank O'Neill, editor of *Carpet & Rug Industry*, said, "Shaw Industries has done two things of significance with this move. First, it has already increased its industry-leading market share. Secondly, it has eliminated one of its own best competitors." As *Georgia Trend* magazine noted, "Shaw Industries, once a tiny carpet-finishing operation, suddenly was selling four times more carpet than its next biggest competitor, Burlington Industries."

Any approach to develop an understanding of the spectacular success of Shaw Industries must begin with Bob Shaw and those close to him. Bob, Bud and Vice President Warren Sims grew up in the industry. Bob and Warren's mothers went to Georgia State College for Women together. Bud and Warren were often pushed in their baby carriages while the mothers walked and talked. Bob and Bud's father was totally engrossed in Star Dye as they grew up and was an extremely hard worker. Their father, Clarence, was a graduate of Georgia Tech and a holder of the 100 yard dash record there. While in the Navy in World War I he lost his hearing. Though personable in private, this disability caused him to be shy in public. His wife Essie was remembered as a delightful teacher by Bill Bowen Jr. until she retired to raise her children.

Helen Shope said, "Mrs. Essie Shaw was the finest teacher I had at Dalton High School. She made Latin a very enjoyable experience. She was a real Victorian lady, but I never expected her to marry, she was too good a teacher." Helen said that Bob told her that his mother had told him that he definitely was not a Latin student.

Warren Sims remembers that Mrs. Shaw filled in for his Latin teacher and gave him a "C" because "she decided that I didn't know it as well as I should." Emily Davies remembered the parents as being fine persons and very active in the Presbyterian church. Warren's step grandmother was Mrs. Harry Lee Jarvis. Harry Lee's dental office was on the first floor of their home and the attic contained her spread table. On Sunday afternoon she made Harry Lee drive her around the countryside delivering sheeting to be tufted. Warren spent as much time as he could in his early years with his grandmother. When he returned in 1953 from his service experience in the Korean War, he already had his degree in business from Davidson College and went to work for First National Bank of Dalton. Daily, the old timers of the tufting industry—Judd Brooker, Jessie Bates, Lamar Westcott and others—drank coffee at First National and shared stories while Warren listened. One of his favorite uncles was Bob McCamy who had started Cabin Crafts, and Lamar Westcott was like a second father to him.

Bob, Bud and Warren all grew up knowing and listening to the early leaders of the industry. When Bob took over Star Dye, he went to Bob McCamy to get advice on the business. Harry Saul sold all the boys of that time their scout uniforms at Saul's Department Store, before he started Queen Carpet. This is one reason why Harry and Julian Saul are such good friends of Bob while being competitors. The Shaws learned at the feet of the masters.

Equally important to Shaw's success is the very competitive attitude of the Clarence Shaw children, even the two girls. Whether the result of their father's demands of the best or a mother who believed in and supported them, they are all aggressive. Bob is the most competitive of them all. He was little and wiry as he grew up and was always having to prove himself. Warren remembers Bud forever coming to Bob's rescue and getting him out of fights. Bob, however, doesn't remember Bud getting him out of fights. "Bud was a lover, not a fighter." Bob does remember a lot of fights that they had with each other, since Bud was only twenty months older. As Bob grew older he always had to be the best. In sandlot football he had to be the quarterback, even if he was small. His leadership ability, competitiveness, and persistence are balanced well in his gifts. He has an infectious, even inspirational spirit. Warren Sims says that he has the ability to turn your view around and get you excited about new possibilities.

Because the leadership of Shaw is first generation it can move faster than most companies its size and make quick decisions. This experience in the industry and a shared vision of their future gives them a sense of what the others in Shaw's corporate leadership feel. Yet at the very center Bob has the firmness, the goal-orientation, the drive and the respect which holds it together. While other companies have lost their leadership to corporate shuffling once going public or a desire to enjoy the good life, the heart of the corporation is still there in Bob Shaw. He has kept everyone in tune with each other, rather than competing for power. Someone has likened Shaw to a good used car which has always had the same driver. The company has expanded its management structure, but has not changed the model.

Michael Berns in *Carpet & Rug Industry* notes that Shaw's approach to production, finance, and marketing has altered the industry. Shaw has set new and higher standards of efficiency. In an industry that is now thoroughly modernized, Shaw was one of the first to automate. As Berns points out, "Shaw has shown the inclination and ability to purchase and rapidly deploy any equipment that results in a savings of labor, material or other efficiencies." Secondly, it has created a "new definition of competitive pricing combining "blockbuster" prices in some areas while selling a substantial amount at full price. It uses a complex mix to entice buyers and yet insure profitability. In addition, its extensive warehousing operation and computer network brings a "new standard of reliability." Its performance as a formidable low cost producer and a reliable supplier of a wide range of popular styled carpeting has enabled the corporation to become an effective "niche" marketer. Finally, Berns points out that Shaw's growth in sales and earnings has given it "new credibility on Wall Street."

John Baugh, an analyst with Wheat First Securities in Richmond, Virginia, underlined this in a statement in the *Atlanta Journal,* "There is a shortage of capital in this business and Shaw is one of the better capitalized companies in this industry." Its strong cash flow and access to low cost sources of financing has allowed it to buy when other mills came up for sale. Glenn Ruffenach in *The Wall Street Journal* (June 12, 1991) feels Shaw's success partially comes from embracing what many companies either shunned or mishandled in the 1980s: "debt, and lots of it. More than $600 million in capital improvements and acquisition costs have left Shaw with long-term debt that represents a chilling 56% of total capital." But that investment has helped Shaw become the industry's lowest-cost producer.

Finally, Shaw is successful because they have kept a central idea at their approach to the market, the expansion and the future. Everyone's primary responsibility is to produce a satisfactory return for the shareholders of Shaw Industries. They are not there to earn a salary or have a good time, but to produce a profit. They feel that this should be true from the sweepers in the plant to the vice presidents at the top. An exclusive interview by Bob Shaw to Dan Alaimo in *Flooring* dealt with the question as to whether, as the largest, they had a responsibility to the industry. Bob clearly responded, "My responsibility is to who pays my salary. My responsibility is to Shaw

Industries, its customers and employees. Now, if we can help the industry by doing things that we think are responsible, that's fine." As *Georgia Trend* pointed out, "Whatever Shaw buys, he will buy for the sake of efficiency. Any acquisition will have to enhance the company's prowess as a low-cost producer. Low-cost production, efficiency, is Shaw's gospel." Bob Shaw is number one in the industry, but he does not plan to wait on anyone to catch up. As in a track meet, he intends to set the pace and let the others respond.

Possibly the best overview of Shaw's drive to dominance in the 1980s and position for the 1990s are found in Frank O'Neill 1990 synopsis of the industry in *Carpet & Rug Industry*. He sees Bob Shaw as a maverick, in the tradition of other mavericks of the industry. "Almost everything he did in the past ten years went against the conventional wisdom. He stopped going to markets, stopped selling primarily through distributors, integrated 100% into yarn making, hired a salaried sales staff, even changed the traditional terms he gave to retailers. But as we've seen, being a maverick didn't stop Bob Shaw from being successful in the 80s. It's not likely to stop him in the 90s, either."

So much for other people's analysis for his success, Bob sees the reason for Shaw Industries phenomenal growth from a slightly different viewpoint. He did not have a grand design from the beginning. "I am a great believer that when you put the building blocks together and get up on the building blocks, you can see a little further. Then the horizon gets bigger every time you put another building block up," said Bob. If he did have a goal, it was to be "a major U.S. corporation," not just a major U.S. carpet corporation. Then the goal grew larger than that to be "a world class corporation," and he began to instill that in his people. To accomplish this, the foundation had to be built on cornerstones that were very, very sound. "First of all, you've got to be ethical, number two you've got to be honest and you've got to be moral. And the fourth part of that cornerstone is that the people have got to be all those things." Most companies do not speak of ethical cornerstones, but profitability, market power and results. But Bob learned much from his hard-working, strait-laced Presbyterian parents. "I don't think parents have to teach children moral values, it's like vaccination. If parents live it and believe it, the children will come back to their parents. If they have respect for their parents, they'll come back. I'm as much like my mother and daddy and their moral structure."

On this ethical basis Bob began to build his small company. "I had a vision to build the stair, build the people, build the ability in the people and one of these days we could say we built a world class company." As they began to grow, he discovered that the world class corporations weren't too tough. Their professional managers were greedy. They were primarily interested in their brief tenure of 5 to 8 years, their bonuses and retirement benefits. "And they didn't give a tinker's damn what was going to happen to their company." So it became an easy thing for an entrepreneur to put himself in their class. This meant that his finances were right. He had the right technology and did all the things they were doing. But then he planned to build his company over 20 years, rather than 5 years and sell out. Once he had control of his balance sheet, he could put his profits together and grow through geometric progression.

Moreover, Bob feels that to be successful you have got to be a dreamer—"think or dream bigger than you can see." Most people are locked into a desire for security above all—from the cradle to the grave. Everyone would like to be rich, but no one wants any risks to be involved. You are paid for being responsible, but that involves making decisions that could put you out of work. "The risk-taker has to take the responsibility on his back. And they've got to be willing to do, as they do in Las Vegas. You're going to push your career to the center of the table and grab the dice and throw them." The entrepreneur is not just a gambler, he's a risk-taker. "If you can figure out what the downside is and if you can live with that downside, then you can make decisions. The upsides will take care of themselves." And since no company had ever grown to 1/2 billion or a billion or 2 billion, it was new ground to plow and a lot of risks.

Bob feels that part of his success or anyone's success relates to charisma. It can be defined many ways, but he believes that it comes when "people have enough respect for whoever that person is that they are willing to follow." His dream and loyalty to that vision gave him and the company the determination and commitment to succeed. His athletic experience colors his words when he says, "WE PLAY THE GAME TO WIN." And the reason that they do is very understandable. "If you're going to work for 25 years for a company," and it goes broke or the leaders make a killing through a leverage buy-out, "that's bad loyalty." Bob has yet to sell the first share, although he has given some to churches and hospitals. "I think I should get it out like the rest of the stockholders, in the form of dividends. I have an obligation to my employees, to my stockholders." This dedication has brought tremendous loyalty on the part of Shaw employees, but Bob is quick to point out the loyalty is a two-way street.

In the boom days of the carpet industry, when demand outreached production, it was easy to become successful. But to become number one in the eighties has demanded a lot of hard work. But that is not foreign to Bob. Bud and Bob might have played football on Friday night for the Dalton High Catamounts, but by 7:00 the next morning they would be sacking groceries at Piggy-Wiggly, after throwing a paper route. And their father did not drive them to work. Success has not slowed his demanding schedule. Bob usually begins the day with a four mile walk about day-break with Norris Little, one of his vice presidents, as they plan the day. And he gets home to dinner and the paper between 5:30 and 8:30, depending upon what's on his mind or somebody else's. Also most of Bob's business knowledge came from the school of experience. "I wasn't interested in what I could learn from a book." He "was much more interested in learning on a one-on-one basis. You get burned and you become a quick learner." He has learned well as history shows.

He has also learned well from the early leaders of the industry and this has led to a commitment to the community. He feels a strong responsibility to Dalton. "Dalton, Georgia gave a lot of people the opportunity to be millionaires. They were not brilliant enough to create that. A couple of ladies trying to make a living did that." Others have made fortunes and have fled the community; Shaw will not. It has chosen to make its national headquarters and future there. "When you get down to it, if Shaw Industries doesn't succeed, Dalton doesn't succeed. And Dalton will go back to be being a sleepy little country town, whose ground is not worth farming and where there is a little bootlegging." But as Shaw succeeds, it draws the BASF and DuPonts and the best of our college graduates to work for a world class corporation that they can stay with until they retire.

It is interesting to note that when Lamar Westcott returned to Dalton in 1931 to help run Cabin Craft, he told his partners that he was going to give one half of his time to the community so they were to base his salary on that fact. Years later at the age of 94 his widow, Mrs. G.L. Westcott, would recall, "He felt very strongly that if you made a living in a community that you owed that community something." Bob Shaw has learned well from his mentors, from his experience, and he's in for the "long haul."

Possibly the best way to sum up the Shaw Story is to let Bob do it himself. "My story is pretty simple. It didn't have anything to do with talent. It didn't have anything to do with anything but taking the building blocks and looking at a larger horizon. That doesn't end."

Shaw Industries, National Headquarters

Bob Shaw

# *Chapter Thirteen*

## NEW PLAYER ON THE FIELD

As the visitor walks into the offices of Beaulieu of America in Dalton, they are greeted by a thought-provoking saying.

> Every morning in Africa, a Gazelle wakes up. It knows it must run faster than the fastest Lion, or it will be killed. Every morning a Lion wakes up and it knows it must outrun the slowest Gazelle or it will starve to death. It doesn't matter whether you are a Lion or a Gazelle when the sun comes up, you'd better be running.

It may be difficult to tell which is Beaulieu and which is the carpet industry in the analogy, but it is clear that Beaulieu is running.

When the Beaulieu Group of Belgium in the mid 1970's bought the Dalton facilities of the bankrupt Barwick Industries, the company appeared to be out of its element. The international corporation, headed by Roger De Clerck, chose to begin making woven polypropylene rugs in the tufted carpet capital. Carl & Mieke Bouckaert's arrival to begin the new U.S. operation, Beaulieu of America, began an incredible success story. In a comparatively few years, the North American Beaulieu operation is the continent's second largest broadloom carpet producer, and one of the largest producers of small rugs.

In 1982 the firm became the first North America company to extrude its own polypropylene rug yarns. In 1988 Beaulieu built the first independent nylon chip producing plant in the United States. Sometime before that plant was built, the Bouckaerts formed a business partnership with Ed Ralston, the owner of D&W Carpets and a major Georgia commission tufter. In 1988 Ralston and Bouckaert bought Conquest Carpet Mills, a fast growing producer of base grade carpet with annual sales of about $120 million at the time. Conquest became a major user of Beaulieu's solution dyed nylon and polypropylene fiber, which had grown to about 60 million pounds in production.

In early 1990, Beaulieu attempted to gain controlling interest of Horizon Industries (the sixth largest in U.S. production) by acquiring 17.7% of Horizon's outstanding stock. When thwarted by a poison pill stock initiative from Horizon, Beaulieu acquired Coronet Carpet, the seventh largest carpet manufacturer in North America.

In 1991 a joint venture between the Bouckaerts and a Pennsylvania compounder created Epsilon Products to produce about 270 million pounds of polypropylene resin. The resin is used to make both carpet yarn and a variety

**Beaulieu Trio: Carl Bouckaert, far right poses with business partner Ed Ralston and wife Mieke during the recent Atlanta winter market**

of extruded plastic parts for the automotive industry, packaging and other applications.

*Carpet & Rug Industry* magazine in its June 1993 issue noted that in the previous fiscal year the International Beaulieu Group's worldwide carpet sales were approximately $2 billion. The same magazine listed Beaulieu's America operations annual sales at $752 million, second only to Shaw Industries' sales of $2,035.9 million.

Beaulieu of America is the second largest producer of mill extruded polypropylene fibers. It is the only U.S. mill which makes its own nylon chip and extrudes solution-dyed nylon. The company manufactures medium-priced commercial carpet under the Dimensions and Cambridge labels, tufted rugs under Beaulieu and produces needlepunch floor and wall products through Murray Fabrics and its Surfaces division. It has both residential and commercial broadloom products through Interloom.

Unlike Shaw, Beaulieu of America has not acquired or merged with the various companies in which its principals have a financial interest. *Carpet & Rug Industry* pointed out in its June, 1991 issue that each of the firm's carpet making operations "are tied together by little more than their common parent and by the fiber making facilities which supply all the separate operations."

Each firm operates as a separate profit center with its own sales operation. Although these separate entities give the firm a somewhat helter skelter appearance, the same magazine indicated that "its informal management style also allows each of those separate entities to use the resources of any other when the need arises." The Beaulieu Group's North American operations, like its European counterparts, are integrated from fiber making through finishing. The company has the capability to make polypropylene filament and staple, solution dyed nylon, and primary and secondary backing.

Beaulieu of America is the result of the evolving dream of Carl Bouckaert. Born into the home of a Belgian surgeon and the oldest of seven children, Carl's values, goals and ways of dealing with people developed in this environment. His father was a gentlemen who taught him discipline, the value of family relationships and respect for money. His parents were strong Catholics who kept the family together, particularly through a common interest in horses. Most weekends the family would go on trail rides through fields and jump ditches and their mother would follow in the car with sandwiches and snacks. This love for horses later led them into competitive jumping, but the overall result was greater. "We had a lot of fun, the family stayed together and we didn't spend any time on the streets," recalled Carl.

His early education taught him hard work and discipline. Carl and Thomas, his younger brother, went to a Jesuit high school which demanded rigorous work habits. Six hours of Latin, five hours of Greek as well as French and German were added to math, sciences, and religion each week in a demanding boarding school schedule. Carl then began a very exacting engineering program, which taught him the need to tenaciously apply himself for later rewards.

While in college Carl began to date Mieke De Clerck whose father was the leader of the largest carpet business in Europe. Carl was impressed by his style. " Mr. De Clerck is a very direct man who could cut through all the smoke, cut through all the politics and cut through all the complications," Carl remembers, and get a matter resolved. Roger De Clerck quickly became Carl's mentor and he was amazed that De Clerck would talk to a "twenty-two-year old boy" about millions of dollars in equipment and investments while sharing his business philosophy. Carl's father had taught him a healthy respect for the value of money, but in the De Clerck environment "the numbers were staggering."

In 1977 Carl became involved in the De Clerck decision to expand into America. In 1966 Roger De Clerck had come to a Barwick convention for customers, distributors and salesmen at the Fontainebleau in Miami and was impressed by the extravagance of the affair. All lodging, food, and drinks were provided by Barwick Industries. Carl related that "Mr. De Clerck, who is a very sober thinker, thought if this is possible, there has got to be a lot of opportunity over here." In 1977 De Clerck returned to America to test the climate.

Carl was invited to accompany Mieke and her father on the trip. In Fred Rosen's empty plant in Cartersville Carl found to "his amazement" De Clerck giving him instructions on how to organize the plant for production. "His genius is so great that he can look at an empty building, and in his mind place machines and envision the complete flow of product from raw materials to finished goods." Carl realized that De Clerck was planning on he and Mieke tackling this project and carrying it to completion. There was no question about whether Carl or Mieke had any interest in coming to America. Upon return to Belgium De Clerck daily checked with Carl on how the plans were taking shape. Carl found himself "following up this extremely interesting project as a twenty-two year old kid."

On February 11, 1978, Carl and two engineers came to Dalton to set up the operation in the old Barwick 5th Avenue plant. The ceilings of the Rosen plant in Cartersville were too low so with the help of Truett Lomax of the Carpet & Rug Institute Beaulieu of America began, ironically, in the bankrupt facilities of the company which had originally drawn them to America. The beginnings were simple. Carl remembers going to Dalton Supply to buy their first tool box, complete with five screwdrivers, four hammers, metric wrenches and other items.

The woven polypropylene Oriental rugs which the company began to make did not seem to be a major challenge for the Dalton carpet empires. Neither was there a market for the product. Carl recalled that "at the time we began the total polypropylene market in the United States was $1,000,000 at retail done by Sears Roebuck." Reflecting on this, Carl added, "De Clerck could care less. He is not the kind of guy who believes in market studies. There are 250,000,000 people here with buying power and Oriental style rugs, if offered at the right price, will sell here. Period. End of the argument. And you guys prove that I'm right. So we did."

By 1981 the company, which had been buying its polypropylene rug yarns from Phillips Petroleum, decided that they were strong enough and that they should follow the example of their European counterpart and extrude their own yarn. The next three years were a testing period for the company as they struggled to make a successful product. The Belgium engineers, who helped them, could not figure why the machinery produced a quality product only in the spring and fall. They didn't realize that the climate was so severe in comparison to Belgium conditions. Carl finally figured out that the dry winters and 100% summer humidity were the problem. Against their technical advice, "the kid, the son-in-law who didn't know anything about carpet or yarn" invested $300,000 in air conditioning equipment. Only then did the machines perform as intended. This also occurred in the early Reagan years when the dollar soared (70 Belgium francs to a dollar), making imported rugs very inexpensive. The tenacity which he had learned as a child paid off. "We just hung on, hung on, hung on" and finally the monetary squeeze and the yarn production problems resolved themselves, by being creative and persistent.

At this time Carl also decided to take his most loyal lieutenant, Skip Johnson, out of the production of rugs and had him focus all his time and attention on yarn manufacturing. Throughout the years he and Carl have made their way through turbulent waters and Skip continues to concentrate on those responsibilities.

When they began to make more yarn than they needed, they began to look for independent users. They worked with Bob Flick at Interloom to produce the first successfully blended Berber yarns in the business. There were a few nylon Berbers on the market, but the yarn was shiny and looked synthetic.

As a result of working with Bob Flick, Carl came in contact with Ed Ralston, owner of D&W Carpets, a commission tufter and package provider to the industry. Carl was attracted to Ed's personal style and business approach and they began to work together very successfully in 1985. In 1988 the Bouckaerts and Ed Ralston bought Conquest Carpet Mill which became another user of Beaulieu's growing yarn-producing capacity. This further cemented his relationship with Ed as he became partners with his best customer. In 1989 they bought Interloom from Bob Flick and in 1990 Coronet Industries. In 1991, Interloom was merged into Coronet. Along with Beaulieu Carpets which began in 1984 this completed a broad, but totally integrated structure.

The partnership concept was not a planned structure, but it simply evolved because of the synergy created by these two son-in-laws of the most successful carpet men of two continents. (Ed Ralston was formerly the son-in-law of Gene Barwick.) They complimented each other and, as Carl added, "Ed is such a strong business thinker and our relationship works very well."

This is in comparison to Beaulieu's relationship to his European business parents. In correcting a false impression, Carl pointed out that "the Beaulieu group as an international entity does not exist. My European brothers-in-law, the De Clerck sons, each have their own companies which they own and operate separately." They have technology exchanges and family meetings, but the "commonality comes from the fact that we come from one family." From an economical, financial, and ownership standpoint, they are six different companies. They work well on technology, all try to be the low-cost producer and learn from each other. They exchange ideas, but in the marketplace they are competitors. Beaulieu of America does not have an exclusive on the United States and it also does sell in Europe.

Carl's business style is an interesting combination. More than just concern for being the low cost producer and totally integrated, he feels, "any business brought in must provide maximum synergy. If we don't see synergy two ways, we are less interested." His management style is modeled after "one of my super great mentors, Sam Walton." "He kept everything simple, worked real hard, was committed to low cost and the continuous improvement of his system and his company and the tremendous motivation of his people." His wealth never changed his lifestyle nor his approach Carl pointed out.

Besides reading Sam Walton's life, he reads avidly, "but not enough." His bible is *Atlas Shrugged* by Ayn Rand which, from his point of view, may be the most important piece of literature ever written.

His management philosophy is an interesting combination of nuances learned from a blend of life experiences. His close family taught him to consider his partners and company leaders as brothers and family. In 1980 Carl and three others ran the 26.2 mile Huntsville, Alabama marathon. "As I think about my business career, I think about that marathon a lot," Carl adds. "At different points in that race, different ones of us felt bad." At the 20th mile Carl "hit the wall," but the others were able to cheer him on, while he was able to boost another at the 22nd mile. The management team at Beaulieu works as a unit to support and motivate each other.

Carl is a strong motivator. He brightens as he says, "I really get a kick out of being able to conceive good ideas and see them implemented. I get a tremendous satisfaction out of hiring the right people and putting them in the right spot and see that work." He feels that they have a management group second to none. When he is not in top form, he has so many good people around him that he soon bounces back.

His brother Thomas, who heads up Conquest, actually got into textiles before Carl. When medical school did not work out for him, he began working in one of the De Clerck warehouses. After six months he was promoted to plant manager of one of the new needlepunch plants. When De Clerck bought Nate Lipson's bankrupt company, Venture Carpet in England, Thomas took over its management. Living for 5 years in a little apartment over the plant Thomas created the English market for the Beaulieu group. Thereafter Thomas very successfully ran the Belgium upholstery division of De Clerck for five years. Finally, Carl persuaded him to come to America in 1987. Piet Dossche, who had worked with Thomas in England and Belgium, married Carl and Thomas' sister, Sabine. After eight years in the United Kingdom as General Manager of Venture Carpet, Piet came to the United States in 1990. He is now president of Murray Fabrics. Instant Turf was merged into Murray Fabrics in 1992 and in 1993 Murray merged with Grassmore.

Larry Swanson, president of Coronet, is an "extremely unusual top-notch individual," and representative of all the management team that Beaulieu has. Carl is a strong believer in the capability of people. He believes that people are employed at levels beneath their abilities. "I am a true, true believer in giving people that you wouldn't think could handle it, the chance to do it. And you will be surprised that 80-90% will come through with flying colors," he explains.

Finally, Carl thinks that Mieke is a major reason for his success. Besides being mother to their four children, she is a sympathetic ear to his concerns and dreams and a gracious hostess at a moment's notice. Her quietude is a pleasing balance to Carl's contagious enthusiasm. His elegant dress style and slight European accent are blended with personal skills that make him equally at home with accomplished horsemen who frequent their showcase farm or business leaders and associates. He may be a comparatively new player in the industry, but his rug and carpet empire is a force with which the other players must reckon and he is an accomplished spokesman for new directions into which the industry will be advancing.

## *Chapter Fourteen*

# CHENILLE LIVES ON

The demand for cotton tufted goods soared in the postwar period as indicated by the records of the Tufted Textile Manufacturers Association (TTMA). The number of tufted bedspreads went from 5,044,323 in 1940 to 19,312,567 in 1951 with a value of $72,422,100. This was a startling amount of yearly cash inflow for the Dalton area. Tufted bath mats, scatter rugs and carpets increased from 1,209,340 in 1939 to 40,821,200 in 1951, and tufted robes jumped from 860,400 units in 1939 to 10,859,523 in 1951. The total gross volume of the Dalton industry was $195,038,440 in 1951.

In the period after World War II tufting plants mushroomed up all over Dalton. All it took was a single needle machine, women to sew and a building. Pete Sims' map of Dalton in the late 1940s shows only a small number of the cotton tufting businesses producing bedspreads, robes, scuffies, toilet covers, dolls, and scatter rugs. Plants worked around the clock and owners hired anyone who applied, regardless of experience. They walked or car pooled from the surrounding communities to fill the vacuum for workers. The boom time for the industry was beginning.

Although companies such as Cabin Craft met the combined demand for chenille goods and carpet by splitting into two companies, most other companies concentrated on one or the other. Although most moved to the higher profit margin of carpet, some, like the Judd Brooker family, focused on chenille.

Judd had a seventh grade education from the Berry Schools in Rome. To pay for his education he had to walk five miles everyday to stoke a boiler. When he was sixteen his father put him in the woods directing a crew of men to provide timber for Brooker Lumber Company. It was natural that Judd would take over the family business. Later, he was persuaded to run for political office and he served as ordinary for twelve years. It was actually his wife Maude who started the chenille business.

In 1932 she and William Westbrook, a family friend, set up a sewing shop in a grainery alongside the house. They made simple draw string beach capes on a single needle machine. The product mix rapidly grew from capes to house coats to spreads. Business for Brooker Spread grew so quickly that they bought a "honky-tonk" roadhouse up the Cleveland Highway; later Brooker moved to the basement of Crown Laundry in Dalton.

In 1944 a fire temporarily put Brooker out of production. In the unique Dalton spirit, J.T. Bates, whose wife started J.T. Bates Candlewick chenille business, offered them space to continue. Actually, Judd and J.T. had previously bought the merchandise and machines of a bankrupt spread company to sell. As they tufted up the extra yarn they became partners. So Brooker Spread moved

SIMS TEXTILE COMPANY'S MAP OF
DALTON, GEORGIA
"THE TUFTED TEXTILE CENTER OF THE WORLD"
THIS MAP LISTS AND LOCATES IN THE DALTON AREA A CONCENTRATION OF APPROXIMATELY 82% OF THE TUFTED TEXTILE MANUFACTURING PLANTS IN THE UNITED STATES. All Friendly Competitors and Contributors to the Sound Growth, Progress and Prosperity of this Fast Growing Industry and Area.
Included Are Manufacturers Of:
Tufted Floor Coverings, Wide Carpet and Rugs
Tufted Bedspreads and Tufted Draperies
Tufted Bath Mats, Bath Sets and Curtains
Tufted Robes, Dusters, Jackets and Coats
Tufted Upholstery and Drapery Fabrics
Tufted Slippers, Mops and Novelties
Tufted Automotive Fabrics
Tufted Toweling
DALTON — U. S. HIGHWAY 41 SOUTH
J. W. Bray Company
Tom Gillian's Peacock House
Malone Chenille Co.
Patcraft Tufted Products Co.
Lyncraft Chenille Co.
R. P. Bailey Chenille Co.
Thomason Chenille Co.
Mostella Chenille Co.
J. M. Muse (Sugar Valley, Ga.)
Whitener Chenille Mfg. Co.
A. J. Lewallen Chenille Co.
Starks Chenille Co.
Beckler Chenille Co.
J. L. Pinion Chenille Co.
Chastain Chenille Co.
Sloan-Johnson Chenille Co.
To RESACA, GA. — 14 Miles
Chitwood Rug Co.
Buford Rug Co.
To CALHOUN, GA. — 20 Miles
C. & H. Bedspread Co.
Calhoun Rug & Spread Co.
Caldwell Chenille Co.
Deaton Spread Co.
Dixie Belle Spread Co.
Georgia Textile Corporation
Georgia Tufters, Inc.
H. & B. Textile Co.
Herbcraft Textiles, Inc.
Hy-Way Arts, Inc.
C. M. Jones & Co.
Mayfair Chenille Co.
O'Jay Spread & Rug Co.
Velvetone Mills, Inc.
Forrest Mills, Inc.
To ADAIRSVILLE, GA. — 30 Miles
Adairsville Garment Co.
Kuhlman Chenille Co.
To ROME, GA. — 42 Miles
Dellinger, Inc.
Tex-Tuft Products, Inc.
Rome Tex. & Fin. Co.
To CARTERSVILLE, GA. — 46 Miles
Kingston Carpet Mills
Textilon Chenille Co.
To CAVE SPRINGS, GA. — 57 Miles
Jack Sutton Co., Inc.
To ROCKMART, GA. — 67 Miles
Ru-Nell Mfg. Co.
To CHAMBLEE, GA. — 85 Miles
E. T. Barwick Mills
To ATLANTA, GA. — 90 Miles
Berry Bedspread Co.
Williams Chenille Co.
To ROCKY FACE, GA. — 6 Miles
B. J. Boyd Chenille Co.
Fields Coverlet Co.
Foremost Chenille Co.
To TUNNEL HILL, GA. — 9 Miles
A. B. C. Chenille Co.
Annette Chenille Co.
J. L. Bonner Chenille Co.
Cheney Chenille Co.
Colonial Crafts
Cottonwood Mills, Inc
Crump Chenille Co.
Dixie Chenille Co.
Edgewood Chenille Co.
Lake View Chenille Co.
Lone Star Chenille Co.
Midway Chenille Co.
Mt. View Chenille Co.
North Ga. Chenille Co.
Putnam Chenille Co.
Roslyn Products Co.
The Rug House
Wayside Chenille Co.
To RINGGOLD, GA. — 15 Miles
Golden Pheasant Shop
Hackett Chenille Co.
Summit Hill Chenille Co.
Sweetwater Rug Company
To FT. OGLETHORPE, GA. — 23 Miles
Croft Carpet Mills
Crown Chenille Mfg. Co.
To LA FAYETTE, GA. — 23 Miles
E. T. Barwick Mills
To CHICKAMAUGA, GA. — 33 Miles
Heirloom Carpet Mills
To SUMMERVILLE, GA. — 41 Miles
Georgia Rug Mills
(Bigelow-Sanford)
To CHATTANOOGA, TENN. — 31 Miles
Carter Bros., Inc.
Carolyn Chenille Co.
Farragut Carpet Mills
Heritage Carpet Mills
(Roxbury Carpet Co.)
Principal Offices Only.
Map does not show subsidiary manufacturing plants, Dye Houses, Latex and Finishing Plants, nor storage and shipping warehouses.
16 Anita Textiles, Inc.
6 Artrich Mfg. Co.
50 E. T. Barwick Mills
25 Barwick-Monarch
13 Barwick-Morrill
42 J. T. Bates Candlewicks
37 Beacon Rug Mills
20 Bellcraft Chenilles, Inc.
21 Bellcraft—5th Ave.
55 Bettilee Chenille Co.
35 Blue Ridge Spread Co.
52 Brooker Spread Co.
62 Dixie Chenilles
29 Dixie Doll Company
45 Duchess Chenilles, Inc.
8 Eleanor Rug Mills
37 Empire Tufting Co.
22 Evans Manufacturing Co.
53 Fashion Crafts, Inc.
58 F. & H. Chenille Co.
56 Georgianna Chenille Co.
27 Georgia Mat Company
11 Gold & Company
30 Loomtex Mills, Inc.
3 Looper Tufting Co.
61 Majestic Rug Co.
24 Marbeth Carpet Co.
18 Mason Chenille Co.
5 McKinney Tufting Co.
12 Modern Tufting Co.
25 Monarch Rug Mills
13 Morrill Mfg. Co.
51 National Chen. Prod. Co.
60 Needletuft Rug Division
49 Painter Carpet Mills
12 Peach State Rug Co.
39 Perma-Tuft Rug Co.
46 Pickering Mills
17 Price Carpet Mills
44 Proffitt Textile Co.
28 Queen Chenille Co.
DALTON is a good town!
It's a good place to live
. . . . and make a living.
We're proud of all of our diversified industries, our civic enterprise and public utilities, our churches, schools and fine friendly people.
We're especially proud of TUFTED TEXTILE INDUSTRY. It's continued growth and development has expanded our borders, increased our population and added much to our prosperity and our happy American way of life.
We have a fortune to share . . . in pleasant living . . . in Dalton and our neighboring towns and cities. We welcome all who may come and share it with us.
SIMS TEXTILE COMPANY

into the basement of J.T.'s building. Then Lewis Card, with Tuftco Machinery Company, offered to supply them with machines and suppliers and even competitors helped them continue.

In 1943 Bettilee (named for and run by his two daughters Bettie and Ruby Lee) began production on war contracts. They made mountains of "those ugly khaki wash cloths." Judd's brother, Clifford Brooker, became a partner on the condition that he use his mechanical skills to keep the machines humming. Very early, they made a practice to operate on credit or bank loans and not use factors, which they felt eliminated their profit.

With the onset of peace in 1945, the two companies tended to concentrate on different segments of the chenille market. Brooker Spread focused on the general market of spreads, house coats, and rugs. Bettilee began to make crimped spreads for baby beds and then added full spreads. In the early 1950s Judd, along with Bettie's husband, Joe Billy Denson; Ruby Lee's husband, John Hugh Hackney; and the plant superintendent of Brooker Spread J.E. Harbuck opened Fashion Craft which concentrated more on speciality accounts with spreads and small rugs. Bedspreads and scatter rugs were sold to S & H Green Stamps, JC Penny, Montgomery Ward, Sears, Gold Bond and Top Value Stamps. With the growth of demand each increased the ability of their machines and color possibilities. Cobble and Card were developing big machines so small companies turned to Irby Passons of Broad Street Machine Shop in Chattanooga. Bettie' s husband, Joe Billy Denson, was actively directing Fashion Craft and developing the printing capabilities with the use of electrically operated cellinoids and photoelectric printing. During the heyday of chenille in the late 1940s and early 1950s Brooker Spread alone had over 250 ladies working to fill the demand.

Unfortunately, in 1985 even the Brooker family quit producing spreads and went out of business. The competition with the carpet companies for quality yarn and backing was forcing them to pay higher prices for the materials or produce inferior goods. Financially, they could not do the former and they would not do the latter. They had come a long way from the wedding ring and double wedding ring patterns with which they started and Bettie and Joe Billy and John and Ruby Lee Hackney had tried to carry on the tradition and quality of Maude and Judd Brooker. The demand was vanishing and so were the companies.

Norman Reints began in bedspreads and progressed into a very successful business in scatter rugs. In 1936 Norman came to the area to find work with TVA, since he had helped build Grandview Dam out west. There was no work available and he did not like Chattanooga, so based on a flip of a coin, he chose Rome, Georgia. He could not get a bus there, but he could get transportation to Dalton. He ended up staying with Mason Treadwell, who was sitting on the back seat with him. After working for a couple of years with Cabin Craft, he and Mason opened in 1938 a bedspread plant, Mason Chenille.

TUFTED TEXTILE MANUFACTURERS
ASSOCIATION
THIRD ANNUAL CONVENTION
SHERATON-PLAZA HOTEL
DAYTONA BEACH FLORIDA
MAY 27-28-29
1948

"He had the money and I had the ability," Norman recalled. It was a 50-50 partnership.

They used single needle machines and had to teach every woman how to sew or at least how to use a power machine. "They'd pump the paddle, thinking it would go like an old Singer," he noted. It was the beginning of the New Deal wage and hour regulations. In 1938 the women worked forty-eight hours a week and were paid thirty-five cents an hour. The next year it dropped to thirty-seven cents for forty-four hours a week and in 1940 the schedule was forty cents for forty hours a week. As an incentive they were paid on piece rates. "We'd either deduct for errors or the girls on their own time would pick out the bad work," Norman remembered.

Working conditions were far from ideal, but they were like plants all over Dalton. Everything was done in cotton. Short-fiber lint covered the walls and the girls' hair was white with it. It was clearly a fire hazard, but none ever occurred. Radios, cokes and slacks were not allowed. Nothing should distract from work.

As the competition began to increase, Norman can remember laying on the design tables at night trying to come up with a new design, a new way to tuft or a new product. For a couple of years in the early 1940s they made children's wear. They made a lot of 1, 2, and 3 size robes. The material was all cut on a size 2 pattern and then sewed either tighter or looser to create the other sizes. They later expanded the idea to women's sizes, using 12 to 18 sizes as their margins. The demand for new items would grow the closer Christmas came and then the orders dried up after the holiday. Cotton robes and open fires in the home were not compatible and by 1945 fire laws curtailed that product's production.

Shortly after World War II they began to make small 18 x 30 inch scatter rugs. They sewed enough passes on small machines to make them as wide as necessary. If they wanted a design, it was overlaid just like they had done with bedspreads.

In 1956 Norman started his own scatter rug business, Menor Rug, to meet an emerging demand. At the time a survey indicated that people were using some 27 rugs in an average home. They would have 3 or 4 in each bedroom and 2 in every bathroom. The plant worked two shifts seven days a week and produced over 100,000 rugs a week. A knotted basal fringe which they created for the sides helped with its appearance and sales' appeal.

One evening, while walking in a Chattanooga K-Mart there was a round dining room tablecloth with fringe, hanging from the wall. When he saw it, he thought it was a rug and told his wife, "God, why didn't I think of that rug?" When he discovered it was a tablecloth, he began to make six foot round rugs. It was a pregnant idea as "we sold millions and millions of those."

In 1971 Norman sold out to Gene Barwick. He had started with 14 employees and by the time the ownership changed, 553 employees not only tufted the scatter rugs, but also coated, laundried and dyed them. In retrospect, Norman feels that the business got so big so fast that he was losing control without a good management team. He retired while the company was still one big family and profitable.

Del Rube Chenille concentrated solely on scatter rugs. In 1945 Odell Edwards returned to Dalton after working in war-time construction. While waiting for his machinery to open a cabinet shop to become available , he visited with his brother-in-law Chester Wilson. Chester was in business with George Hanson building table-top machines. Odell discovered that he could repair the single needle tufting machines. He bought a dozen machines and started making scatter rugs. His mother-in-law Ruby Tatum provided the land and he built the building. Together they created the company and shared the name—Del Rube. He hired women who had made bedspreads and they started making bath sets.

Initially, Odell sold all his products to Pilgrim Chenille which dyed them different colors and sold them to consumers. Later Del Rube began to sell to Rich's in Atlanta, Sears and Roebuck and others. Each operator would receive about 50 rugs and sew into the cotton backing all the colors and patterns. Later, using a line shaft to run the machines and a conveyor belt, 10 to 12 operators would do specific tasks to complete a single rug. Initially, the rubber backing was hand sprayed and the yarn was predyed. As the demand multiplied through the 1970s Odell was forced to set up his own laundry, then buy his own dye machines, add curing ovens for the rubber backing and ship world-wide. His most successful scatter rugs were the Snoopy series.

Odell's success can be attributed to his strong work ethic, his natural mechanical ability and good employee relations. His father taught him to be a carpenter and by the time he was 15 years old he could build a house expertly. He remembered his father saying, "If you're not going to do anything but dig a ditch, dig it straight and level." He worked hard and was very conscientious. George Rice at First National Bank recognized this and loaned him every dollar he ever requested.

Odell's mechanical ability helped him build and repair his machines in the early days. Even when he had mechanics developing new machines, he continued to work with them. Finally, he was proud of scatter rugs and as the only representative of that tufting area on TTMA, he constantly reminded "the big boys" of their presence. He also sought to make every operator proud to see their work on store shelves, something a carpet worker could not claim.

Lawtex is one of the success stories of area rugs for bath rooms. Seymour Lorberbaum began a small bedspread and housecoat business in a little warehouse on King Street in Dalton. They along with Carolyn Chenilles, which later developed into Art Rich Manufacturing Co, and Bell Textiles made the transition through the war and tended to dominate the market.

As other companies became successful in carpet, Lawtex decided to expand into that area. That choice almost put them out of business by 1970. They bought a small carpet mill in Chickamauga, Georgia, but did not have the knowledge, experience or marketing know-how to make it in carpet. In the 1950s their chenille bedspread business was dwindling just like everyone else's and they finally discontinued it. With the carpet line unsuccessful and the bedspread business fading they changed to the production of room-size rugs. By the late 1970s Lawtex was the largest room-size manufacturer in the market.

**Officers and Directors of the Tufted Textile Manufacturers Association are, left to right, seated: Henry C. Ball, executive vice president; R.E. Hamilton (Cabin Crafts, Inc.), vice president; G.H. Rauschenberg (G.H. Rauschenberg Co.), out-going president; Ira N. Nochumson (Monarch Rug Mills), newly-elected president; J. Raymond Bates (J.T. Bates Candlewicks), vice president. Standing W.H. Sparks (Sparks, Inc.), Paul Shoffner (Hy-Way Arts, Inc.), J. Ires Akers (Dalton Spread Laundry), Harry I. Saul (Queen Chenilles), Paul Conley (Alabama Bedspread & Bamatuft), Arthur N. Richman (Art Rich Manufacturing Co.), and Said Shaheen (Katherine Rug Mills), directors**

Their success, Seymour's brother Leonard says, can be attributed to three factors. First, they had the greatest merchandise in the world so it was not difficult to sell it. In addition, they put in very tight administrative controls. Much of this can be attributed to Tom Neal who came in as senior vice president in charge of finance. Leonard pointed out, "He knew where the money was going, that the receivables were coming in, and that the inventory was under control." He was "the financial doctor" who helped make the company financially healthy. Finally, Lawtex had integrity. Leonard did all the buying and he was motivated by one thing: "What was best for Lawtex." Even if sales were slow, if new machinery would produce a superior product, they bought it.

Lawtex also helped the industry by participating in the formation of the Tufted Textile Manufacturing Association in 1946 and Leonard even served as president (1964-66). They might be competitors from 8 AM to 5 PM, but they were the best of friends after hours. Then when carpet began to relegate rugs to surrogate position in the new Carpet & Rug Institute, Leonard led in a movement to create a rug division.

On February 28, 1979 Lawtex was acquired by Springs Mills, but the Lawtex division has continued to be the leader in the production of area rugs for bath rooms. Members of the family stayed on to continue the success as a part of the larger textile power Springs Industries Inc.

The Rosen family and LaRose Bedspread Company was one of the local tufting operations that decided it was better to switch than fight the tide. In World War II the youngest son Fred had gone through the same PT Boat Training program as John F. Kennedy, but when he returned to Dalton in 1946 things had changed. During the war LaRose had produced duffle bags and mosquito nets, yet they quickly converted to producing bedspreads and robes. Their own mechanics built a 120-inch wide machine for bedspread tufting and they sold their spreads as fast as they could make them.

However, in 1954 they decided that the tide had shifted and tufted carpet was the wave of the future. Woven looms could weave 100 yards in 24 hours, while tufting could produce 5,000 yards in the same time. The cheaper tufted carpet had the power to seize the floor covering business which was surging with the post-war boom. LaRose Bedspread Company was replaced by Northwick Mills which produced carpet on the first engineered carpet knitting machine. Northwick continued to produce until 1982 when it sold out to Cannon Mills.

The bedspread, house coat, scatter rug and toilet cover business put Dalton on the map, provided its payroll for nearly a century and employed its labor. The rug business has survived and now companies like Shaw and Beaulieu are developing rug programs. However, the demand for raw materials by tufted carpet, a dwindling market, and competition for labor has forced the bedspread industry to nearly vanish. In late 1992 Reatha Quinton sold her Soft Goods Chenille Company to The Limited of California leaving only Painter Chenille

**Painter Chenille**

south of Dalton making a few spreads. Soon, the only place you will be able to find a tufted bedspread in Dalton will be Crown Gardens and Archives.

## *Chapter Fifteen*

# FROM SPREADLINES TO INTERSTATE MARKETING

In the period following World War II one of the most apparent aspects of the cultural landscape of north Georgia were the "spreadlines," known as Bedspread Boulevard, Peacock Alley, or Bedspread Row. Bedspread lines were principally found between Cartersville and Chattanooga, although there were other sites throughout North Georgia and East Tennessee radiating out like spokes of a wheel from the center of tufting. However, the primary area of diffusion was Dalton and it spread mostly north and south along U.S. Highway 41.

The appearance of spreadlines and gift shops upon the north Georgia landscape ties together two phenomenon—developments in roads and transportation and the mechanization of the chenille industry. Although Ford and the Model A allowed even the common man to afford a car, his travel through north Georgia was not only hindered by poor roads, but also by the financial burden of the Great Depression in 1929.

Spread Line

Plans to build a road between Atlanta and Chattanooga, known as the Johnson-Sherman route or Dixie Highway, were finalized in 1911. It was not completed until early 1917 and was still only a gravel surface. Drivers were threatened by clouds of dust in the summer and muddy red clay in the winter. Finally, the paving of U.S. Highway 41 was completed in 1929, about a week before the stock market crash.

In 1935, Thurman Chitwood was one of the first to open a bedspread line business in his home on Dixie Highway. He and his wife would stamp designs onto the spreads on the living room floor, their neighbors would tuft them, and he would hang them on clotheslines to attract the tourists. Gradually, Thurman expanded into chenille housecoats and ventured into scatter rugs. Some tourists reordered and others sold his spreads once they returned home from vacation. In 1937, business was so good that he was able to buy his first Model A. Previously, he had delivered his tufting materials to local women by foot. The business grew until the scarcity of materials brought on by World War II stopped much of his production.

The great heyday of the spreadlines took place between the end of World War II and the opening of Interstate 75 in 1965, yet the method of roadside—selling had already evolved. After a bedspread was tufted, it was usually washed in a large iron pot to clean and bleach it. Then it was hung on a clothesline to dry and fluff up the tufts.

Tourists on Highway 41 saw the spreads drying on lines, and recognized them as ones that they had seen in stores. Many of these travelers stopped and bought them. The word of easy money from bedspread lines traveled fast in the small farm community and so lines began to appear frequently. Traffic increased with the prosperity of the postwar period, and Dalton's market expanded.

There were many people in the area who still hand tufted goods to sell, but the postwar period brought on extensive use of sewing machines adapted to produce tufted spreads, bath sets, throw rugs, scuffies, and housecoats.

Soon spread houses, where products were not only manufactured or collected, but were also processed, and shipped cropped up, as well as textile mills which had sprouted up all over Dalton and the surrounding area. The flow of tourists, coupled well with the increasing supply of goods helped create a new medium of sale, the spreadlines.

A typical farm house was set back from the road, primarily to keep both the house and cooking from road dust. However, the distance was not conducive to the customer nor to the seller, so new buildings, closer to the highway, were constructed. Early buildings were small, tin-roofed huts dotted against the roadside with clotheslines tied to nearby trees and the spreads blowing in the breeze.

As the product mix was expanded to include other items, small gift shops and covered porches were added. Some were more elaborate and others were just shelters thrown together, sometimes shops were built in conjunction with tourist cabins. Today, there are only a few active roadside shops on this famous stretch, but there are a number of remaining structures where the marks of a time past are still visible.

The characteristics of a spreadline shop are:

1. Its closeness to the road.
2. Gravel across the front marks places where customers could park.
3. Some posts, to which lines were hung, still remain.
4. Some old signs, either on the side of a building or hanging from posts, still advertize tufted wares.
5. Long covered porches, to protect the spreads, still remain.
6. Houses have been build both behind the shops to meet the needs of both selling and living quarters.
7. Some still sell bedspreads in addition to other Southern souvenirs.

Between 1952 and 1965 more than a hundred small chenille-type shops dotted the road between Atlanta and Chattanooga. Clothes-lines sagging under the weight of spreads, housecoats, bath sets, scatter rugs and pillows advertised each shop's treasures. However, the feature attraction was the peacock bedspread.

Double Peacock Spread: Crown Gardens and Archives

Minnie Hite Moody, writing for the *Saturday Evening Post* in 1946, wrote that when asked its cost, the proprietor responded, "Yes suh! Peacockses? Well, the wife says she wants seven and a half for the full-size spread with peacockses. Twin sizes comes lesser." Fred Rosen, who continued to manufacture chenille rugs after tufted carpet took over most of Dalton, said it was a joke, only Yankees bought peacock spreads. "No decent Southerner would want one of those gaudy, bright things in their house," said Rosen.

Jack and Willene Morgan were in the chenille business from April, 1952, until late 1992, the longest continuous spread retailer, and their story gives a picture of this quaint era. Willene was clipping bedspread tufts at the age of five, and by fifteen she was working on spreads for G.H. Rauschenberg. Jack, whom she met at the local swimming pool, started working in a laundry at fifteen, weighing and dyeing spreads. After serving in World War II, Jack spent six years in back-breaking labor at a Chattanooga foundry. When his doctor told him work demands were too great, he joined the chenille business which he had established for Willene. On the edge of U.S. 41, just south of Tunnel Hill, they built a single room store next to their home so that she could sell spreads as a hobby. It looked easy compared to foundry work, and the chance to make money while working with his wife and meeting lots of different kinds of people was attractive to Jack.

Morgan Chenille Company

Although they were one of the first spreadlines whose heyday lasted into the early 1960s, competition came quickly. The thickest concentration of spread houses was between Rocky Face, just north of Dalton, and Tunnel Hill. Jack remembers being able to stand on his front porch and see ten different competitors. The struggle for business was so fierce that everyone seemed to cut the price as low as possible and use every means available to draw in customers.

Jack and Willene worked seven days a week for twenty-eight years until illness forced Jack to take some time off. During the holiday season and Florida racing times, they kept the shop open 24 hours a day, sleeping on the rugs, under the tables or in their car. Sometimes they would be awakened by a trucker who wanted a spread or housecoat for the family, or by a "tater" farmer from the Midwest, or a Yankee who always seemed to want to "hanker" on the price more than anyone else.

They sold the Peacock pattern most often, but they also had Flower Garden, Floral Basket, Princess, Texas Rose, and others. Princess, made by Beckler Chenille, was the most expensive ($15), and the Morgans sold all of the ornate patterns that they could get.

Interestingly enough, it was Burch Beckler, a competitor south of Dalton, who really helped the Morgans in the early days. They started with $375 worth of goods on consignment from Burch. When they tried to pay him back, he counseled them to put it back into their business to build it and pay him back later. Burch actually wanted them to work for him, but they had worked all these years for themselves. Now the opening of the interstate and a greatly reduced demand for tufted materials has driven just about everybody out of the chenille business. Several times Jack tried to retire only to find that he could not be lazy, but in late 1992 cancer forced Jack and Willene to close their doors.

Some of the spreadline shops expanded their market potential into rugs and ultimately made the transition to carpet companies perched on the edge of Interstate 75 or U.S. 41. They broadened their clientele from tourists to retail customers from Michigan to Florida as well as carpet distributors throughout the nation. Beckler at one time had eight gift shops with spreadlines stretching between Cartersville and Tunnel Hill. Beckler's company survived the travel pattern changes to become an interstate retailer and wholesale supplier. Its huge red and white Beckler Carpet sign south of Dalton attests to its success.

Burch and Claudell Beckler and their son Randy are good examples of those who made the transition in a developing tufting industry. As the industry grew, bedspread boulevard gave way to interstate marketing. Some business principles remained constant, while others had to be modified, until only the hardy and the persistent survived.

At the age of thirteen Claudell tufted bedspreads by hand for ten cents a spread for G.L. Westcott of Cabin Craft. Burch grew up in textiles as a mechanic for Real Silk Hosiery Mills in Dalton. When the depression slowed the textile business, he sought work in Detroit. Homesick for Dalton, he returned in 1942 and using a single needle machine, Claudell began to create bedspreads whose intertwined border design "looked like a black snake." Burch returned to Real Silk as a mechanic.

Working out of the home of their aunt, he and Claudell serged together remnant sheeting from Crown Textiles of Dalton, since World War II shortages almost eliminated available sheeting. They added a design and sold it to the tufting plants. After six months Burch and Clarence Thompson, a restaurant owner famous for his nickel hamburgers, pooled their assets to start a small plant.

**Claudell Beckler: tying fringe on spread**

"Good money" led them to construct a small building next to their rental home on Ashworth Drive. They were becoming well enough known that salesmen like Fred Lloyd of Lloyd Linoleum & Rug Company were buying every peacock spread they could produce. Soon they were buying more machines and leasing them to women who sewed spreads in their homes. Backing was added to the sheeting and a design was printed at the plant; then Burch would carry out the spreads twice a week. Later he would take the completed ones to Crown Laundry for finishing and return them to the plant for inspecting and shipping.

By 1950, they built a small gift shop next to their new home and a plant behind it at Valley Point on U.S. 41, south of Dalton. Slowly the shop expanded to eight gift shops up and down the Dixie Highway. Each gift shop was individually owned, usually by relatives, but Burch provided the tufted goods. They sold chenille spreads, housecoats, bathroom sets, pillows, house shoes from J.W. Bray Company and even chenille dolls. The dolls were stuffed with lint, had a plastic face, and were made by a local barber, Henry Hall, and his wife. Each shop was in competition with the others, although they were generally run by relatives. Yet all benefited from Burch's heavy commitment to a variety of road signs advertising all the beautiful treasures awaiting within each store.

Beckler Ad

When World Carpet opened its doors on Green Street, Burch began to buy carpet remnants from Shaheen Shaheen, cut them into small rugs, and sell them to his eager customers. Soon it was rolls of carpet. In 1960, the Becklers moved to Huntsville, Alabama, to help a struggling store they had begun there.

In 1963, Burch returned home to retire, but he could not settle down. He rented a building from James Thompson just a short distance off an exit on the new Interstate 75. He also expanded to stores in Jackson, Mississippi; Huntsville, Alabama, and the Tri-Cities of East Tennessee. Just prior to Burch's death it was decided to concentrate on the Dalton operation, and Randy and his mother began to handle primarily World, Queen, and Galaxy Carpets. Since July 1981, they have operated on the edge of the interstate. Ten years ago 80%

of their business was wholesale to dealers, but currently, his sales have completely reversed in the direction of retail.

Advertising has continued to be a hallmark of Beckler's success. Burch initially peppered the tourists with catchy signs immediately before each gift shop: "Chenille Spreads Just Ahead on Left," "Chenille Robes and Pillows," and "Bath Mat Sets and Slippers." Even if people did not shop at the first store, it prepared their minds for the next Beckler store down the road. Today, the largest billboard between Chattanooga and Atlanta towers over their beautiful showroom while others dot the interstate.

Finally, the support of Shaheen Shaheen from the start, and particularly at the time of Burch's death, provided a stable force in crucial times. In the early days, Claudell can remember Burch and Shaheen sorting remnants on July 4th for the gift shops. When Burch died in 1975, Shaheen and his wife Piera were in Chicago, but early the next morning they arrived in the Beckler driveway. They told 24-year-old Randy, "We'll stick by you and your credit line is good with us." With that vote of confidence and the successful business left by his father, Randy has worked with his mother to expand the operation and develop "as much as he can say grace over." The Beckler story goes on.

Carpets of Dalton is an example of a successful interstate carpet outlet whose owner began solely in the carpet field and then branched out to associate items like grandfather clocks and furniture. Lamar Hennon combined hard work and long hours with the opportunities that carpet offered a Daltonian in the 1960s. His parents worked at Crown Cotton Mills and the American Thread Mill and he grew up in Thread Mill Village. As a teenager, he delivered Chattanooga newspapers and worked as a bag boy at O. & H. Grocery. A baseball scholarship helped his parents put him through Lincoln Memorial University in mountainous East Tennessee, then he returned to Northwest Whitfield High School in 1959 to teach and coach. For three years he taught General Science and Physical Science while coaching three sports. However, he resigned when the school tried to increase his General Science classes, which he did not like and felt unqualified to teach. Looking back, Lamar feels that if he had been in a situation that he liked, he'd still be coaching. But, when he started counting the days until the end of the school year, he knew that he needed to get out. He was making $4,400 a year when he resigned.

While playing summer softball with Ed Green, they decided to open a carpet business. Advertisements in the Atlanta newspapers prompted potential customers to send in coupons or call collect to their office over the Oakwood Cafe in Dalton. Then armed with samples they would travel all over the state selling carpet which later they installed. Often Lamar would leave Dalton at 3 AM and return 24 hours later after calling on residences in Macon, Dublin and Vidalia. Since they were offering carpet at $5.99 a square yard, they would sometimes get 300 to 400 responses to a single ad.

In the fall of 1962, they opened Carpet & Rug Mills of Marietta, Georgia, which was the first of a string of outlets they started in Atlanta, Macon, and later Columbia, South Carolina. He sold these and repeated the process from a base in Decatur, Georgia, before returning to Dalton in February, 1967 to start Direct Carpet with Bob Daily down on old Highway 41. In 1970, they sold the four stores they had founded to a conglomerate, Equity National. Finally, in December, 1971, Lamar started Carpets of Dalton and moved to his current site on the edge of Interstate 75 in July, 1972.

Using a small group of suppliers, including Shaw Industries, Queen, Coronet and Salem primarily, he stocked 32 items in all dye lots, having as many as 6,000 rolls in his 130,000 square foot modern showroom and warehouse. Although he is on the interstate just south of Dalton and, therefore, convenient to drive-in customers, only $4 million of his $22 million volume in 1984 was made with this irregular demand. Most of his business is with distributors who recognize his ability to give individual attention and service. By calling ahead, the wholesaler can pick up his small or large order in a matter of minutes.

Lamar is also a leader and innovator in advertising. Carpets of Dalton was the first to add an electronic carpet sign on the interstate and is a magnet to the eye of the traveler. This is just one example of the advertising supplementing the use of newspapers, radio, business journals and Cable TV. His flexibility, in spite of his size, coupled with excellent relations with the mills, seems to be the key to his success. Lamar is just another example of the individuals who rose from a very modest background to seize success from the opportunities of the boom times of carpet growth.

These companies represent Dalton area retail marketing, but they are small in comparison to the total retail volume of the industry. Frank O'Neill, editor of *Floor Focus,* notes that the floorcovering industry (carpet, vinyl and hardwood) is a $11.9 billion business with 22,700 floorcovering retailers in the U.S.

In the decades of the 60s and 70s these retailers enjoyed the enormous popularity of broadloom carpet. The retailer could sell anything without really trying, but sales have flattened out and retailer's profit margins have dropped recently. As an attempt to draw the consumer back to the showroom, many retailers have lowered their prices to absurd levels. Steve Keiser of DuPont has pointed out that between 1967 and 1991, the real price of all consumer products rose 229%, while the average price of carpet rose 80%. The problem does not appear to be with the product, which is better looking and better made. In the past, the retailer depended on the supply sector to create an image and market their product with skillful advertising. DuPont's Stainmaster has greater recognition than any carpet style or manufacturer. Consolidation in both the mill and fiber sectors has made it difficult to provide retailers with marketing and merchandising support.

## FLOOR FOCUS 100 RETAILERS

1. COLOR TILE & CARPET, Fort Worth,TX $490
2. NEW YORK CARPET WORLD, Southfield,MI $315
3. SEARS, Chicago, IL $290
4. SHERWIN WILLIAMS, Cleveland,OH $120
5. CARPETLAND, USA, Munster,IN $90
6. CAPETERIA, Valencia,CA $83
7. CARPET EXCHANGE, Seattle,WA $67
8. ABC CARPET & HOME, New York,NY $53
9. AIRBASE CARPET MART, New Castle, DE $51
10.KMART, Troy,MI $49
11.GIANT CARPET, Moonachie,NJ $45
12.LOWES COMPANIES, North Wilkesboro,NC $45
13.HOME DEPOT, Atlanta,GA $44
14.DAYTON-HUDSON, Minneapolis,MN $39
15.TIM HOGAN'S DALTON CARPET,Cincinnati,OH $36
16.ETHAN ALLEN, Danbury,CT $35
17.PAYLESS/CASHWAYS, Kansas City,MO $32
18.PLYWOOD MINNESOTA, Fridley, MN $30
19.CONKLIN BROTHERS, San Mateo,CA $29.5
20.DON'S CARPET BARN, Independence,OH $29
21.FLOOR COVERINGS INT., Forest Park,GA $28.8
22.SANDLER & WORTH, Springfield,NJ $28.5
23.DEAN'S FLOOR COVERING, Rockaway,NJ $28
24.STANDARD BRANDS, Torrance,CA $28
25.McSWAIN CARPETS, Cincinnati,OH $27
26.RICHLAND INDUSTRIES, Rochester,NY $27
27.CENTURY SUPPLY, Lombard,IL $26
28.NEBRASKA FURNITURE MART, Omaha,NE $26
29.J.C. PENNEY, Dallas,TX $26
30.KINNAIRD & FRANCKE, Louisville,KY $25.5
31.CARPET FAIR, Baltimore, MD $25
32.FLOOR COVERING ASSOC. Shorewood,IL $25
33.LEONARD'S, Anaheim,CA $25
34.PARVIZIANA, Chevy Chase,MD $25
35.BURDINES, Miami,FL $24
36.EINSTEIN-MOOMJY, Pine Brook,NJ $24
37.THE BROADWAY, Los Angeles,CA $23
38.RICH'S/GOLDMIT, Atlanta,GA $23
39.CARPETS OF DALTON, Dalton,GA $22
40.LAZARUS STORES, Cincinnati,OH $22
41.RITE RUG, Columbus,OH $22
42.TILE CITY & CARPET, Pittsburgh,PA $22
43.BUILDERS SQUARE, San Antonio,TX $21
44.FAIN'S Seekonk,MA $21
45.OLSON RUG CO., Chicago,IL $21
46.WAL-MART, Bentonville,AR $21
47.WOODWARD & LOTHROP, Washington,DC $20
48.BUDDY'S CARPET, Franklin,OH $19.6
49.CALIFORNIA CARPET OUTLET, San Carlos,CA $19
50.PRIZANT'S CARPET, Pittsburgh,PA $19
51. BUILDER'S SHOWCASE, San Diego,CA $18.5
52. BAKER BROS., Tempe,AZ $18.4
53. A&S/JORDAN MARSH, Brooklyn,NY $18
54. CARPET TOWN, Los Angeles,CA $18
55. G. FRIED, Westbury,NY $18
56. GEORGIA CARPET, Montgomery,AL $18
57. MMM CARPETS UNLIMITED, Santa Clara, CA $18
58. REDI-CUT CARPETS, Bronx,NY $18
59. SPIEGEL, Chicago,IL $18
60. BANNER CARPETS & DRAPES, Anaheim, CA $17
61. BECKLER'S CARPET, Dalton,GA $17
62. STAR LUMBER, Wichita,KS $16.5
63. BECKWITH-EVANS, Troy,MI $16
64. CAMPBELL'S CARPET, Benecia,CA $16
65. GROSSMAN'S, Braintree,MA $16
66. HOUSE OF CARPETS, Albuquerque,NM $16
67. LASHER/WHITE, New York,NY $16
68. COGDILL'S, Columbus,SC $15.5
69. J.M. BENSON, Hartford,CT $15.5
70. FAMOUS BARR, St. Louis,MO $15
71. HECHINGER'S, Landover,MD $15
72. MONTAUK RUG & CARPET, Farmingdale,NY $15
73. S&G DISCOUNT OUTLET, San Jose,CA $15
74. VILLAGE CARPET, Largo,FL $15
75. FLOOR TO CEILING, Rochester,MN $14.5
76. CARPET CORNER, Kansas City,KS $14.2
77. CADILLAC CARPETS, Westbury,NY $14
78. CARPET KING, St. Louis Park,MN $14
79. ESSIS & SONS, Mechanicsburg,PA $14
80. MILES CARPET, Baltimore,MD $14
81. PEDIAN RUG, Lincolnwood,IL $14
82. SERGENIAN'S, Madison.WI $14
83. UNITED CARPET, Sterling Heights,MI $14
84. McINTYRE-MANN, Kansas City,MO $13.75
85. TERRY'S FLOOR FASHIONS, Cary,NC $13.5
86. MACY'S/CALIFORNIA, San Francisco,CA $13
87. MACY'S, New York,NY $13
88. POLK BROTHERS, Melrose, Park,IL $13
89. STANDARD CARPET, Baltimore,MD $13
90. AMERICAN CARPET, Honolulu,HI $12
91. BOB'S CARPET MART, Largo,FL $12
92. COLES, San Diego,CA $12
93. DEAN'S CARPET ONE, Manchester,NH $12
94. NEILSEN BROTHERS, Seattle,WA $12
95. PIERCE FLOORING, Billings,MT $12
96. RUSMUR FLOORS, Bridgeville,PA $12
97. WOODMONT CARPET, Rockville,MD $12
98. CARPET WORLD, Oklahoma City,OK $11.5
99. GIANT FLOOR & WALL, Wilkes Barre,PA $11.5
100. MASSAU'S FURNITURE, South Windsor,CT $11.5

*In millions of dollars

*Floor Focus*, November 1992

Whereas the tufted business started with roadside stands or personal marketing to department stores, the old-line industry used distributors which sold to speciality shops and furniture stores or they created dealers who handled their woven goods exclusively. The *Floor Focus* list of its top 100 retailers includes independent retailers, large chains, and franchises. Nearly one-third are not exclusively floorcovering enterprises. Fourteen of these firms are either home centers or building supply chains and eleven are department stores. One-half of the leading players are clustered on the coasts, but that is not unusual since almost half of all floorcovering sales are generated within a 100 mile corridor of the coasts. Yet the industry's Top 100 retailers account for only 29% of total sales, which indicates that the industry is still quite fragmented.

As competition has increased and profits continued to decline, more and more retailers are joining buying groups. In 1992, more than 30% of all retail sales were made by dealers who belonged to buying groups. Frank O'Neill predicts that the figure will increase to 50% in the next few years.

"Until recently, all the retail groups that have formed since the late 80s could legitimately be called buying groups, " notes Frank O'Neill. The lure of group buying power drew in the independent retailer. However, as competition for their financial commitment increased, training and services began to be offered as further incentives. Private labeling became nearly universal to block comparison shopping by the consumer. Beyond that, some groups are packaging support services such as sales and management training, advertising support, and merchandising.

The first franchisor Abbey Carpet (1958) targeted the small retailer who owned one or two stores and offered them the whole gamut of hard and soft floorcoverings. The others, like Carpet Max, Color Tile, New York Carpet World, and Georgia Carpet Outlets, also cater to niches, charge franchise fees beginning at $12,000 as well as royalty fees, and develop supply and training services.

Carpet One is the largest of the nation's retail groups and targets the nation's largest independent retailers who usually dominate market areas. This network of over 500 stores is the carpet industry's only co-op. Each member, its initial fee is not publicly available, is involved in the ownership of the organization and each member receives regular dividends on his investment. In 1991 Carpet One returned $4.5 million to store owners in dividends.

They draw from thirty-five major suppliers in ten different business: carpet, rugs, support products, hard surfaces, wall coverings, and window treatments. Each member signs a written agreement to relegate at least 50% of their store purchases to Carpet One products. Most dedicate more and are excited about their success. Its Interiors 2001 in-store design package creates a total merchandising package and focuses on selling carpet from the customer's point of view. This is supplemented by its training program through its traveling Carpet One University and "Internet" which brings a unique expertise to contract selling.

# CARPET ONE CONNECTION

Carpet One is the creation of President Sandy Mishkin and co-founders Alan Greenberg of St. Louis and Howard Brodsky of Manchester, New Hampshire. Sandy learned a strong work ethic from his parents who were immigrants from Europe. After he graduated from New York University in economics he was hired as a management trainee and later floorcovering buyer by E.J. Korvette, a forerunner of the discount floor covering industry. In 1969 Nate Lipson invited him to become Director of Marketing at Trend Mills in Rome, Georgia. Within ten years he was vice president. Peter Spirer then lured him to Horizon as Vice President of Merchandising where he stayed until the company went public. In 1984 he left to open his own retail stores, only to sell out a year later. In late 1985 he joined with Allen Greenberg and Howard Brodsky to form Carpet Coop of America, whose trade name is Carpet One.

He feels that their success is due to the cooperative being committed to the success and profitability of its members as opposed to the larger personal profits which go to a few individuals in a franchise relationship. Their vision is a creative network which offers high quality independent structure while providing quality marketing and management opportunities for Carpet One members, allowing the co-op member to maximize the profitability of his retail carpet business.

Quantity buying results in rebates, which are returned to the members in the form of dividends for supporting the co-op program. All product programs are offered under the Carpet One private label. Bill Krueger, a member since 1990, said it pays to buy from Carpet One suppliers. "I have never had a mill give me money back, but with Carpet One, I actually got money back that I could not have gotten on my own."

Carpet One has attempted to fill a void created by the mills. The manufacturers sold to anyone who could open a store, but failed to provide further marketing aid. Besides the tools for marketing, store design and advertising promotion, Carpet One markets its own flexible credit program that is available to both consumers as well as its builders through its Business 4 Business credit program. All this is evidence of the vision that the leaders have used to propel Carpet One to the lead in this wave of retailing for the future.

Finally, the concept of shopping at home has also emerged in the floorcovering industry. Floor Coverings International was the first of the shop-at-home carpet van franchises and is today the largest and most successful. Franchisees go through a four week training program initially, which is supplemented by special sales presentation programs every 90 days. Decorating Den, which is the largest shop-at-home interior decorating service in the United States, and Lifestyle Mobile Carpet Showrooms are also catering to a purchasing public who likes to compare styles and colors with the furnishings and decor of their own home.

In the past there were too many ugly, non-consumer oriented floorcovering stores dotting the downtown areas of America's cities. The scramble for the consumer dollar in a shrinking economy also is forcing the retail industry to become innovative in marketing. The larger stores and the buying groups are sharpening their image and the smaller Mom-and-Pop stores must offer better personal services in order to survive. It appears that retailing is adapting and will make a successful transition.

## *Chapter Sixteen*

# SUPPLY, SERVICE AND SUPPORT

Although most people concentrate on the success of carpet companies, these companies' profitability catapulted numerous supply groups into prosperity. This is one of the interesting things about the industry. There are so many ways to become a millionaire.

Printing and samples were the venue which James Brown chose to pursue. His father was a local grocer, while his mother was a floor lady for Brooker Spread Company and later Bates Spread. After a stint in the cadet corps in the Merchant Marine in World War II he returned home to seek his fortune. While a salesman for Gregory Printing Company he and Jimmy Hair started Tufted Sample, a sideline business making up samples for carpet mills. They worked at nights cutting up samples and putting them in binders that they bought out of town. Then Brown and Carl Griggs started Southern Binders so that they wouldn't have to buy the sample binders from someone else.

In 1958, he quit his salesman job and with Don Martin, who had handled the actual printing of most of his jobs, started Brown Printing. James did most of the sales, while Don ran the inside business. They worked night and day for years to get the company going. One day James brought Don a heat-set label from Cabin Craft and challenged him with success for the company if he could create one. He first tried rubber plates as labels but they stretched. A letter press on cloth was also unclear and inadequate. Finally, the labels were printed on rayon satin fabric with a gutta-percha backing. Gutta-percha is the same base as chewing gum and in order to use it, they had to refrigerate it. Don developed a cooling process for the presses until synthetic materials replaced it. Currently, Brown Printing is the largest printer in the United States of heat-seal labels for carpet samples.

Next James started a company to build display equipment for carpet showrooms and then a swatching operation in Cartersville. There were hundreds of people working in each of these five companies in 1970 when he sold out to National Services Industries of Atlanta. This division then started an advertising agency and two new swatching operations and bought the biggest carpet sample business on the West Coast. James remained as CEO and president for the Dalton operations for many years and for the last eighteen years he has been chairman of Marketing Services.

Another dimension of James Brown is his character and civic concern. He is not an excitable person, but as one described him, "He is a man of few words, but strong, consistent action." If people start arguing, he simply walks away. Don Martin adds, "In the forty-four years that I have known him, I have never heard him use the Lord's name in vain." James provided such strong support in helping start and develop the Dalton Recreation Center that he served as the first chairman and a park was recently named for him. He currently serves as a Regent on the Board of Regents of the University System of Georgia and has helped present the community's case for four year status for Dalton College.

Masterpiece Finishing is representative of the companies which came into existence to provide dyeing and finishing for tufters who needed their services. Its founder, Vernon Foster, grew up in a family which hand tufted bedspreads to supplement their Murray County farm income. If it was fringed and the work was satisfactory, he remembered that they received 15 cents per spread. In high school he worked nights for Lawtex in the shipping department and later ran a yardage machine for Art Rich. Upon graduation he went to work for DuPont in its nylon processing facility in Chattanooga which gave him an invaluable learning experience in fibers.

In 1955 he began to work alternative jobs with Southern Railroad and in the carpet industry. The railroad needed him in the summer months and then when their needs slowed, the carpet industry was gearing up for its major production period. He worked 12 hour shifts for his brother, Smith, at Dalton Carpet Finishing. Often during peak season he would work 84-hour weeks. He then went to Advance Finishing and next Foremost Processing. In each job he handled processing, lab work and dyeing.

In 1960 he was only making $1.40 an hour, but when he started to leave Foremost they offered him an opportunity to own stock in the company. The fact that he was in demand gave him the confidence to start his own company. First National Bank of Dalton recognized the need for another dye house and agreed to loan him the money to get started. Masterpiece grew rapidly from that point, but a stroke forced him to leave the pressure and excitement of the industry. Today, his brother Smith Foster runs Masterpiece and Vernon enjoys a more leisured existence selling log homes.

The chenille bedspread industry was the training ground for Zach Norville. In 1943 his mother moved to Cartersville to join her sister Mavis Slaughter and start Southern Chenille. Mavis's husband Walter was one of the founders of Candlewick Yarn Mills. He convinced them to buy the yarn rejects and "you can trade part of the yarn for sheeting and then you'll have yarn and sheeting. Buy machines and you can make bedspreads and make money." While looking for products to replace the goods ordinarily imported by their family's Chicago company, Said Shaheen stopped by their small operation. Impressed by the Bible on his mother's desk, Said decided to trust them with an order and a check for $10,000. The orders continued until he moved to Dalton to start Katherine Rug Mills.

With the end of the war in 1945 Mavis returned home to Watkinsville and started Norville Chenille Company. Zach learned the industry by installing and fixing machines. When a machine would break down, they would call the Varsity, a student fast food restaurant, at the University of Georgia and leave word. Zach would check between classes and if necessary, skip a class and drive the six miles to solve the problem. Unfortunately, the business was miles from the closest dyehouse, experienced labor and the sources for yarn and sheeting. It closed after four years and Mama Norville went back to school teaching.

However, Zach's mechanical interest continued. He transferred to Georgia Tech and upon graduation in 1950 he went to work for Uncle Walter Slaughter with Candlewick Yarn Mills. He started by unloading trucks, but then began to run the night shift in the Cartersville plant. After a stint with Uncle Sam in the Korean War, he returned to find that Dixie Mercerizing owned his uncle's operation. Using his technical skills Zach began to travel all over the country as a Nylon Technical Service Representative for DuPont. Tired of traveling he decided to settle his new family in Dalton and become a sales representative for Kraemer Textile of Nazareth, PA.

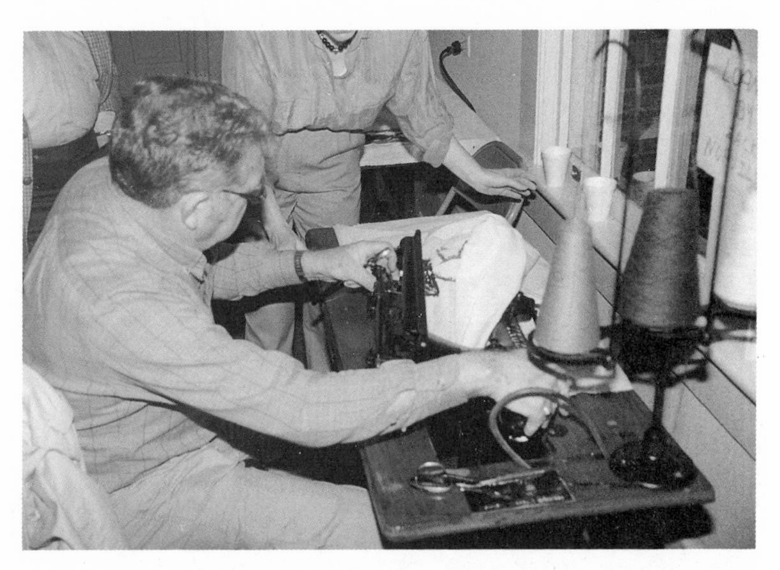

**Zack Norville repairs early machine**

In 1954 Dalton had limited facilities and comforts. There was one pay telephone at which the salesmen lined up to make their calls. Zach's first call was to Doc Williams whose Modern Tufting Company was one of the first broadloom producers. It was perhaps the first carpet mill to be sold to a major company outside the industry, Scripto Pen and Pencil. He did not get a sale, but he did get a job offer. Quickly Zach saw the opportunities that tufting offered. In 1955 he and his wife Merle founded Textile Supply Company to provide the tufted industry with a local source for necessary goods and services. They shared space in the old Flour Mill with Pete Sims and his tube and supply operation, and Harvey Howalt and his latex mixing. In 1956 they bought Sims Textile Company and moved into a chicken house, since space in town was at a premium. They stamped patterns on colored sheeting by night and peddled yarn by day. Gradually, they expanded into novelties such as doilies, Aunt Lydia's heavy rug yarn in 60 colors, spool cotton thread, and zippers. Then they began to represent suppliers of sheeting, burlap, jute, infrared heating units and ovens. As times changed, Norville Industries expanded and changed, even buying Doc Williams Speciality Company and others. As Zach moves toward retirement, he is doing the unusual thing of turning his creation over to his daughters, except for Debbie who is in the broadcasting industry.

Also providing service to the carpet industry are the regional markets and design centers. The Chicago Market was the most important market and its Winter Market, which usually was the first week of January, set the styles and the tones for the total industry. The Summer Market was not as important, but they both were the site of the deals and contacts of the industry. One major buyer remembers that at the Chicago Market major distributors could meet with the president of the various companies and begin the process of pricing their carpet buys. The parties were in grand style and Hollywood entertainers and stars such as Dick Van Dyke, Lucille Ball and Carol Channing appeared.

**Showroom at Atlanta Market**

The New York Market occurred the second week of January and the other major markets were Atlanta, Dallas, Los Angeles and San Francisco. Denver, Minneapolis, Miami and even Dalton have served as smaller markets.

Recently, the Western Carpet Manufacturers market at Las Vegas has become the "glitzy" event for exhibitors, distributors and retailers.

The carpet industry also has spawned a number of fashion programs such as Clem Stein's International Academy of Merchandising & Design in Chicago's Apparel Center. Clem had been in merchandising all his adult life. Fresh out of Ohio State University, he joined Sears as a trainee in a store in Middleton, Ohio. Literally, he started at the bottom. The store manager consigned him to the receiving room. The receiving room boss told him to forget about his college degree and grab a broom and clean out the pit of the elevator shaft. He progressed through a variety of jobs in a number of stores before arriving at Sears headquarters in Chicago where he filled a number of posts in retailing, buying, and merchandising. Using Walter Guinan as a role model Clem played a pivotal role in making Sears floor covering departments a styling and financial success in Sears 51 major market areas.

Finally, in the fall of 1978 his vision of The Academy as Chicago's answer to Manhattan's Fashion Institute of Technology became a reality. The school's three basic courses are: fashion merchandising, fashion design, and interior design. The visitor to the school is greeted by the words of Daniel Burnham—"Make no little plans. They have no magic to stir men's blood." This school, along with other independent and university related schools, have helped marketing and design programs focus on each other.

The industry has also sought to serve itself with trade associations. In the early 1930's an unnamed group of key bedspread manufacturers met to discuss registration of bedspread patterns or designs. The codes of the National Recovery Administration of President Franklin Roosevelt forced the manufacturers to work together. Led by Pete Lumpkin, B.J. Bandy, Sam Hurowitz and Fred Westcott a select group hurried to Washington to protect themselves against wage and hour laws.

The Tufted Bedspread Manufacturers Association (TBMA), formed in July, 1938, was a natural outgrowth of their fears. The first president was Otis Moore and he was followed by Fred Westcott of Cabin Craft. Among the early problems of TBMA in the late 1930's and early 1940's were "the evils of over production," "low profits," "consumer problems," quality control and product testing. They also prodded the members to concern themselves with improved styling, merchandising and advertising.

Near the end of World War II War Production Board Order M317 Directive 9, which concerned the allocation of raw materials, seemed to "condemn the chenille industry to death." In response to this order, TBMA became the Tufted Textile Manufacturers Association (TTMA) on May 16, 1945 with Dalton Attorney R. Carter Pittman as president. The initial need of the organization was to represent the industry to the Office of Price Administration and the Civilian Production Administration. In 1946 when the latter agency was about to take away half of the sales yarn formerly available to the industry, statistics gathered by TTMA and political support marshalled by its members saved the industry again from the government.

One of the early tasks of the organization was consumer concern. Cotton housecoats and robes were very prone to catching on fire when they came in contact with gas heaters, floor furnaces and fireplaces. When the flammable fabric legislation became law, the group set up testing equipment in a laboratory to test chenille robes and housecoats for association members.

Woven carpet manufacturers initially met together early in the 20th century to solve pricing and transportation rates. Prices had declined annually since 1880 and historical records indicate that the Carpet Manufacturers Association came forward to try to stabilize prices. The Carpet and Rug Traffic Association was formed to create community action concerning transportation rates and traffic regulations. The Institute of Carpet Manufacturers of America (ICMA), formed on July 29, 1927, primarily was created to pull the smaller groups together to sell carpet and rugs. Manufacturers were anxious to have barriers against foreign carpet, while others in the industry wanted lower import costs on Indian jute. The Hawley-Smoot Tariff Act of 1930 gave carpet manufacturers "the best tariff they had ever had." As the needs for market development, governmental interaction and foreign importation of fiber and carpet increased, the organization evolved into the American Carpet Institute (ACI) in January, 1958.

Both trade associations were concerned with industry statistics, product research, training seminars, public relations and traffic management. ACI's public relations and marketing program was regarded by many observers as "the most complete and ambitious of any trade association."

In September, 1969 TTMA and ACI merged to form the Carpet & Rug Institute, based in Dalton, but with offices in Washington, D.C. George Paules, its first president, summed up what he perceived as its focus. "It's an industry that has grown by accident rather than on purpose. Now we must continue to grow—on purpose." Consumer affairs along with governmental concerns are the two major divisions of focus along with technical development, marketing services, public relations, and installation services.

## CRI OFFICERS AND DIRECTORS

Chairman-Elect
**Paul B. Comiskey**
President
JPS Carpet Corporation

Chairman of the Board
**W. Norris Little**
Senior Vice President Operations
Shaw Industries, Inc.

Vice Chairman
**Julian D. Saul**
Executive Vice President
Queen Carpet Corporation

Immediate Past Chairman
**John J. Riley**
President
Karastan Bigelow

Treasurer
**James R. Jolly**
President
J & J Industries, Inc.

Vice Chairman Associates
**Thomas G. Iversen**
Business Director - Nylon
Monsanto - The Chemical Group

**Carl M. Bouckaert**
President
Beaulieu of America, Inc.

**John C. Carson**
Vice President, Gen. Mgr.
Flooring Systems Division
E. I. du Pont de Nemours

**Steve Dickinson**
President and CEO
Carriage Industries, Inc.

**W. John Dixon**
President and COO
Columbus Mills, Inc.

**Thomas R. Fischel**
Vice President Carpet Fibers
BASF Corporation Fibers Division

**Martin Greenwood**
Chairman
Multitex Corp. of America

**George W. Henderson III**
President
Lees Commercial Carpets

**Wayne Hunter**
Division President
Milliken & Company
Int. Furn. & LaGrange Ind. Div.

**Shirley J. Lorberbaum**
Secretary
Aladdin Mills, Inc.

**John A. Shaheen**
Chairman of the Boad
World Carpets, Inc.

**Robert E. Shaw**
President and CEO
Shaw Industries, Inc.

**C. Edward Terry**
President
Interface Flooring Systems, Inc.

**Ronald E. VanGelderen**
President
The Carpet & Rug Institute

**Lovic A. Brooks Jr.**
CRI General Counsel
Constangy, Brooks & Smith

**Caswell O. Hobbs III**
CRI Regulatory Counsel
Morgan, Lewis & Bockius

**Past Chairmen**

| | |
|---|---|
| 1969-1971 | J. C. Shaw |
| 1971-1972 | Walter Guinan |
| 1972-1973 | Thomas R. Jones* |
| 1973-1974 | Jep Peele |
| 1974-1978 | Frank E. Masland III |
| 1978-1980 | Irwin M. Harvey |
| 1980-1982 | Peter R. Spirer |
| 1982-1983 | Joe B. Maffett |
| 1983-1985 | Burton M. Gold |
| 1985-1987 | Donald W. Kuhn |
| 1987-1989 | David L. Kolb |
| 1989-1990 | Douglas A. Cummins |
| 1990-1992 | John J. Riley |

*Deceased

CRI STAFF

**James Blankenship**
Director
Printing Services

**Dan Cochran**
Director
Member Services

**Judy Elliott**
Administrative Assistant
Technical Services

**Kaye Henry**
Assistant
Accounting Department

**Betty Hickman**
Administrative Assistant
Member Services

**Sarah Hicks**
Director
Public Relations

**Ned Hopper**
Director
Govermental Affairs

**Jerry Hullander**
Controller

**Ann Jones**
Assistant
Publications

**Ken McIntosh**
Director
Technical Services

**Brenda Murry**
Administrative Assistant
Projects

**Peggy Parks**
Administrative Assistant
to President

**Joyce Schuler**
Secretary/Receptionist

**Carroll Turner**
Associate
Technical Services

**Eugene Underwood**
Assistant
Printing Department

**Cindy Walters**
Program Assistant
Technical Services

## *Chapter Seventeen*

# A FEMININE PERSPECTIVE

The early days of the tufted industry was characterized by some aggressive women who seized the opportunity and pursued the future. In the steps of Catherine Evans Whitener, walked Mrs. Eugene Evans, Eugenia Jarvis, Mamie Redwine and Edna Redwine Strain. It was Dicksie Bandy who traveled to Washington and Philadelphia to sell bedspreads, while her husband ran his grocery stores and waited for the spread orders.

However, as machines began to appear, male mechanics were drawn into the plants. Significant profits from bedspreads in the late 1930s and the post-war years were accompanied by men pushing ladies out of positions of control. Today, there are very few women in major administrative roles.

However, one of the women who carved out a niche was Addie Treadwell. She was the first woman to hold the top executive position in a Georgia carpet mill. After high school graduation she took a job folding spreads on the night shift at Kenner & Rauchenberg for $3 a week. When she moved to a day shift job, Addie enrolled for night classes at a business school. Fire destroyed the spread and laundry where she was working, and she became a supervisor with Novelty Mills, a company that made housecoats and bedspreads.

Addie continued her studies with the University of Georgia through evening extension courses. During World War II she was a civilian inspector for the U.S. Army, checking textile products such as bomber chutes. In 1947 she returned to textiles as plant manager of Monarch Mills, while studying textile engineering. When Barwick Mills merged with Monarch, Addie became the assistant to the president of Monarch and started studying promotion, distribution and distributor accounts. After being general manager of Noxon Mills 1958-1967, Addie decided to do something on her own. In early 1968 she started Whit-Ray Mills with $25,000 of her own money and a $148,000 loan from Southern Eastern Financial of Charlotte, North Carolina. The company began small and stayed small, just the way Addie wanted it. They only tufted, leaving the dyeing and finishing to others. She geared production so that annual sales did not exceed $4 million. Her success was based on three almost absolute elements: a good sound administration and good manufacturing, sales management and quality control. By 1981 she had retired and turned the direction of Whit-Ray over to her daughter Glenda and her son-in-law Calvin Dunn.

One lady whose life spans the beginning of the industry to the present is Peggy Baugh Jonas. After graduation from Murray County High School she started working as a "Girl Friday" for $30 for J. M. Feighery Co. Jim Feighery was building machinery as well as repairing and selling used cutters, loopers and tufters. When Peggy was not keeping the books, she would spend time in the shop, learning the technical side from its grassroots. It was a time when the first twelve-foot tufting machines were being created and FHA certification for tufted carpet ushered into the industry a tremendous boom. In 1956 she went to work for Luxury Carpet Mills which was owned by the original owners of Morrill Manufacturing and W. H. Griffin.

By 1958 Dalton was exploding at its seams as salesmen, representatives and agents poured into town. Peggy responded by opening Office Services Unlimited as a combination telephone answering service and office center. The Oakwood Cafe was the social hub around which the industry revolved and she rented the top floor. She provided offices with or without service to salesmen, agents, five trucking firms, Eastern Airlines, and factors such as Walter Heller Company and James Talcott. Peggy represented two carpet magazines and provided public relations for them. She kept books for rubber supply companies like Patchogue Plymouth, and for the Oakwood Cafe, and helped the Rotary and Civilian Club members remember their luncheon dates. It was "a circus," but it was exciting to be at the center of the surge of success, said Peggy.

During this time Peggy met Oscar Jonas who was buying closeouts and renting space with Luke White. A fire at Luke's warehouse forced Oscar to find another space in Dalton and spend more time in town. Peggy and Oscar met in the fall of 1957; they married the following year. In 1958 with a $54 profit Oscar started a business and a merchandising concept called "the One Price Rug Sale." It hit the retailing merchants like a bolt of lighting.

In 1962 Peggy sold her office service to an accounting firm and concentrated on raising their four children. Yet the industry continued to swirl around their home. Dalton was limited in its eating and lodging establishments. Clients were friends and often they were entertained at home. The Jonas' built a guest house just as World, Cabin Craft and others did.

Oscar died in 1968 and Peggy had to devote herself to the family until 1977. Then she returned to become the chairperson and chief executive office of Jonas Carpet, Inc. until the estate sold the company in 1979. She stayed for two years until the new owner liquidated it and Peggy moved to Atlanta to work with the Wool Bureau.

In 1993, she decided to retire, but her background still allows her to walk back into a mill and understand everything that is occurring. The "glass ceiling" which currently blocks so many capable young women had not been erected when Peggy pushed her way upward through the chaos of the surging industry.

One of the legends and pioneers in the carpet retailing industry is a 4 foot 10 inches tall ball of fire, known as "Mrs. B." Rose Blumkin founded Nebraska Furniture Mart in 1937. During her 52 years there it evolved into a massive 700,000-square-foot furniture and carpet outlet. She was known as one of the deepest discounters in the industry, often selling products far below competitors' prices. By 1983, Mrs. B estimated the business was generating $165 million in annual sales. That year she sold out to Omaha billionaire Wallen Buffett, but continued to operate it until March, 1989 when she retired over a family dispute. Three months later the then-95-year-old Mrs. B started Mrs. B's Warehouse directly north of her old business. Within three years the six businesses in the facility were selling a combined total of $30 million.

Mrs. B got a taste of the retail business at the age of 12, when she managed a small dry goods store in Russia. In 1917 she bluffed her way past a Russian border guard and traveled to America on a peanut boat. She settled in Omaha and for several years worked in her husband's small store. In the mid-1930s, she borrowed $500 to hold a furniture sale in a local auditorium, selling furnishings she had purchased in Chicago. Her profit was the seed money to found the Nebraska Furniture Mart.

Mrs. B's success seems to be the result of her drive, her business sense and her desire to give the lower class incredible bargains. Dick McAdams, president of Georgia Carpet Outlet, a retail flooring chain based in Montgomery, Alabama says that she is proof of what hard work can do. "I heard that she was a very good buyer, a tough negotiator. She was known for having tremendous selections and value," remembers McAdams, who first met her when he was Mohawk's Southwestern assistant district manager. Frank De Martini, a sales representative for Cedar Carpets and Homeland Carpet, says that it "wasn't unusual for her to knock $5 off a square yard of carpet to secure a sale. People felt when they bought from Mrs. B they were getting an honest bargain, a good price and a good piece of merchandise."

Her selling style was unconventional and aggressive. She often traveled around the store in a golf cart. Bud Seretean, cofounder of Coronet Industries, recalled that he had to chase around the floor to talk to her and "if a salesman didn't write up an order in five minutes, she went right over there." Her sharp discounts enabled her to create huge volume. Her prices were so low that she was taken to court six times by her competitors. Until declared unconstitutional in the 1950s Nebraska fair-trade laws allowed manufacturers to force retailers to sell at certain prices. However, consumers loved her and remained loyal to her. Mrs. B is definitely a legend and a pioneer. Frank De Martini even went so far as to say, "I think she's one of the seven wonders of the world."

Unfortunately, women have been relegated to creative designers, support services or decorations to attract male buyers. Gene Barwick was the first to use models to draw customers to carpet shows and to entertain clients. Others have copied this in their annual market presentations and printed advertisements.

One of the logical extensions of this approach is the Miss Resaca Beach contest. Resaca is a small town south of Dalton which does not have a beach, but the beauty contest paid greater financial rewards to the winner than any beauty pageant in the state of Georgia. Beauty and physical attractiveness were the primary qualification for selection and much of the money for the

winner was paid for being the hostess for the sponsoring company, Conquest Carpet and later Victory Carpet. The first winner was Marla Maples. The contest is now separate from any carpet company-sponsorship, but still a fixture of Dalton's summer entertainment plans.

Possibly the best example of the Horatio Alger story of success as the result of persistence, hard work and a positive mental attitude is Linda Freeman, president of 1st Choice Carpets Int'l, Inc. Born into a tobacco farming family in Reidsville, North Carolina, Linda learned to work hard for long hours and to compete with her three brothers. She sometimes believed that her mother had wanted another son and Linda worked to prove her own worth. Before she finished high school she married, which ended her dream to be a nurse. She had been working weekends since she was 14 at a retail clothing store, then worked at a bank and went to night school. While teaching kindergarten one of her student's parents talked her into working with customer service and samples for a carpet company.

This was a crossroads in Linda's life. Her husband was unemployed, she was working twelve hour days and Linda began to wake up to the realities of life. She was faced with the question of how could she make a living without an education. Two weeks after she started her carpet job her employer asked her what her goals were. She immediately responded. First she wanted to learn as much as she could as quickly as possible. And with that knowledge to improve her abilities at work, her moneys earned and her benefits due.

One year later she started a company called Speciality Carpet for Mike and Jerry Thomas. She was responsible for putting together what the product was going to be, how it would look, how to market it, and build an agent and customer base. She remembers that she was smart enough to do that, but did not have enough brains to ask for part of the ownership until six months to a year later. The owners laughed at her.

Linda worked 12 hours days building the company which put together carpet packages and did commission tufting to where they were doing $20 million in sales a year. In 1988 she was made Executive Vice President of Sales and Marketing, yet she was not allowed any rights of ownership. Whenever she considered doing anything on her own, the owners discouraged her by comments about how hard the industry was, the worries it involved and the gamble that such a move presented.

After working for 11 1/2 years to build Speciality, she was suddenly made aware of how little thought was given to her value to the company. She had just returned from the Dometex Show in Hanover, Germany where she represented the company when Jerry Thomas announced a merger. The new owners' ethics were totally opposite to hers. At that point she decided she had enough courage, knowledge and direction to start her own company. 1st Choice Carpet Int'l was born. She is doing the same thing that she had been doing for 11 1/2 years, but she has total belief in her work and its success.

Her success is not only built on hard work and experience, but also a strong positive mental attitude. She takes pride in doing a good job. "Part of the rewards of life is knowing you have given everything you can to make what you do successful. I still believe in America and that if you give everything you can, tell the truth and live up to what you said you'd do, success is still there." Whenever she begins to doubt, Linda listens to motivational tapes like her favorite Zig Ziglar and she bounces back. Linda Freeman is an example of the smaller successful mills. She is quick to point out that more people work for the smaller mills than the Shaws and the Beaulieus. As long as the Linda Freemans are starting their own companies, the dream of the industry and America is still alive.

# NOTES FROM THE EDGE

In 1987 Carrie Fisher wrote her autobiography *Postcards from the Edge,* which was her view of life as the daughter of Hollywood celebrities. Living among and studying about the tufted carpet industry for the last fourteen years has given me an interesting perch from which to view the business. I am not employed by it, but intensely interested in it. Whether sitting in the boardroom with Bob Shaw, on the deck overlooking Carl Bouckaert's pool, or at RBI with Reg Burnett I began to listen for the trends being manifested from their perspectives.

Reg Burnett has been predicting the advance of consolidation for the past ten years and his prophecy is coming to fruition. In July, 1993, he told the Carpet Max group visiting at Queen Carpet that "Consolidation is the only way that our carpet industry can continue to supply you with the best value in household products that the consumer can purchase." Reg went on to project that approximately 50% of all existing carpet companies will be either acquired by other mills or fade away. By 2000 there will be three or four mega mills, five to ten large mills and only approximately 40 small speciality carpet manufacturers.

It is true, at this time the wave of acquisition seems to be subsiding. Shaw might have acquired all that it needs domestically, although its recently released 10-year plan envisions growing to a $10 billion dollar sales level. Beaulieu seems to be getting its total integration plans resolved, therefore it seems to be maintaining its position.

Therefore, of the three mega mills only Mohawk seems to be interested in adding to its empire. Mohawk's summer 1993 acquisition of Bigelow-Karastan virtually monopolizes woven production. Reports are that it is trying to add a contract commercial carpet company to its regime as it moves its market-place position forward.

These mega companies will force the other mills into niche marketing as well as focusing their attention to service in order for survival. Collins & Aikman has turned totally to the contract market, leaving the broadloom market to others. C & A is turning full attention to courting customers with tours of the plant, customizing presentations, and providing a total service and performance program. C & A is leading the contract industry in the concept of selling a total service and performance package to the customer. Attention to detail whether it is design, application, or maintenance is the wave of things to come.

Package selling to large commercial accounts makes any program more attractive. Airports, hospitals, and municipal buildings are the focus of this approach. Carpet is styled to particular requirements, installers are provided and maintenance programs for long-term care are detailed. Unfortunately, the resources of small companies will be strained by these demands.

Residential carpet is under pressure for restructure also. In the 1980s the consumer might brag about his $100 per square yard floor covering, but now the focus has shifted. Now he might very well point out that he got this exquisite carpet for an extremely low price. The carpet industry has always prided itself as being the best investment for the dollars spent in the house. Now companies must compete with the economically-directed customer and the rapid advancement of quality tufted rugs replacing broadloom sales. Rugs are currently the fastest growth sector in floor covering as evidenced by Shaw and Mohawk's movement into this area once dominated by Beaulieu.

Another direction for the future for both manufacturers and dealers is to become a partner with one of the well-known buying groups. The advantages of becoming a member of such a buying group or franchise are lower prices from the manufacturer as well as the expertise in marketing and advertising, promised by most buying groups. With these buying and technical helps the small retailer is promised a larger profit margin.

An increase of direct marketing by major mills is also on the horizon. In the past, retailers often promised the manufacturer that their carpet was the product of choice for a major commercial installation. At the last minute a cheaper product by another mill would replace it, as price became the major consideration. The fickle distributor or retailer, besides a desire for larger profits, is forcing manufacturers to go directly to the quality purchaser. If direct marketing does not fit their plans, then companies like Shaw may create or buy their own retail outlets.

Ecological concerns are even being felt in Dalton, an area which prides itself with clean water. Earl Whittaker of Collins and Aikman points out to the commercial customer that C & A has a strong commitment to recycling which is cost-saving to the customer and better for the environment. Image Carpets in Armuchee, Georgia has been a front runner for the past few years in making carpet from recycled plastics. Also Carpet One has a mill making carpet for them from recycled materials.

Finally, the industry is slowly recognizing that their male-dominated industry must open the doors of upper management to qualified women. More and more residential buying decisions and many commercial design choices are in the hands of women. Government and other companies are under guideline pressures to elevate women to administrative positions. Therefore, these women will tend to look more favorably toward companies whose commitment is beyond a token representation. There are extremely qualified women in the industry who have been held back by a glass ceiling. Hopefully, the industry will respond to the pressures of the male and female marketing world rather than wait for government mandates.

In conclusion, the philosopher Voltaire said that the only thing that we learn from history is that we never learn from history. This is still an industry in which hard work, creativity, and inventiveness pay off in dollars.

Professional managers and college-educated trainees are in increasing numbers, but the demand for creativity transcends these artificial barriers. The tufted carpet industry is still the great American dream at work.

## *Appendix I*

# 1992 TOP FIFTY NORTH AMERICAN CARPET & RUG MANUFACTURERS BY SALES
## ($ in millions, U.S.)

| | | | | | |
|---|---|---|---|---|---|
| 1. | Shaw | $2,035.9 | $1,607.4 | $1,475.3 | $1,275.9 |
| 2. | Beaulieu of America Group | 752.0 | 600.0 | 590.0 | – |
| 3. | Interface | 594.0 | 582.0 | 623.5 | 581.7 |
| 4. | Collins & Aikman | 405.0** | 226.1** | 238.0** | 242.0** |
| 5. | Aladdin | 397.0 | 330.0** | 285.0** | 240.0** |
| 6. | Peerless/Galaxy | 392.0 | 383.6 | 430.0 | 394.0 |
| 7. | Queen | 390.0** | 340.0** | 345.0** | 290.0** |
| 8. | Mohawk | 352.5 | 279.0 | 288.0 | 275.0 |
| 9. | Burlington Lees | 346.0 | 390.0 | 439.7 | 518.1 |
| 10. | Milliken | 20.0** | 300.0** | 280.0** | 250.0** |
| 11. | Diamond | 290.0** | 245.0** | 235.0** | 220.0** |
| 12. | World Carpet | 280.0 | 225.0** | 276.0 | 275.0 |
| 13. | JPS Stevens | 269.6** | 245.1** | 258.0** | 272.)** |
| 14. | Fieldcrest | 267.4 | 281.8 | 343.1 | 351.3 |
| 15. | Horizon | 259.0 | 278.4 | 288.5 | 298.6 |
| 16. | Tuftex | 145.0 | 150.0** | 168.0** | 170.0** |
| 17. | Columbus | 142.0 | 130.0** | 158.0** | 160.0** |
| 18. | Carriage | 133.3 | 106.0 | 111.0 | 94.1 |
| 19. | Mannington | 127.5** | 120.0** | 140.0** | 135.0** |
| 20. | Bentley | 125.4 | 119.8 | 134.5 | 140.0 |
| 21. | Soreltex Cumberland/Harding | 120.0 | 152.1 | (previously reported separately) | |
| 22. | Springs Industries | 118.5** | 105.0 | (previously reported separately) | |
| 23. | Kraus | 100.0** | 94.0** | 96.0** | 102.0** |
| 24. | Image | 98.0 | 85.0 | 80.0 | 85.0 |
| 25. | Marglen | 94.0 | 88.0 | 95.0 | 110.0 |
| 26. | Royalty | 90.0 | 90.0 | 77.8 | 81.4 |
| 27. | Sunrise | 89.0 | 68.0 | 66.0 | 62.0 |
| 28. | J & J Industries | 85.2 | 93.5** | 95.5** | 95.0** |
| 29. | Masland Industries | 80.0** | 75.0** | 77.5** | 77.5** |
| 30. | Hollytex | 68.0 | 48.0** | 91.0 | 115.0 |
| 31. | Magee | 64.0 | 59.0 | 63.0 | 78.0 |
| 32. | Wunda Weve | 61.5 | 60.0** | 70.0 | 73.0 |
| 33. | Atlas | 55.7** | 54.1** | 58.0 | 62.0 |
| 34. | Masland Carpet | 55.6 | 62.0 | 69.0 | 70.0 |

| | | | | | |
|---|---|---|---|---|---|
| 35. | DWB | 55.0 | (previously reported separately) | | |
| 36. | Blue Ridge | 50.8 | 47.5** | 44.0 | 50.0 |
| 37. | Venture | 50.2** | 48.7** | – | – |
| 38. | Durkan | 45.0 | 35.0 | 34.48 | 36.5 |
| 39. | American Rug Craftsmen | 44.5** | 28.0 | – | – |
| 40. | Downs | 44.0** | 42.7** | 45.0 | 47.0 |
| 41. | Princeton | 43.0 | 53.0 | 50.0 | 40.0 |
| 42. | Victory | 40.0 | (not previously listed) | | |
| 43. | Prince Street | 38.5 | (not previously listed) | | |
| 44. | Grassmore | 38.2 | 40.7 | 34.4 | – |
| 45. | Crossley | 37.2** | 36.1** | 38.0 | – |
| 46. | E.T.C. | 35.6 | 36.0** | 35.5 | 35.8 |
| 47. | Fabrica International | 35.5** | (not previously listed) | | |
| 48. | Regent/Patrick | 35.0** | 42.8** | 45.0 | 53.0 |
| 49. | Bloomsburg | 34.3** | 33.3** | 35.0 | 33.0 |
| 50. | Capel | 33.0** | 32.0** | 31.0 | – |

**Estimated    Carpet & Rug Industry, June 1993

## *Appendix II*

# GLOSSARY OF CARPET TERMS

**Acrylics** - Acrylic and modacrylic carpet fibers. Acrylic fiber contains at least 85% by weight of acrylonitrile units. Modacrylic fiber contains between 35 and 85% by weight of acrylonitrile.

**Axminster** - A carpet weave. Pile tufts are individually inserted from colored yarns arranged on spools making possible an enormous variety of colors and patterns.

**BCF** - Bulked continuous filament. Continuous strands of synthetic fiber formed into yarn bundles of a given number of filaments and texturized to increase bulk and cover. Texturizing changes the straight filaments into kinked or curled configurations.

**Backing** - Materials (fabrics or yarns) comprising the back of the carpet as opposed to the carpet pile or face.

(1) Primary back—in tufting, a woven or nonwoven fabric in which the pile yarn is inserted by the tufting needles. Usually woven or nonwoven polypropylene or woven jute for carpet and often cotton duck for scatter rugs.
(2) Secondary back—Fabric laminated to the back of carpet to reinforce and increase dimensional stability. Usually woven jute or woven or non-woven polypylene.
(3) Backings of woven carpets are the "construction yarns" comprising chain warp, stuffer warp, and shot or fill which are interwoven with the face yarn during carpet fabric formation.

**Bulking** - Processing yarn, usually by mechanical means, to fluff it up and give more coverage with the same weight. Also known as texturizing and lofting.

**Carpet Cushion**- A term used to describe any kind of material placed under carpet to provide softness when it is walked on. Not only does carpet cushion provide a softer feel underfoot, it usually provides added acoustical benefits and longer life for the carpet. In some cases the carpet cushion is attached to the carpet when it is manufactured. Also referred to as "lining," "padding" or "underlay," although "carpet cushion" is the preferred term.

**Continous Dyeing**- The process of dyeing carpet on a continuous production line, rather than piece-dyeing separate lots. Most often done on continuous dyeing equipment which flows on dyestuffs, as distinguished from submerging carpet in separate dye becks.

**Continuous Filament** - Continuous strand of synthetic fiber extruded in yarn form, without the need for spinning which all natural fibers require.

**Cornrowing**- A term used to describe matting that occurs in plushes and shags where some of the yarns that do not mat form "rows" usually across the width of the traffic lanes. These "rows" are caused when groups of tufts lie down horizontally against the primary backing, while adjacent tufts overlap, causing an appearance similar to rows of corn or waves in the ocean. Can often be prevented by changing vacuuming directions frequently.

**Cotton** - A soft, white, fibrous substance composed of the hairs clothing the seeds of an erect, freely branching tropical plant (cotton plant).

**Crimp** - In fiber, a nonlinear configuration, such as a sawtooth, zig-zag or random curl relative to the fiber axis. In woven fabrics, nonlinear yarn configurations caused by three-dimensional displacements such as the zig-zagging of warp yarn over fill yarn. Most synthetic fibers, both staple and filament, used in carpets are crimped. Fiber crimp increases bulk and cover and facilitates interlocking of staple fibers in spun yarns.

**Cut Pile** - A fabric, the face of which is composed of cut ends of pile yarn.

**Denier** - A yarn count unit. It is the weight in grams of 9000 meters. Denier is a direct yarn numbering system; the higher the denier, the larger the yarn.

**Density** - The weight of pile yarn in a unit volume of carpet. U.S. government FHA density (D), expressed in ounces per cubic yarn, is given by the formula

$$D = \frac{W \times 36}{T}$$

in which D is density, W is pile yarn weight in ounces per square yarn, and T is pile thickness or height in inches.

**Dry Rot** - A condition caused by attack by microorganisms on fibers, textiles, carpets or other materials, characterized by loss of strength and integrity. Attack on carpet backings permits carpet to break and tear easily. Cellulosics such as jute are susceptible whereas polypropylene and most other synthetics are virtually immune.

**Dyestuff** - (or Dye) - A highly colored substance capable of permanent physical or chemical attachment to textile fibers; coloration of fibers occurs upon attachment of small quantities. Most dyes are applied from water solutions or dispersions.

**Fading** - Loss of color. Caused by actinic radiation such as sunlight or artificial light, atmospheric gases including ozone, nitric oxide, and hydrogen sulphide, cleaning and bleaching chemicals such as sodium hypochlorite, and other household and industrial products, chlorine chemicals or swimming pools, and other factors. Commercial installations in areas where such exposures occur require extreme care in selection of colorfast carpet.

**Fibers**- Natural or man-made objects having very high aspect ratios, that is, having lengths hundreds of thousands of times greater than their widths. Useful textile fibers have high tensile strengths, flexibility, and resistance to heat, light, chemicals, and abrasives.

**Filler**- A low cost material used for extending rubber, plastic, or other polymers. Fillers are generally powders of very small particle size. Carpet latex laminating compounds and foams contain large amounts of fillers. The most common filler in carpet latex is finely powdered calcium carbonate, often called whiting, produced by grinding limestone.

**Filling Yarn** - In weaving, any yarn running across the width of the fabric perpendicular to the warp yarns. In woven carpet, filling yarns are part of the group of construction yarns which also include chain and stuffer warp and form the backing. Woven carpet fill and chain warp yarns interface to secure the pile yarns. Filling and other construction yarns usually are fibrillated polypropylene, jute, kraftcord, or similar materials.

**Finishing** - A collective term denoting processing of carpets and textiles subsequent to tufting, weaving, and dyeing. Carpet finishing processes include shearing, brushing, application of secondary backing, application of attached foam cushion, application of soil retardant and antistatic chemicals, back beating, steaming, and others.

**Flocking** - Short, chopped fiber or flock is adhered, usually by electrostatic processes, to a base fabric, resulting in a short pile material with a velvety texture.

**Gauge/Pitch** - The number of ends of surface yarn counting across the width of carpet. In woven carpet, pitch is the number of ends of yarn in 27 inches of width; e.g., 216 divided by 27 = 8 ends per inch. In tufted carpet, gauge also means the number of ends of surface yarn per inch counting across the carpet; e.g., 1/8 gauge= 8 ends per inch. To convert gauge to pitch, multiply ends per inch by 27; e.g., 1/10 gauge is equivalent to 270 pitch, or 10 ends per inch x 27. One-eighth gauge is 8 ends of yarn per inch x 27 = 216 pitch.

**Greige Goods** - (Pronounced "gray goods") - Undyed carpet or other textile materials.

**Hand** - The tactile aesthetic qualities of carpets and textiles. Factors determining how carpets feel to the hand include weight, stiffness, fiber type and denier, density, backing and latex.

**Heat Setting**- Process of stabilization of carpet yarns by exposure to heat. Conventional autoclave heat-setting treats yarns in relaxed skein configuration with pressurized steam, usually at temperatures in the 240-300 degree F range, often 270 degrees F for nylon. Some continuous heat-setting machines employ dry heat. The principal benefits are twist retention in plied yarns in cut-pile carpet and general stabilization of yarn configuration.

**High Low** - Multilevel carpet style comprising high and low loop pile areas or high cut-pile and low loop areas. The latter is also called a cut and loop style.

**Indoor/Outdoor** - Type of carpet, regardless of construction, which is made entirely of components (surface yarns, backing, adhesives, or laminating materials) which have been especially designed or treated to withstand moisture, extremes of temperature, ultra-violet rays and other types of exposure.

**Jute** - A natural cellulosic fiber made from certain plants of the linden family which grow in warm climates such as found in India and Bangladesh. Jute yarns are used for woven carpet construction (backing) yarns and twine. Woven jute fabrics are used in tufted carpet as primary and secondary carpet backing. The latter are similar to burlap fabrics commonly used for carpet wrap and sewn burlap bags.

**Knitting**- A fabric formation process comprising interlacing yarns in a series of connected loops with needles. Some carpet is produced by knitting, but is a very small fraction of total carpet. In carpet knitting, as in weaving, pile and backing are produced simultaneously. Multiple sets of needles interlace pile, backing, and stitching yarns in one operation.

**Kusters Dyeing** - Continuous dyeing used the kusters dye applicator and range. (See Continuous Dyeing)

**Latex**- A water emulsion of synthetic rubber, natural rubber, or other polymer. In carpet, latex is used for laminating secondary backings to tufted carpet, back-coating carpet and rugs, and for manufacturing foamed cushion. Almost all carpet latex consists of styrene-butadiene synthetic rubber (SBR) compounded with large quantities of powdered fillers. The latter are most often whiting, which is calcium carbonate.

**Loom** - Machine which produces woven fabrics. In weaving, lengthwise yarns (warp) are interlaced with yarns (fill) inserted at right angles to them by the shuttle (or other device such as gripper or rapier).

**Loop Pile** - Carpet style having a pile surface consisting of uncut loops. May be woven or tufted. Also called "round wire" in woven carpet terminology.

**Mending** - Hand repair of carpet after tufting and weaving to replace missing tufts, remove knots and loose ends, etc.

**Metallic Fiber** - Synthetic fiber made of metal, metal coated plastic, or plastic coated metal sometimes used in small amounts in carpet to dissipate static electricity, thus preventing shock.

**Mill End** - A short piece of carpet roll goods having a length less than that of a full shipping roll or short roll but greater than a remnant. Quality standards differ among mills, but a mill end length specification of nine to twenty feet is typical.

**Nap** - Carpet or rug pile surface.

**Needle Punching** - A method for manufacturing felt fabrics in which fiber batts or fleeces are compressed by the entangling action of barbed needles. Needle-punched carpet made from solution-dyed polypropylene is often used as outdoor carpet. Needle-punched nylon carpet is often printed and foam backed for indoor use.

**Nylon** - The generic name of a fiber in which the fiber-forming substance is any long chain synthetic polyamide having recurring amide groups as an integral part of the polymer chain. There are numerous types of nylon, but the two used to produce carpet fibers are nylon-6 and nylon-6.6.

The history of nylon in the carpet industry is often expressed in terms of generations or advancements in the performance of the nylon hiding properties and built in static protection, the latter brought about by metallic or carbon based conductive filaments incorporated within the nylon fibers. Fourth generation nylon has built-in soil and stain resistance achieved by the addition of certain fluorochemicals during fiber formation.

**Olefins** - Any long chain synthetic polymer composed of at least 85% by weight of ethylene, propylene or other olefin units. Polypropylene yarns are used in carpets.

**Outdoor Carpet** - Carpet which may be used outdoors without rapid fading or deterioration. The principal requirements are resistance to sunlight and water. Most outdoor carpet pile yarns are solution dyed polypropylene containing ultraviolet stabilization additives. Coatings and backing materials are synthetics that are water and rot resistant.

**Pattern** - Artistic decorative design on the surface of carpet. It may be printed, woven with colored yarns, or sculptured in multiple pile heights.

**Pattern Streaks** - Visually apparent streaking in patterned carpet resulting from linear juxtaposition of pattern elements in one direction. It is usually most visible in the length direction. It is not a carpet defect, but is inherent in certain designs. Contract specifiers should view rolls of carpet laid out on a floor to evaluate geometric or other busy patterns for this characteristic which may be objectionable in long corridors and other large areas but not visible in small rooms.

**Pigment** - Highly colored insoluble powdered substance used to impart color to other materials. White pigments, e.g., titanium dioxide, are dispersed in fiber forming polymers to produce delustered (semidull and dull) fibers.

**Pile**- The visible wear surface of carpet, consisting of yarn tufts in loop and/or cut configuration. Sometimes called the face or nap.

**Pile Height** - The length of the extended tufts measured from the primary backing top surface to their tips. Pile tufts should be gently extended but not stretched during this measurement. This specification is usually expressed in fractions or decimal fractions of an inch in the U.S. and sometimes in millimeters elsewhere.

**Plush Finish**- A smooth carpet surface texture in which individual tufts are only minimally visible and the overall visual effect is that of a single level of fiber ends. This finish is normally achieved only on cut-pile carpet produced from non-heatset singles spun yarns by brushing and shearing.

**Polyester** - A fiber-forming thermoplastic synthetic polymer used in some carpet fiber. Essentially all polyester carpet fiber is staple and the yarns are spun yarns. Polyester for carpet is made from terephthalic acid and ethylene glycol and is known as poly (ethylene terephthalate).

**Polypropylene** - Synthetic thermoplastic polymer used for molded items, sheets, films, and fibers. FTC (U.S. Government) classification is Olefin. The polymer is made by stereospecific polymerization of propylene. Most polypropylene carpet fiber is solution dyed and sometimes contains ultraviolet stabilizers for outdoor use. Printable modifications are available but not extensively used. The carpet fiber is available as both bulked continuous filament yarns and staple for spun yarn production.

**Primary Backing** - A component of tufted carpet consisting of woven or nonwoven fabric into which pile yarn tufts are inserted by the tufting needles. It is the carrier fabric for the pile yarn and should not be confused with secondary backing which is a reinforcing fabric laminated to the back of tufted carpet subsequent to the tufting process. Most primary backing is either woven or nonwoven polypropylene, although woven jute is still sometimes used. Some synthetic primary backings have nylon fiber attached to their upper surfaces to make them union dyeable with nylon pile yarns.

**Printed Carpet** - Carpet having colored patterns applied by methods analogous to those used for printing flat textiles and paper. These include flatbed screen printing employing woven fabric screens, rotary screen printing with perforated sheet steel screens, Stalwart printing employing sponge rubber pattern elements on wooden rollers, and modern computer programmed jet printing.

**Random Sheared**- A carpet texture created by shearing either level loop or high-low loop carpet lightly so that only the higher loops are sheared. The sheared areas are less reflective than the unsheared loops which appear brighter and lighter in color. Random shearing of high-low loop carpet produces a texture somewhat similar to cut and loop.

**Rebonded Urethane Cushion** - A carpet cushion made from trim generated from urethane foam product manufacture which has been granulated and bonded to form a porous foam material and fabricated into foam sheets.

**Remnant** - A short piece of carpet roll goods usually less than nine feet long.

**Saxony** - A cut-pile carpet texture consisting of heatset plied yarns in a relatively dense, erect configuration, with well defined individual tuft tips. Saxonies are denser and have more erect tufts than shags. Their tip definition is more pronounced than in singles plush, which is another dense cut-pile carpet style. Saxonies have generally displaced singles plush styles from the market place, and many dealers call their smoother finished saxonies "plushes."

**Secondary Backing-** Woven or nonwoven fabric reinforcement laminated to the back of tufted carpet, usually with latex adhesive, to enhance dimensional stability, strength, stretch resistance, lay-flat stiffness, and hand. Most secondary backings are woven jute, woven polypropylene, or nonwoven polypropylene. The term is sometimes used in a broader sense to include attached cushion and other polymeric back coatings. Because secondary backing is visible, whereas primary backing is concealed under the pile yarn in finished carpet, most dealers and installers refer to the secondary backing simply as "backing."

**Seconds** - Off-quality, defective, or substandard carpet normally marketed at substantial price discounts as "seconds" or "imperfects" by manufacturers. If manufacturers' first quality standards are high, seconds may represent excellent values.

**Selvage** - Carpet edges at sides of rolls.

**Shearing-** Carpet manufacturing process for producing a smooth carpet face, removing fuzz, or creating random sheared textures. Carpet shears have many steel blades mounted on rotating cylinders which cut fibers on carpet surfaces in a manner analogous to a lawn mower cutting grass. Depth of shearing may be indicated by a modifying word, e.g., defuzz and tip-shear suggest a shallow cut of the shear, whereas a full shear would imply a deep cut as used for producing mirror-finished plush.

**Sisal-** Very strong, smooth, yellowish leaf fiber yielded by the Agave Rigida of Central America and the West Indies; used for cordage. It was first imported to the U.S. about 1860.

**Skein Dyed Yarn** - Pile yarn dyed while in the form of large loosely wound skeins

**Solution Dyed** - Fiber colored by pigments dispersed in the polymer melt or solution prior to extrusion into synthetic fiber (Same as Dope Dyed or Spun Dyed).

**Space Dyeing** - Process whereby different colors are "printed" along the length of yarn before it is manufactured into carpet.

**Spinning** - A term for yarn or fiber production. To the fiber manufacturer, spinning is synonymous with extrusion of polymer through the small holes of the spinneret into synthetic fiber. To the conventional textile yarn mill, spinning is the conversion of staple fiber into spun yarn.

**Staple Fiber-** Short lengths of fiber which may be converted into spun yarns by textile yarn spinning processes. Also simply called staple. Staple may also be converted directly into nonwoven fabrics such as needle-punched carpet. For carpet yarns spun on the common modified worsted systems, most staple is six or eight inches long.

**Stock Dyed Yarn** - Colored spun yarn produced from fibers dyed in staple form. The term does not include yarns spun from solution dyed staple.

**Streak** - Any lengthwise narrow visual defect in carpet. Dye streaks may be caused by a single pile end having different dye affinity from the others. Other streaks may be yarn defects such as tight twist, stretched yarn or yarns larger or smaller than the others.

**Swatch** - A small carpet sample. Carpet specifiers should retain swatches to verify color, texture, weight and other quality factors when carpet is delivered.

**Tak Dyeing** - A continuous dyeing process for producing random multicolor patterns which are usually less sharply defined than printed patterns. Colored dye liquor is applied to the carpet in a controlled pattern of droplets.

**Total Weight** - Weight per square yard of the total carpet pile, yarn, primary and secondary backings and coatings.

**Traffic** - The passing to-and-fro of persons with special reference to carpet wear resulting therefrom.

**Tufted Carpet** - Carpet manufactured by the tufting process, which comprises insertion of pile tufts by a row of eyed needles which penetrate a primary backing fabric, thus forming tufts from the yarn threaded through the eyes of the tufting needles. More than ninety percent of all carpet sold in the United States is tufted.

**Tufts** - The cut or uncut loops of a pile fabric.

**Twist** - A yarn term describing the number of turns per inch and direction of twist of either the singles or plies around their axes. Twist direction is either right or left handed, also called Z or S-twist. Carpet yarns usually have rather low-twists, in the 2.5 to 6.0 turns per inch (TPI) range, with the majority in the 3.5 to 5.0 TPI range.

**Velvet Carpet** - Woven carpet made on a loom similar to a Wilton loom but lacking the Jacquard motion. Velvet carpets are generally level loop or plush in solid or tweed colors.

**Weaving**- A fabric formation process, used for manufacturing carpet, in which yarns are interlaced to form cloth. The weaving loom interlaces lengthwise (warp) and widthwise (filling) yarns. Carpet weaves are complex, often involving several sets of warp and filling yarns. (See Axminster, Wilton and Velvet.)

**Weft or Woof** - Yarns which run widthwise in woven cloth or carpet, interlacing with the various warp yarns. See Filling Yarn.

**Wilton** - A type of woven carpet and the loom used to manufacture it. Wilton looms have Jacquard pattern mechanisms which use punched cards to select pile height and yarn color. The carpets are often patterned or have multilevel surfaces.

**Wool** - The most important animal fiber, the outer covering of the sheep.

**Woven Backing** - A tufted carpet term for primary or secondary backing manufactured by the weaving process. Secondary backings are usually woven jute or woven polypropylene. Primary backings are usually woven (or nonwoven) polypropylene.

**Yarn** - A continuous strand composed of fibers or filaments and used in tufting, weaving, and knitting to form carpet and other fabrics. Carpet yarn is often plied and may be either spun or continuous filament.

**Yarn Dyeing**- Dyeing yarn before tufting or weaving it into carpet.

*Definitions provided by The Carpet and Rug Institute*

# BIBLIOGRAPHY


## BOOKS:

Andrews, Mildred Gwin. *The Men and the Mills A History of the Southern Textile Industry.* Macon, Georgia: Mercer University Press, 1987.

*Carpet & Rug Institute Annual Reports*

Edge, Arthur B., Jr. *Fuller E. Callaway (1870-1928) Founder of Callaway Mills.* Newcomen Society in North America, Princeton University Press, 1954.

Ewing, John S., and Nancy P. Norton, *Broadlooms and Businessmen,* Cambridge, Mass: Harvard University Press, 1955.

Kriegel, Robert J., and Louis Patler, *If it ain't broke... BREAK IT!.* New York: Warner Books, 1991.

*Man-Made Fiber and Textile Dictionary,* Celanese Corporation

Norville, Zack. *Zack's Book.* Dalton, Georgia: Norville, Industries, 1992.

Plice, Steven S. *Manpower and Merger: The Impact of Merger Upon Personnel Policies in the Carpet & Furniture Industries.* Harrisburg, PA: University of Pennsylvania Press, 1975.

Reynolds, William A. *Innovation in the United States Carpet Industry, 1947-1963.* Princeton, N.J.: D. Van Nostrand Company, Inc., 1968.

*Tufted Textile Manufacturers Association Directory and Yearbook*

Shaheen, Shaheen. *World Carpets, the First Thirty Years.* Dalton, Georgia: Lee Printing, 1984.

Taylor, Elaine. *I've Had A Millionaire's Fun, The Mose Painter Story.* Chattanooga, TN: Painter and Taylor Manuscript Co., 1982.

Ward, Derek T. *Tufting: an introduction.* Manchester: Textile Business Press, Ltd., 1969

Windham, Roy H. *The Tufting Machine, A Practical Text of Instruction for Machine Fixers.* 3rd Edition. Rome, GA: Southern Craft Company 1941.

## ARTICLES:

"Associations of the Carpet and Rug Industry in the United States leading to The Carpet and Rug Institute." *CRI Reports,* Special Issue, September 30, 1971, pp. 1-22.

"A People Man," (Tom Jones), *Floor Covering Weekly,* May 14, 1973, pp. 1, 32.

Coram, Robert. "Towns that Tell the Story of Textiles, Dalton, Georgia." *Textile World,* April, 1968.

Corbett, Jim. "An 1895 Wedding Present Started Whitfield Bonanza." *The Chattanooga Times,* February 10, 1980, pp. G-1.

"Dalton on the Move." *Georgia Progress,* (Atlanta, Georgia), November, 1969, pp. 9-11.

Darby, Edwin. "School fashions a good fit here." *Chicago Sun-Times,* January 31, 1979.

"Eye on the Goal." (J.C. "Bud" Shaw), *Floor Covering Weekly,* May 14, 1973, pp. 1,32.

"4-Year-Old CRI Traces History to 1927 Through Predecessors." *Floor Covering Weekly,* May 14, 1973, pp. 1, 30

Gavin, Kimberly. "Mohawk/Horizon Merge to Create Industry Giant." *Floor Covering Weekly,* November 2, 1992, pp. 1, 9

Gunter, Ron. "Spring Signals - Joseph McCutchen, Jr." *Home Furnishings Daily,* December 27, 1968, p. 16.

Hamilton, R.E. "Bedspreads are Big Business." *Christian Science Monitor,* March 15, 1941, pp. 5, 15.

Hamilton, R.E. "Bedspread Bonanza." *Reader's Digest,* April, 1941, pp. 41-44.

Jonas, Peggy Baugh. "Early Days of Industry Recalled." *Citizen News,* Dalton, Georgia, February 27, 1978, pp. 5-6D (Reprinted from *Floor Covering Weekly.*

Kary, Lee. "Hamilton: Dynamic Man." Dalton *Daily Citizen-News.* June 12, 1964, p. 3.

Kary, Lee. "Hampton: Master Craftsman." Dalton *Daily Citizen-News,* June 26, 1964, p. 3.

Kary, Lee. "Jolly: Soaring Salesman." Dalton *Daily Citizen-News,* August 19, 1964, p. 3

Kary, Lee. "Turner: Man of Action." Dalton *Daily Citizen-News,* September 10, 1964, p. 3

"Main Issues: Consumerism, Marketing." *Floor Covering Weekly,* May 14, 1973, pp 1ff.

McGregor, John R., and Robert H. Maxey, "The Dalton, Georgia, Tufted Textile Concentration." *Southeastern Geographer,* Vol.XIV, No.2, pp. 133-144.

O'Neill, Frank. "Focus 100 Retail." *Floor Focus,* November, 1992, pp. 8-30.

O'Neill, Frank. "Retail Alliances." *Floor Focus,* November, 1992, pp. 31-39, 43.

"The Early Days of Candlewick." *Dixie Yarns, Inc. Report,* Fall, 1979, vol. 34, No. 3, pp. 4-9.

Oliver, Thomas. "Designer Craze Hits Carpet Industry." (Horizon), *Atlanta Journal and Constitution,* July 26, 1981, pp.15c

"On Top of it All." (Walter Guinan), *Floor Covering Weekly,* May 14, 1973, pp. 1, 26, 29.

Parker, Barry. "Bandy Sees Demand for Carpet in Next Decade." *Chattanooga News-Free Press,* Dalton Supplement Edition, December 12, 1976, pp. 1-2.

Sapp, W.M. "The Genesis of a Great Industry." *The Dalton News,* Archives of Dalton-Whitfield County Historical Society.

St. John, Wylly Folk. "Georgia Bedspreads Cover the Country." *Atlanta Journal Magazine,* pp. 16-17.

Ruffenach, Glenn. "Wall to Wall." *The Wall Street Journal,* June 12, 1991, pp 1ff.

"Tufting History of the Carpet Capitol of the World." *Citizen News,* Dalton, Georgia, June 22, 1979, p. 10.

Valero, Greg. "The Legendary Mrs. B Just Keeps Selling." *Floor Covering Weekly,* August 10, 1992, pp. 1-2.

Whaley, Peggy. "At Queen Carpet it's 'teamwork' that counts!" *Carpet & Rug Industry,* December, 1980, pp. 12-14.

Whaley, Peggy. "Coronet Carpet, 25 Years of Success." *Carpet & Rug Industry,* August, 1981, pp. 12-14.

Whaley, Peggy. "Patcraft Mills Inc., That's Real Living." *Carpet & Rug Industry,* June 1981, pp. 10-12

Whatley, Peggy. "The Chairman is a Lady." *Carpet & Rug Industry,* November, 1981, pp. 10-12.

"The Top 25." *Carpet & Rug Industry,* June, 1989, pp 34ff.

"The Top 25." *Carpet & Rug Industry,* June, 1990, pp 11ff.

"The Top 25." *Carpet & Rug Industry,* June, 1991, pp. 25ff

Walters, Billie J., and James O. Wheeler. "Localization Economics in the American Carpet Industry." *The Geographical Review,* Vol. 74, No. 2, April 1984, pp. 183-191.

Whitener, Catherine Evans. "Mrs. Whitener Recalls Beginning of Bedspread Industry." *The Dalton News,* Dalton, Georgia, March 11, 1937, pp. 1ff.

## INTERVIEWS:

Albright, Stan. Masland Carpet Company, Alabama, July 13, 1993, August 6, 1993.

Babb, Carl. Hauler, Dalton, Georgia, March 22, 1979.

Bandy, Jack. Co-founder, Coronet Industries, Dalton, Georgia, July 3, 1979; January 28, 1980.

Barrow, Hugh. DuPont Laboratories, Dalton, Georgia, October 12, 1979.

Barwick, E.T. (Gene). Barwick Industries, Atlanta, Georgia, April 8, 1980, Dalton, Georgia, March 26, 1981, September 8, 1990.

Barwick Reunion Interviews. Dalton Parks & Recreation Center, September 8, 1990.

Boggess, Polly. Crown Gardens & Archives, Dalton, Georgia, September 9, 1979, and following.

Howell Brook. Barwick employee, Dalton, Georgia, August 24, 1990.

Brock, Gary, Director of Materials Management, Horizon, Calhoun, Georgia, by Michael Smith, March 4, 1982.

Browan, Don. Barwick Industries, Eton, Georgia, July 13, 1992.

Brown, Maxine. sister of James Brown, Atlanta, Georgia, June 7, 1993

Brown, Tom. Georgia Textiles, Calhoun, Georgia, December 11, 1979.

Burnett, Reg. RBI International Carpet Consultant, Dalton, Georgia August 26, 1980, various speeches, July 14, 1993.

Caldwell, Mrs. Fred, and Calvin Caldwell. early bedspread business owner, Calhoun, Georgia, December 10, 1979.

Chandler, I.V. Patcraft Mills Inc., Dalton, Georgia, September 9, 1979

Chitwood, Thurman. early pioneer, Dalton, Georgia, May 14, 1981.

Cobble, Albert. Cobble Industries, Chattanooga, Tennessee, September 9, 1979.

Card, Lewis. Tuftco Machinery, Chattanooga, Tennessee, May 21, 1979.

Carmical, Bobbie. industry writer with *Floor Focus,* Dalton, Georgia, throughout 1993.

Clark, Mike. Patchogue Plymouth, Dalton, Georgia, September 22, 1989.

Cofield, Charles, *American Emulsions*, November 30, 1979.

Dennard, Lindsey. Jute King, Dalton, Georgia, April 30, 1981.

Denson, Joe Billie, and Bettie Denson. Dalton, Georgia, August 26, 1980, July 23, 1993.

Dickson, Mary Stuart McCamy. Dalton, Georgia, 1979.

Dorian, Dick. RBI, carpet consultant, Dalton, Georgia, December 15, 1979.

Eitel, Charlie, president, Collins & Aikman Floor Covering Division, Dalton, Georgia, September 22, 1993.

Evans, W.R. son of Mrs. Eugene (Addie Cavender) Evans, and nephew of Catherine Evans Whitener, Dalton, Georgia, January 22, 1980.

Edwards, Odell. Del Rube Chenille, Dalton, Georgia, October 29, 1979.

Evans, Addie. bedspread tufter, Dalton, Georgia, January 22, 1980.

Feightery, J.M. J.M. Feightery Company, Dalton, Georgia, January 22, 1980, July 24, 1989.

Ferguson, Edith. North Georgia resident during Great Depression and early tufting days, by Lynda Loudermilk, April 24, 1986.

Foster, Vernon. Masterpiece Carpet, Dalton, Georgia, May 12, 1979.

Gibson, Bryan. Dixie Yarns, Barwick Industries, Rossville, Georgia, May 26, 1981.

Giddens, Janey. Sec. to Gene Barwick, Dalton, Georgia, May 26, 1981.

Guinan, Walter. Sanford-Bigelow, Atlanta, Georgia, January 21, 1983.

Hall, Lucille, and Pink Hall, bedspreads, Dalton, Georgia, January 19, 1980.

Hamilton, R.E. Executive Sec., Tufted Textile Manufacturers Association, August 5, 1972

Hanson, George. Hanson-Painter Carpet Co., Dalton, Georgia, May, 1989.

Hennon, Lamar. Carpets of Dalton, Dalton, Georgia, July, 1984.

Howalt, Harvey. Textile Rubber & Chemical Co., Dalton, Georgia, August 24, 1979.

Jolley, Paul. Cobble Tufting Machine Co., Dalton, Georgia, May 30, 1991.

Jonas, Peggy Baugh. Jonas Corp., April 8, 1981 and June 28, 1993.

Jones, Tom. president, J&J Carpet, Dalton, Georgia, May 6, 1983.

Lidderdale, T.W. (Tanc). Jute, Dalton, Georgia, May 30, 1991.

Lomax, Truett. Carpet & Rug Institute, Dalton, Georgia, July 15, 1993.

Lorberbaum, Leonard. Lawtex Corp., Dalton, Georgia, April 21, 1981.

Manly, Jean. Crown Gardens & Archives, Dalton, Georgia, April 9, 1993.

Martin, Don. former president, Brown Printing, Dalton, Georgia, June 8, 1993.

McCarty, Frank. McCarty Chenille, Dalton, Georgia, May 19, 1981.

McCutchen, Joseph, and Christine McCutchen. Universal Carpet, Ellijah, Georgia, July 10, 1979.

Meltzer, Lou. Patchogue Plymouth, Dalton, Georgia, July 12, 1979.

Mishkin, Sandy. Carpet One, Atlanta, Georgia, August 11, 1993

Moench, Ernest J. early inventor and owner of Tennessee Tufting, Nashville, Tenn. June 20, 1980; July 21, 1980.

Neal, Tom. Lawtex (factoring), Dalton, Georgia, April 22, 1981.

Painter, Mose. inventor, Painter Carpet Co. Dalton, Georgia, April, 1979.

Passons, Irby. Main Street Machine Co., Chattanooga, Tennessee, May 17, 1979.

Petty, Campbell. Cabin Craft, Dalton, Georgia, February 21, 1980.

Rice, George. First National Bank of Dalton, Dalton, Georgia, May 21, 1979.

Roberts, Ed. early hauler, Dalton, Georgia, February, 1979.

Rosen, Fred. Dalton, Georgia, February 28, 1980

Rogers, Herb. Rogers Dye Finishing, Dalton, Georgia, December 3, 1979.

Saul,Harry. Queen Carpet, Dalton, Georgia,

Saul, Julian. Queen Carpet, Dalton, Georgia, May 10, 1983.

Secord, Al. Banker, Dalton, Georgia, April 15, 1981.

Seretean, Bud. founder, president Coronet Carpet, Dalton, Georgia, January 28, 1980.

Shaheen, Said. Carolyn Chenille, Dalton, Georgia; Shaheen Carpets, Resaca, Georgia, May 21, 1979.

Shaheen, Shaheen. founder, president, World Carpet, Dalton, Georgia, August, 9, 1979, October 2, 1986.

Shaw, Bob. Shaw Industries, Dalton, Georgia, May 10, 1983, May 30, 1991.

Sims, Warren. Shaw Industries, Dalton, Georgia, October 5, 1990.

Sobelman, Sandy. Barwick Industries, Atlanta, Georgia, March 18, 1980

Stark, Daniel. Vice President of Style and Design, Horizon, by Michael Smith, Calhoun, Georgia, March 4, 1982

Spirer, Peter. Horizon Industries, Calhoun, Georgia, January 7, 1981 and Horizon Pacific, Atlanta, Georgia, June 8, 1993 also by Michael Smith, Calhoun, Georgia, March 4, 1982.

Stein, Clem. International Academy of Merchandising & Design, Ltd., Chicago, Ill., April 3, 1980

Strain, Jack. Redwine-Strain Company, Dalton, Georgia, August 5, 1972.

Talley, Buford. President, Barwick Industries, Dalton, Georgia, May 10, 1983.

Turner, Jack. Cabin Craft, Dalton, Georgia, August 9, 1979.

Walters, Robert W. The Mill Store, LaGrange, Georgia, November 15, 1990.

Weissenberger, Margaret. daughter of Glenn Looper, California, June, 1980.

Westcott, Mrs. G.L. (Lulu). wife of founder, Cabin Craft, Dalton, Georgia, April 23, 1991.

Whittaker, Earl. Collins & Aikman, Chattanooga, Tennessee, August 15, 1993.

Wiegand, Bill. former president, Collins & Aikman Floor Covering Division, Dalton, Georgia, June 11, 1993.

Williamson, Fred. President, Hardwick Bank, Dalton, Georgia, May 20, 1981.

## MAPS:

Sims Textile Company Map of Dalton, courtesy of Dalton-Whitfield County Historical Society. c1946.

The National Association of The Carpet, Rug and Tufting Industry. c1971.

# INDEX